EUROPEAN POLITICAL, ECONOMIC, AND SECURITY ISSUES

ECONOMIC AND POLITICAL DEVELOPMENTS IN POLAND

EUROPEAN POLITICAL, ECONOMIC, AND SECURITY ISSUES

Additional books in this series can be found on Nova's website under the Series tab.

Additional E-books in this series can be found on Nova's website under the E-book tab.

EUROPEAN POLITICAL, ECONOMIC, AND SECURITY ISSUES

ECONOMIC AND POLITICAL DEVELOPMENTS IN POLAND

MAUREEN P. LARSEN
EDITOR

Nova Science Publishers, Inc.
New York

For permission to use material from this book please contact us:
Telephone 631-231-7269; Fax 631-231-8175
Web Site: http://www.novapublishers.com

NOTICE TO THE READER

Library of Congress Cataloging-in-Publication Data

Economic and political developments in Poland / editor, Maureen P. Larsen.
p. cm.
Includes index.
ISBN 978-1-61209-951-4 (hardcover)
1. Poland--Economic policy--1990- 2. Poland--Economic conditions--1990- I. Larsen, Maureen P.
HC340.3.E293 2011
338.9438--dc22 2011004596

Published by Nova Science Publishers, Inc. † New York

CONTENTS

PREFACE*

This new book presents and discusses political and economic developments in Poland. Topics discussed include Polish industry in the transformation period; the economic base of the major cities in Poland in the political and economic restructuring period; foreign investment capital in Poland; regions and regionalism in Poland; privatisation of the Polish economy and Polish public opinion and the changing euro-debate.

Chapter 1 – One of the most important processes crucially affecting the course of the economic transformation in Poland was the change in its ownership structure. It consisted mainly in the privatisation of so far state-owned enterprises (de-nationalisation) and the establishment of new, private economic entities. The effect has been the dominance of the private sector in various economic structures and a decreasing role of the public sector.

Chapter 2 – This chapter presents changes that have occurred in the industry of Poland during the economic transformation which started in 1989. The changes described concern the branch and spatial structure of industry as divided into the extractive and processing sectors. Special attention is paid to factors accounting for the processes taking place.

Chapter 3 – This chapter refers to the classical conception of economic base, which determines theoretical and methodological basement for research on functions of major cities in Poland. Besides updating on empiric knowledge about size and structure of the cities' economic base, there were attempts on defining direction of its rearrangement during system transformation, as well as on the cities' functional types.

Chapter 4 – The aim of the chapter is to characterize selected components of contemporary regionalism in Poland. Manifestations of regionalism are analysed against the backcloth of historical processes, changes in the administrative structure, and ethnic issues.

Chapter 5 – The current stage of development of the service sector in Poland is the consequence of many factors. Some of the factors are those that influenced the organization of services during the time when the centrally planned economy was in place, while the other factors are those that brought about the changes in the service sector during the socio-political transformation beginning in the late 1980's. In the first group of factors, it is impossible to overstate the effects of: services being counted in the national income, forced industrial investments being prioritized over other sectors of the economy, many services being

---

* Versions of chapters 1-7 were also published in *Current Politics and Economics of Russia, Eastern and Central Europe*, Volume 23, Issues 1-6, edited by Frank Columbus, published by Nova Science Publishers, Inc. They were submitted for appropriate modifications in an effort to encourage wider dissemination of research.

intentionally internalized within government-run businesses, as well as the low level of the society's assets. In the second group of factors, one should look at the current picture of the service sector in Poland and take into account the effects of new processes: the development of private enterprise, privatization, the deregulation of many service markets; the nature and scale of foreign direct investment, as well as the increase in the gross national product and changes in household consumption behavior.

During the last decades, development of the service sector has been accompanied by the creation or the widening of local inequalities in the development of service infrastructure (supply-side), as well as by changes in reported demand for business services and for consumer services (demand-side). It should be noted that attempts at portraying the changing role of the Polish economy's service sector, as well as changes within the sector, have not had much success due to a lack of satisfactory and official statistical data. Statistics concerning the service sector are still disproportionately meager in comparison to the sector's significance in the Polish economy. In addition, in many instances it is impossible to trace changes over a certain period of time, due to changes in data-collection methodology and changes in the industrial classification system. In those cases in which it was possible, an attempt was made nonetheless to show variation in the indicators for the longest-possible time period. Sometimes this was possible only in the qualitative sense.

Chapter 6 – In 1989 Poland was the first among the post-communist states of Central and Eastern Europe to start a deep, fundamental systemic transformation that has changed the country's political, social and economic conditions irrevocably. The Polish economy had to grapple with a host of problems, largely posed by its communist heritage, especially in the initial period of the transformation. They included an obsolete economic structure, a worn-out stock of machines, high unemployment, soaring inflation, low accumulation, a budgetary deficit, foreign debt, and other. Poland still needs capital badly to continue the opening of the economy and its restructuring, but suffers a deficiency of domestic sources of financing. This is a major obstacle reducing the pace and range of the systemic changes, given the fact that the country is still striving to make up for its civilisational backwardness, modernise and supplement the existing manufacturing potential, and create an efficient, growth-enhancing infrastructural system. But first of all, it has to build an efficient economic system meeting the standards of advanced countries.

Poland's present capital resources are inadequate to deal with its economic situation, hence the country has to look for and employ external sources from which to finance developmental processes. One of them is the inflow of foreign capital, especially foreign direct investment (FDI), which is treated as the most advantageous form of capital flow. The change of regime in 1989 has made it possible for Poland to join in globalisation processes, including its opening to foreign investment, which has become a new development moulding the country's economic processes. This is due to the fact that the inflow of foreign capital is accompanied by additional elements highly significant for economic growth: the transfer of new technology and know-how, and modern, more efficient methods of labour organisation, management, and marketing. Foreign direct investment is also connected with access to foreign markets and the creation of new jobs. Among the many benefits associated with the inflow of foreign investment capital, especially worth mentioning are the acceleration of the systemic transformation and enhancement of the competitiveness of the Polish economy. Foreign investment promotes the stability of the country's economy, the building of market institutions, privatisation, the restructuring of its industry and foreign trade, and its integration with the world economy. That is why foreign direct investment can be a major factor of socio-economic development in Poland and the other post-socialist states.

The aim of this study is to present the inflow of foreign investment capital to Poland since the beginning of the transformation period, spatial differences in investment processes, barriers to investment, and the role of foreign investment in the transformation of the Polish economy.

Chapter 7 – Recent years have seen a significant fall in support for Polish EU membership and the emergence of a sizeable bloc of anti-EU public opinion. While, the new ex-communist led government elected in September 2001 adopted a more flexible approach to the accession negotiations this produced a mixed public reaction and the fact that they have been forced into a coalition with an agrarian party will constrain their room for manoeuvre during the negotiating endgame. Nonetheless, overall levels of support for Polish EU membership appear to have consolidated at a relatively high level and it is extremely likely that most Poles will vote Yes in the 2003 accession referendum. The only real threat to a Yes vote appears to be if the referendum is turned into a plebiscite on the socio-economic transition as a whole. However, the greater concern for the pro-EU camp is that the referendum fails to achieve the turnout required by the Polish Constitution for it to be valid.

The September 2001 Polish parliamentary election received considerable comment both domestically and internationally because of its perceived impact on the EU accession negotiations. On the one hand, the election led to the formation of a new government committed to adopting a more flexible negotiating strategy in order to accelerate the EU accession process. On the other hand, it also saw parties and groupings that had expressed hostility or even outright opposition to Polish EU membership win a significant share of the vote. At the time of writing (July 2002) Poland's EU accession negotiations are entering their final, decisive stage. In autumn 2002 they are scheduled to enter their 'endgame' when the most difficult and controversial issues (regional aid, agriculture and the budget) are due to be discussed. These negotiations must be completed successfully before the end of the year in order for Poland to be admitted in the next enlargement wave scheduled for 2004. In autumn 2003, therefore, Poles will have to vote in an EU accession referendum.

This chapter examines the state of Polish public opinion and the changing euro-debate at this critical conjuncture for Polish-EU relations. It begins by examining and accounting for changing patterns of support for Polish EU membership over the last few years. Section two moves on to examine the impact on the Polish euro-debate of both the new government's negotiating strategy and the presence, for the first time, of a sizeable anti-EU bloc of parliamentary deputies. Finally, section three considers how public attitudes towards EU membership are likely to evolve over the coming period in the run up to the referendum.

The chapter argues that the new ex-communist led government's more flexible negotiating strategy produced both a hostile political and mixed public reaction. The fact that the September 2001 election saw parties and groupings critical of and even hostile to EU membership obtaining a substantial share of the vote and significant parliamentary representation has also, to some extent, polarised the terms of the Polish euro-debate. Moreover, the fact that the former communists and their allies fell short of winning an overall parliamentary majority and have been forced to form a government with an agrarian party critical of the EU has constrained their room for manoeuvre somewhat. It will continue do so during the negotiating endgame on issues such as agricultural subsidies where the EU is proposing to phase in payments to Polish farmers over a ten year period.

In: Economic and Political Developments in Poland
Editor: Maureen P. Larsen
ISBN 978-1-61209-951-4

Chapter 1

PRIVATISATION OF THE POLISH ECONOMY

Anna Tobolska
Institute of Socio-Economic Geography and Spatial Management,
Adam Mickiewicz University, Poznań, Poland

ABSTRACT

One of the most important processes crucially affecting the course of the economic transformation in Poland was the change in its ownership structure. It consisted mainly in the privatisation of so far state-owned enterprises (de-nationalisation) and the establishment of new, private economic entities. The effect has been the dominance of the private sector in various economic structures and a decreasing role of the public sector.

PRIVATISATION AS AN ELEMENT OF THE TRANSFORMATION OF THE POLISH ECONOMY

The aim of the systemic change undertaken in Poland in the late 1980s was to transform the national economy into one meeting the standards of a modern economy, capable of facing the challenges of civilisation and international competition. The mainstays of the new economic system were now to be market mechanisms, a stable monetary policy, and the recognition of private ownership (cf. Wilczyński 1994: 65). Private ownership and market competition were to be the antidotes to the compromised socialist central planning and the dominance of state property, regarded as the two underlying causes of 'the economics of shortage'. Private ownership and market mechanisms were expected to bring about a more effective use of the existing potential; they also established profit maximisation as the rationale for the operation of economic entities (cf. Suwalski 1996: 8).

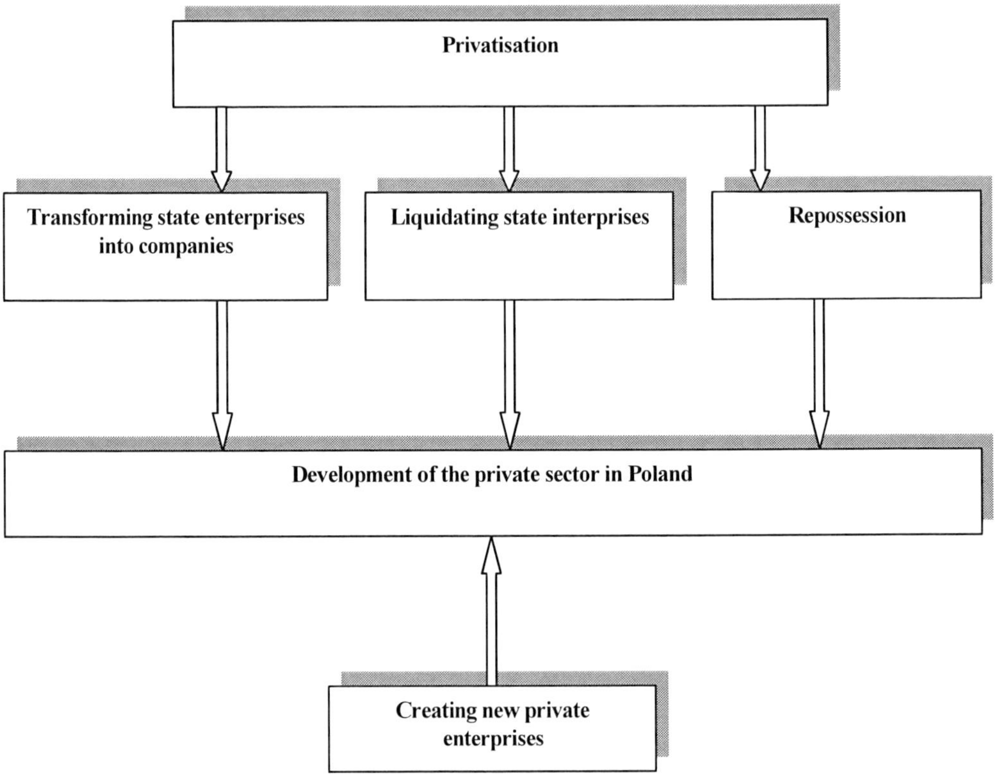

Source: Own compilation.

Figure 1. Building the private sector in Poland – a general diagram.

One of the most important processes crucially affecting the course of the economic transformation in Poland was the change in its ownership structure. It consisted mainly in the privatisation of so far state-owned enterprises (de-nationalisation) and the establishment of new, private economic entities. The effect has been the dominance of the private sector in various economic structures and a decreasing role of the public sector. Thus, the creation of the private sector has taken various paths in Poland (cf. Figure 1): through privatisation, i.e., 'shifting' state enterprises to the private sector (this type of change is termed *top-down privatisation*), and through the introduction of legal regulations allowing individuals to start their own businesses, i.e. creating the conditions for *bottom-up privatisation* (cf., e.g., Surdykowska 1997).

Ownership changes, in fact, started in Poland back in the 1980s with an increase in private handicraft workshops, which was allowed by the Council of Ministers' Development of Small Manufacturing Resolution no. 112 of 8 June 1981. In the years 1980-1990 the number of private handicraft businesses grew from 147,300 to 334,600, and their employment, from 282,700 to 716,100. The proportion of private crafts in total industrial employment rose from 5.4% to 16.3% (cf. Misztal 1993). A symptom of ownership change was also the appearance in the late 1970s of foreign small-manufacturing plants, whose operation was sanctioned by the act of 6 July 1982 laying down the rules of economic activity carried out on the territory of Poland by foreign persons in the field of small manufacturing. The next legal documents that paved the way for ownership changes in Poland were the act of

1986 concerning the establishment of joint ventures with foreign capital and the act of 1988 concerning the free undertaking of economic activity and enabling natural persons to set up private commercial companies (cf. Balicki 1994: 9).

In recent years, privatisation has become one of the global economic processes, but its meaning is totally different in advanced countries reducing their state-run sector (which is often small anyway). In the former centrally planned economies, privatisation is not only intended to improve the performance of the economic system, but also to help build a completely new, market-based economy. In the early 1980s in Poland, 82% of the national income was generated by the state sector, which employed 73% of the total labour force. Private employment was understood as including mainly farmers, who numbered in excess of 4 million (or 87% of employment in the entire private sector), according to the 1980 statistics. However, relations between the private and the public sector (the latter was called socialised until 1989) were changing rapidly, and in 1990, the first year of the systemic transformation, the private sector accounted for nearly 31% of the GDP and 50% of total employment. In 2001, it employed 75% of the total labour force and generated more than 71% of the GDP.

There is now an extensive body of information about ownership changes in Poland collected by many disciplines, including economy, law, sociology, and socio-economic geography. Especially worth noting are the collective study of the various aspects of privatisation in different spheres of the economy edited by Jałowiecki and Mync (1994), and a work by Misztal (1993) dealing with the privatisation of enterprises in a regional approach. Numerous papers on the different aspects of privatisation in industry have also been presented at the annual conferences of the Industrial Geographic Commission of the Polish Geographical Society organised by Prof. Z. Zioło. Important synthetic works on ownership changes in Polish industry involving foreign capital are Domański (2001) and Stryjakiewicz (1999). A synthesis of those changes in agriculture can be found, e.g., in the papers by Szczęsny (1999) and Zgliński (1999).

Forms of Privatisation

To describe privatisation processes in Poland, their types, and the terminology involved, one should start with a definition of the notion of privatisation. The most precise definition is given in the State Enterprise Privatisation Act of 13 July 1990; it is "a change in the form of ownership of an enterprise via its transformation or liquidation and offering its assets to third parties through: sale of shares, sale or bringing into a company of all its assets or their organised part, or offered for use against payment for a specified time".

The fundamental legal act authorising privatisation in Poland was the State Enterprise Privatisation Act of 13 July 1990, in force until 7 April 1997. After this time another document took effect, viz. the State Enterprise Commercialisation and Privatisation Act of 30 August 1996. The remaining acts regulating ownership changes include:

- the State Enterprise Act of 25 September 1981,
- the Treasury's Agricultural Property Management Act of 19 October 1991 concerning the privatisation of state enterprises engaged in farming activities through the inclusion of their assets in the Treasury's Agricultural Property Reserve,

- the Privatisation of State Enterprises of Unique Importance for the National Economy Act of 15 February 1993, and
- the National Investment Funds and their Privatisation Act of 30 April 1993.

Unfortunately, to this day no legislation has been passed in Poland concerning repossession, or the restitution to former owners of property expropriated under the nationalisation act.

On the basis of the above-mentioned legal acts, four basic procedures are employed to privatise state enterprises:

(1) indirect, capital privatisation,
(2) direct privatisation,
(3) liquidation, and
(4) inclusion of the assets of former state farms in Treasury's Agricultural Property Reserve.

Indirect, Capital Privatisation

This form of privatisation is intended for big enterprises which employ more than 500 workers and which are in good financial condition, or can reach this condition as a result of the transformation.

The procedure that precedes capital privatisation and which is the first stage in the privatisation of state enterprises is *commercialisation*. This term is understood to denote the transformation of a state-owned enterprise into a Treasury's sole-shareholder company or a limited liability company; thus, there is no change of the owner but only of the legal status of the enterprise. The legal basis of the enterprise's operation as a Treasury's company is the commercial code. In accordance with the provisions of the new State Enterprise Commercialisation and Privatisation Act, commercialisation also embraces the process of transforming a state enterprise into a limited liability company with the participation of creditors as a result of converting debts into shares.

A commercialised state enterprise can then be privatised (a) through an individual sale, or (b) through sale under the National Investment Funds (NIF) programme (originally, the Mass Privatisation Programme), or (c) until April 1997, also along a special sale path reserved for enterprises of unique importance for the national economy; such enterprises, after having been turned into Treasury's sole-shareholder companies, underwent restructuring and could be privatised individually on special conditions defined by the Council of Ministers.

a) *Individual capital privatisation* consists in the sale of shares in Treasury's sole-shareholder companies by public offer, public tender, or negotiations started on the basis of a public invitation of potential strategic investors, both domestic and foreign. A significant element of the sale of shares to a strategic investor is his agreement to additional stipulations concerning the size, quality and structure of production, outlays on modernisation and technological progress, environmental protection, raising share-capital, or social obligations.

b) *Capital privatisation under the National Investment Funds programme* - this path of privatisation came into operation in 1995 following the implementation of the National Investment Funds Act of 30 April 1993 and the Mass Privatisation Programme declared earlier by the government. The chief idea behind mass privatisation programmes that appeared in the early 1990s not only in Poland, but also in other formerly socialist states was the assumption that a necessary condition of any economic and social reform was the transfer of ownership titles to state property to the widest possible circles of society. The capital privatisation under the NIF programme was intended to spread ownership changes by allowing all adult citizens to benefit from the increase in the value of privatised enterprises. This path of privatisation was devised primarily for big and medium-sized firms in good financial condition. What may be considered a prototype of mass privatisation was the British privatisation strategy pursued by Margaret Thatcher's government. It made use of de-nationalisation as a way of creating popular capitalism, or a capitalist social system in which ownership titles are not concentrated in the hands of a narrow oligarchy, but spread over the entire society (cf. Suwalski 1996: 63). The aims of the Polish Mass Privatisation Programme were to simultaneously privatise and restructure enterprises through an inflow of capital, the opening of new markets, and the introduction of modern management and organisation techniques, and to float, in one go, 15 new companies, the NIFs, on the Warsaw Stock Exchange. Hence, it is another form of indirect privatisation consisting in the bringing of shares of commercialised enterprises into the National Investment Funds and their sale as the next step. In 1995 a list was drawn up of 512 Treasury's companies selected for this type of privatisation. The programme foresaw the following sequence of steps (after *Pakiet Informacyjny* 1995: 10 and *Program NFI - Konferencja prasowa* ... 1995: 3/20):

1. Converting state enterprises into Treasury's sole-shareholder companies (TSSCs);
2. Setting up in December 1994 of 15 National Investment Funds as joint-stock companies, 85% of whose shares were earmarked for exchange for the public's privatisation certificates and the remaining 15% were to be kept by the Treasury;
3. Bringing 60% of TSSC shares into the National Investment Funds. Ultimately, 512 companies took part in the programme, and in July 1995 their shares were distributed among the 15 NIFs. Each of them obtained 33% blocks of shares in selected companies and minority shareholdings in all the others (cf. Figure 2);
4. Emission of privatisation certificates and their distribution among all adult citizens of the Polish Republic (the distributing was done by the PKO BP bank starting November 1995);
5. Floating NIF shares on the stock exchange; and
6. Exchanging privatisation certificates for NIF shares.

The participation of enterprises in the NIF programme does not bar their way to a further ownership transformation. For instance, they can seek a strategic investor, and the capital obtained from the sale stays in the enterprise rather than going to the Treasury. This aspect of participation in the NIFs has been the most frequently emphasised advantage of the programme. To run the Funds, consulting firms (Polish-foreign consortia) have been employed which take over a part of NIF property in return for their services (only the Eugeniusz Kwiatkowski Fund No. 9 operates without the help of such a firm; cf. Mojkowski 1996: 5). Still, the NIF programme has given rise to a lot of controversy (cf. Mojkowski 1996: 5, Suwalski 1996: 77, Kostrz-Kostrzewska 1995, Szulc 1994). All the Funds concentrate on strengthening their position on the market, mainly through the sale of shares of companies that are part of their investment portfolios. Since their listing on the stock exchange, i.e., since mid-1997, there has been a steady decline in the share prices of all NIFs. There have also been some fusions, e.g., in March 2000 NIFs no. 3 and 11 merged, mainly to reduce operating costs and improve management efficiency (cf. Domaszewicz 1998: 32).

c) The State Enterprise Privatisation Act that was in force until 7 April 1997 foresaw *a special privatisation path for enterprises of unique importance for the national economy*. They underwent restructuring and could be privatised individually under special conditions defined by the Council of Ministers.

Among the methods employed in this type of privatisation were *managerial contracts*. This method is known in market economies, but of all the countries in the transition period only the Polish Ministry of Privatisation offered it to selected enterprises late in 1993 on the basis of a 'Privatisation with Restructuring' programme. The enterprises eligible for the programme were ones employing under 1,500 workers that could not be privatised in any other way owing to their bad financial situation. The method consists in closing a contract with a group of managers for restructuring a firm with a view to eventually handing over at least 51% of shares in it to a private investor. The managerial group is motivated to do the restructuring and increase the firm's value over that given in the contract by a specially devised compensation system and the possibility of acquiring shares in the firm on preferential terms. This type of managerial contracts is counted among privatisation methods because their execution results in a change in the enterprise's ownership.

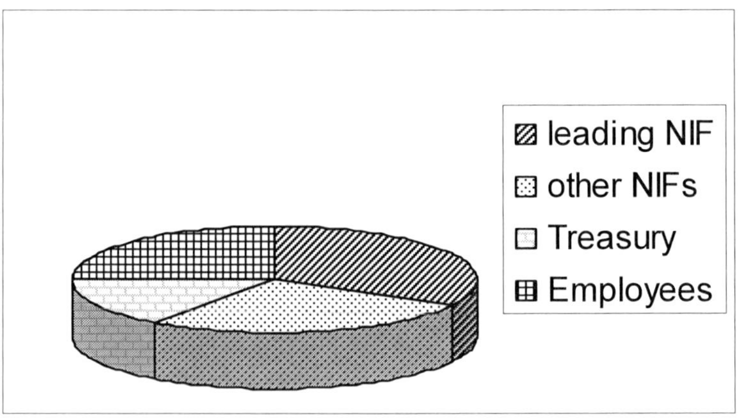

Figure 2. Structure of shares in Treasury's sole-shareholder companies participating in the National Investment Funds (NIF) programme.

Direct Privatisation

In the study period, i.e., 1990-2002, this type of privatisation was carried out on the basis of two acts.

1. The process followed until April 1997 under the State Enterprise Privatisation Act of 13 July 1990 was called *privatisation by liquidation*. It consisted in a formal winding-up of a state enterprise by striking it off the register and then selling or leasing its assets, whole or in part, to a third party, e.g. private businesses, or natural or artificial persons. The temporary transformation of the enterprise into a Treasury's company was not necessary in this case. Two variants of privatisation by liquidation were possible, depending on the market and financial situation of the enterprise:
   - Liquidation under article 19 of the State Enterprise Act of 25 September 1981 if the economic condition of the enterprise was bad and the aim of the liquidation was to terminate its existence as an organised volume of estate. Assets left after the liquidation (unwanted property) were taken over by the Treasury, and the enterprise's founding organ, acting on the Treasury's behalf, could sell them or bring them into a company;
   - Liquidation under article 37 of the State Enterprise Privatisation Act of 13 July 1990 offered the possibility of passing the organised volume of liquidated estate to the new owner through the sale of the entire enterprise or its individual assets to an external investor or leasing them to an employee partnership. In other words, the enterprise was wound up as an artificial person in order to dispose of its assets.
2. The document that came into effect after April 1997 is the State Enterprise Commercialisation and Privatisation Act of 30 August 1996. It defines direct privatisation as an ownership change procedure following the second variant of privatisation by liquidation in force until April 1997. The procedure starts with an enterprise's founding organ issuing a direct privatisation order, and all the assets of the privatised enterprise are transferred to the new owner. The assets can be sold, brought into a company, or put to use against payment. The commonest direct privatisation procedure is the giving of assets to an employee partnership for use against payment (employee leasing). The enterprise is sold by tender or in the course of negotiations opened on the basis of public invitation. The sale offer is addressed to both, domestic and foreign buyers, with preference given to the employees of the enterprise being thus privatised (who have a right to a gratuitous 15% of shares).

Direct privatisation (formerly called privatisation by liquidation in the variant based on article 37 of the Act of 13 July 1990) is only designed for smaller enterprises which can be purchased or leased by domestic investors or employee partnerships. Under section 2 of article 39 of the 1990 Act, a state enterprise could be privatised directly if it employed not more than 500 workers, if its sales (of goods or services) did not exceed a Polish zloty equivalent of ECU 6 million, and if its own funds did not exceed a Polish zloty equivalent of ECU 2 million (cf. Karwowska, Krause 1997: 18).

Liquidation

This is a procedure which the act in effect until April 1997 included among forms of direct privatisation, and which the act currently in force simply calls the liquidation of an enterprise. It is employed in the case of enterprises in bad economic condition. The winding-up takes place under article 19 of the Debt Securing Act. Assets left after the liquidation (unwanted property) are taken over by the Treasury, and the founding organ, acting on the Treasury's behalf, can sell them or bring them into a company. The basic modes of disposal of the assets of enterprises wound up under this act are their sale or transfer to creditors in lieu of the liabilities.

A separate procedure of ownership change is followed in the case of the property of former state farms, which are the principal object of privatisation in rural areas in Poland. Details of this type of privatisation will be discussed in chapter 4.

A diagram of the various pathways of privatisation of Polish state enterprises is presented in Figure 3.

Effects of the Privatisation of the Polish Economy

Regional Dimension of the Privatisation of the Economy

From the start of privatisation in Poland in 1990 till the end of 2002, a total of 6,982 state enterprises underwent various privatisation procedures. The rate of the process was the fastest in the initial period, i.e. till 1993, when 56.3% of the enterprises were privatised. The course of privatisation in the particular years and along the particular routes is presented in Figure 4.

Treasury's sole-shareholder companies created as a result of the commercialisation of state enterprises are as a rule big economic entities largely engaged in industrial processing (54.5%), mainly producing food and beverages (15.2% of the total). At the end of 2002 they employed 352,600 workers, or 35.9% of the labour force of the privatised enterprises. Most, in excess of 40%, worked in companies classified under the mining and quarrying section (primarily mining), usually big firms employing more than 1,000 people. The employment structure in the privatised economic entities by sections of the Nomenclature of Economic Activities in Poland and by workforce is presented in Tables 1 and 2. However, the economic performance of Treasury's sole-shareholder companies developed from commercialised state enterprises was poorer in 2002 than the average for the entire population of privatised entities.

At the close of 2002, the biggest number of commercialised companies were located in the voivodeships of Silesia (315), Lower Silesia (176), Mazovia (154), Wielkopolska (118), and Małopolska (109). A detailed distribution of privatised state enterprises, including companies created as a result of their commercialisation, is presented in Figure 5.

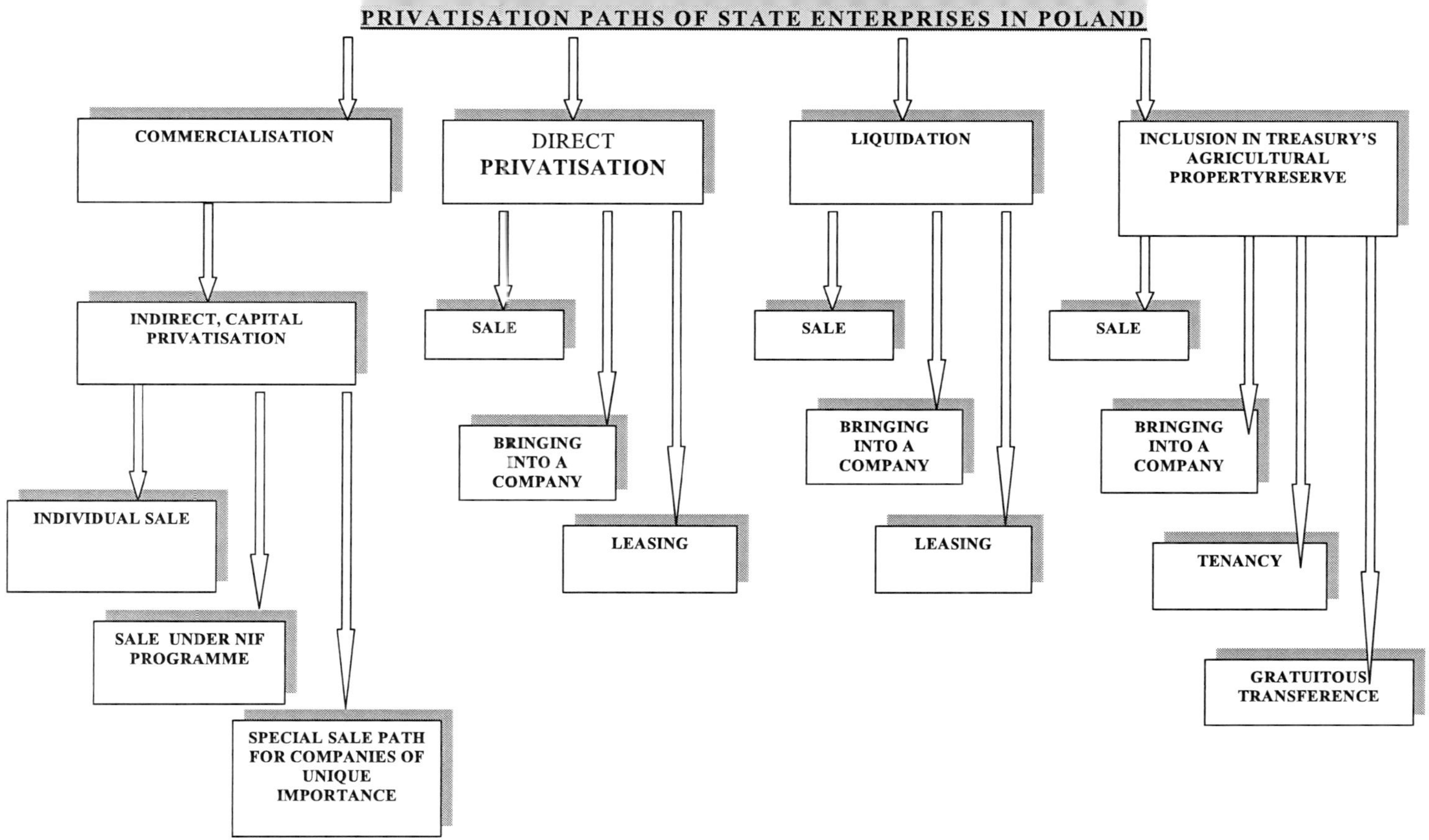

Figure 3. General diagram of the various privatisation paths of Polish state enterprises.

Table 1. Employment in privatised economic entities by sections of the Nomenclature of Economic Activities in Poland (as of 31 Dec. 2002)

Economic entities	Total	of which:				
		Mining and quarrying	Manu-facturing	Production and supply of electricity. gas and water	Construction	Transport. storage and communication
	in thousands					
Total	982.8	174.8	489.6	88.7	70.1	81.6
of which:						
Treasury's sole-shareholder companies after commercialisation	352.6	142.7	98.5	67.4	2.2	21.8
Companies set up after conversion of liabilities	1.9	-	1.7	-	-	-
NIF companies	124.9	3.0	106.8	0.2	11.7	1.0
Capital-privatised companies	242.3	19.9	133.2	14.3	9.4	46.8
Companies with Treasury's participation after direct privatisation	44.1	1.1	35.0	-	1.8	2.7
Employee partnerships	151.2	3.4	63.2	0	44.4	9.2
State enterprises undergoing privatisation	2.5	-	1.2	-	0.2	0.2

Source: *Prywatyzacja* ... (2003)Out of the privatised enterprises, 1,535 were commercialised, i.e., transformed into Treasury's sole-shareholder companies. An additional 14 underwent commercialisation with a conversion of liabilities. Out of the total number of Treasury's companies thus created, 512 were selected for the National Investment Funds programme, while 330 were privatised by the sale of controlling interests in them to strategic investors.

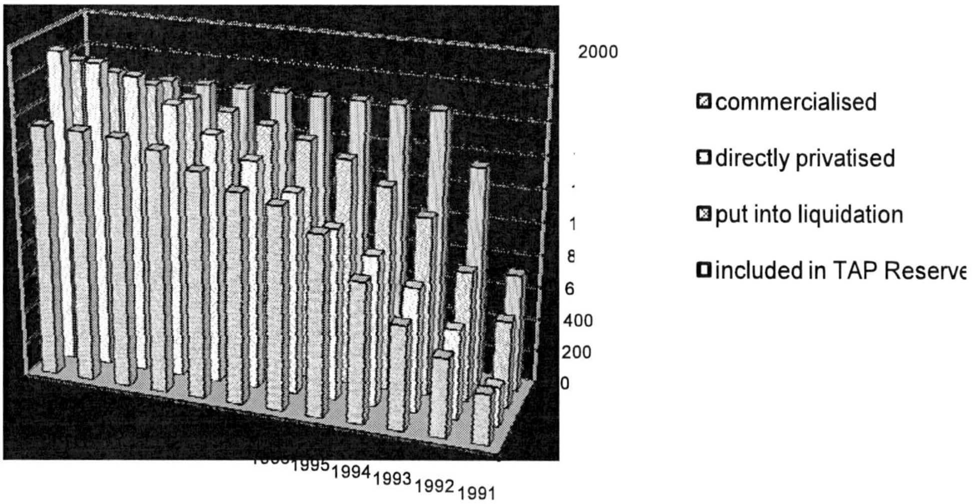

Figure 4. Privatisation of state enterprises in the years 1991-2002.

Out of the commercialised companies, 330 underwent further capital privatisation, i.e., controlling interests in them were sold to strategic investors, including 111 foreign investors. A significant element of this type of privatisation is the strategic investor's agreement to additional stipulations concerning outlays on modernisation and technological progress, environmental protection, increasing initial capital, social obligations, and obligations as to the size and structure of production. Out of foreign strategic investors, Germans were the biggest buyers of capital of Polish companies, followed by those from the USA and France. They were mostly interested in companies manufacturing goods from non-metallic raw materials (11.3% of companies privatised indirectly with the participation of foreign capital) as well as food and beverages (9.3%). At the end of 2002, capital-privatised companies employed a total of 242,300 people (cf. Table 1), of whom 81,500 worked in those with the participation of foreign capital. Those companies, both with foreign and exclusively domestic capital, showed the most successful economic performance out of all privatised enterprises.

Out of the 512 companies selected for the National Investment Funds (NIF) programme, at the close of 2002 the Treasury still had a stake in 348 of them while it had sold all its shares in 146. 24 NIF companies with the participation of the Treasury were actors on the capital market (mostly by being listed on the Warsaw Stock Exchange), 7 were being wound-up, and 82 were undergoing proceedings in bankruptcy. NIF companies employed a total of 124,900 people (cf. Table 1). In terms of size, these were entities much smaller than when the NIF programme had first been launched (cf. Table 2) - more than a half of them employed between 100 and 499 workers, while the enterprises joining the programme had been very large, with more than a half employing in excess of 500 people. However, NIF companies perform poorly in comparison with other privatised units.

Highly effective, in turn, has been direct privatisation which (under the State Enterprise Commercialisation and Privatisation Act of 1997) consists in the sale of the assets of the enterprise being privatised, or bringing them into a company, or putting them to use against payment. By the end of 2002, this type of privatisation had embraced a total of 1,998 state enterprises, of which in 1,911 the process had been completed. Most firms privatised in this way were in the voivodeships of Mazovia (224), Lower Silesia (190), Silesia (172), and Wielkopolska (168); the data for all voivodeships are presented in Figure 5.

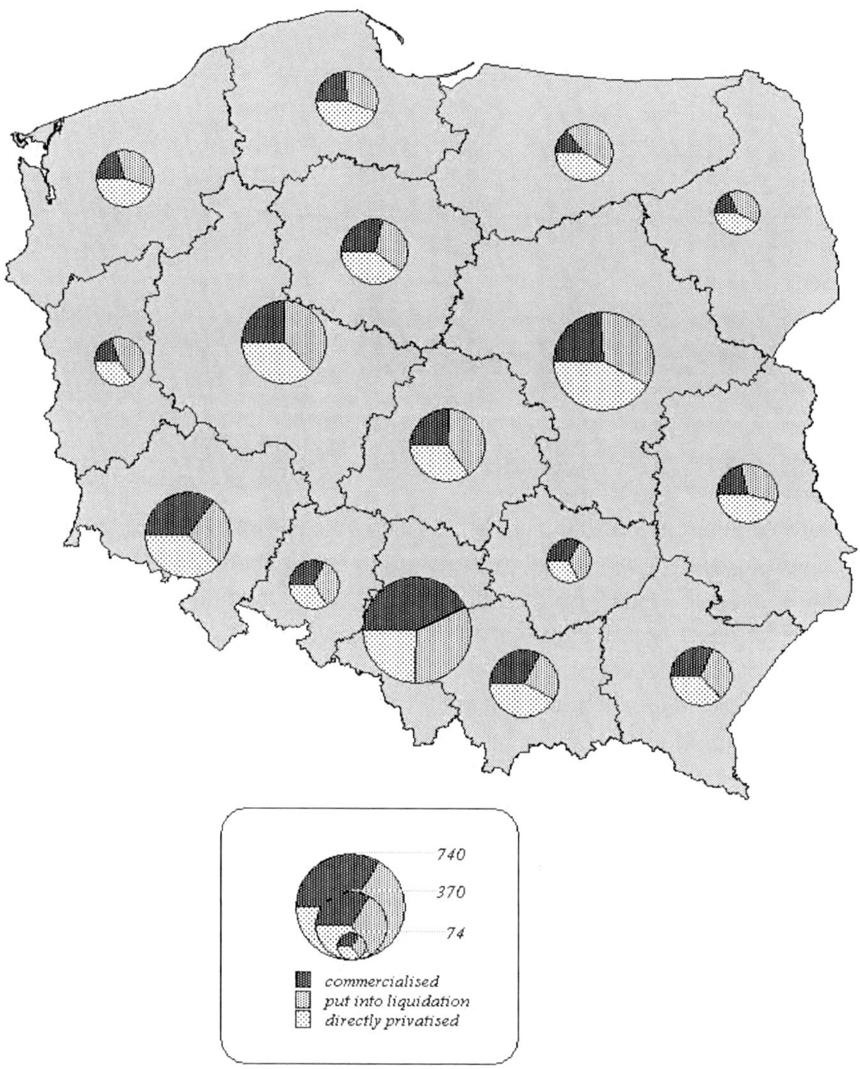

Figure 5. Number of State enterprises privatised by 31 December 2002, by voivodeship.

The direct privatisation path is usually reserved for enterprises whose workforce does not exceed 499 (cf. Table 2). Those forming the greatest proportion in them (36.8%) are ones classed under manufacturing, with 22.2% made up by construction firms, and 16.7% by trade and repair establishments. The most popular way of disposing of the assets of the privatised enterprises was giving them to employee partnerships for use against payment. Over the years 1990-2002 this mode of disposal was employed in 65.4% of cases, i.e. in 1,249 state enterprises. In the case of 193 enterprises, or 10.1% of the total number of units privatised in this way, their property had been brought into mixed companies (i.e. ones with the participation of the Treasury), and in the case of 415 units, or 21.7%, sold. The structure of enterprises privatised in the various direct ways (as of 31 December 2002) is presented in the diagram in Figure 6.

The procedure employed in the case of enterprises in bad economic condition is liquidation. By the end of 2002, 1,795 state enterprises had been put into liquidation, with the proceedings completed in only 852. The biggest number of enterprises were wound up in Silesia (114), Mazovia (87), and Wielkopolska (76) (cf. Figure 7).

The assets of enterprises that had been privatised directly and liquidated were used to set up mixed companies and employee partnerships. Over the years 1990-2002, there appeared 235 mixed companies, including 58 with the participation of foreign investors. The most numerous were manufacturing units (137), with 46 where foreign capital had a stake. By the end of 2002, only 163 of them still carried on (including almost all with the participation of foreign capital), employing a total of 44,100 people (cf. Table 1).

Table 2. Structure of privatised economic entities by employment

Economic entities	**Percentage of entities employing:**			
	up to 19 workers	**20-99 workers**	**100-499 workers**	**over 500 workers**
Total	13.1	30.2	41.5	15.2
of which:				
Treasury's sole-shareholder companies after commercialisation	4.0	11.8	53.8	30.4
Companies set up after conversion of liabilities	7.7	38.4	53.9	-
NIF companies	10.8	16.7	54.6	17.9
Capital-privatised companies	6.3	15.6	40.4	37.7
Companies with Treasury's participation after direct privatisation	14.8	28.0	44.5	12.7
Employee partnerships	14.9	46.8	33.9	4.4
State enterprises undergoing privatisation	47.1	17.6	23.5	11.8

Source: *Prywatyzacja ...* (2003).

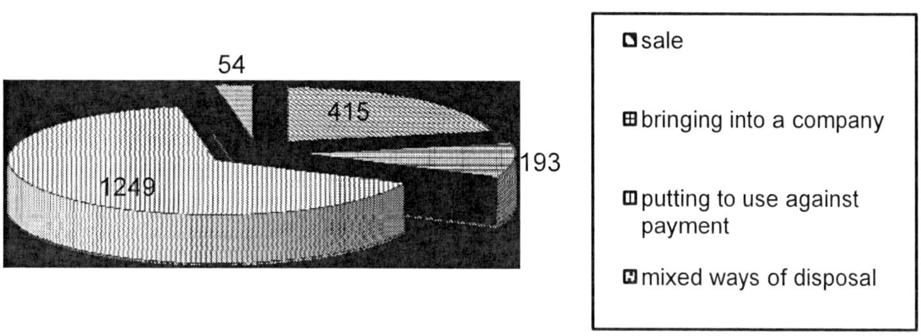

Figure 6. Number of enterprises privatised in various direct ways (as of 31 December 2002).

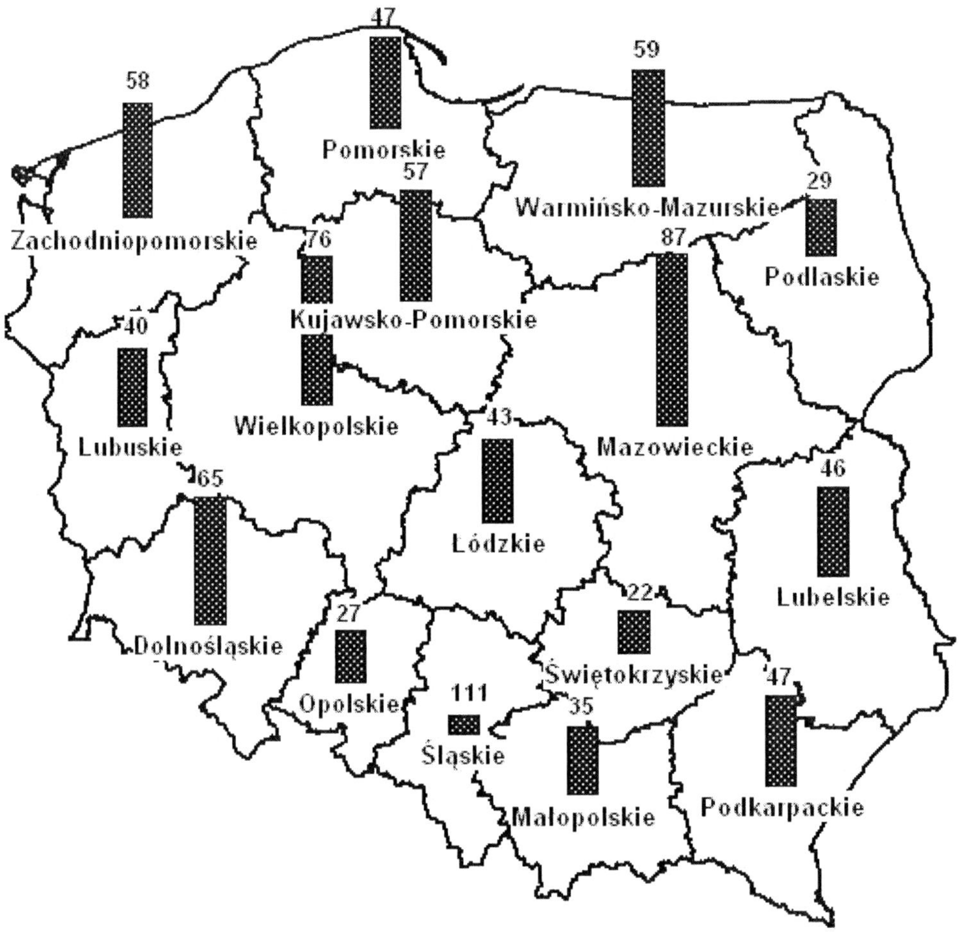

Figure 7. Number of enterprises liquidated by 31 December 2002, by voivodeship.

In the study period, 1,492 employee partnerships were established that used the assets of former state enterprises against payment. The biggest proportion of them were manufacturing units (29.2%), there was also a large share of construction firms (24.6%) as well as trade and repair shops (23.1%). Employee partnerships showed a comparatively good performance among privatisation-generated entities. Regional differences in the number of companies established by bringing in the assets of directly privatised and liquidated state enterprises are presented in Figure 8.

By the end of 2002, there were still 1,411 state enterprises in Poland employing a total of 213,300 people. Most of them (43.2%) were manufacturing plants of medium size, i.e. employing up to 99 workers. According to the Treasury data, their economic condition was very poor; more than a half (763) were being put into liquidation or were undergoing proceedings in bankruptcy. However, in 253, or 17.9%, no restructuring measures had been undertaken. Only 38 were undergoing direct privatisation, and these were small enterprises with a total employment of 2,500 (cf. Table 1). The biggest number of state enterprises can still be found in Mazovia (245) and Silesia (240) as well as Łódź voivodeship (143) and Małopolska (116). The distribution of still active state enterprises in the particular voivodeships is presented in Figure 9.

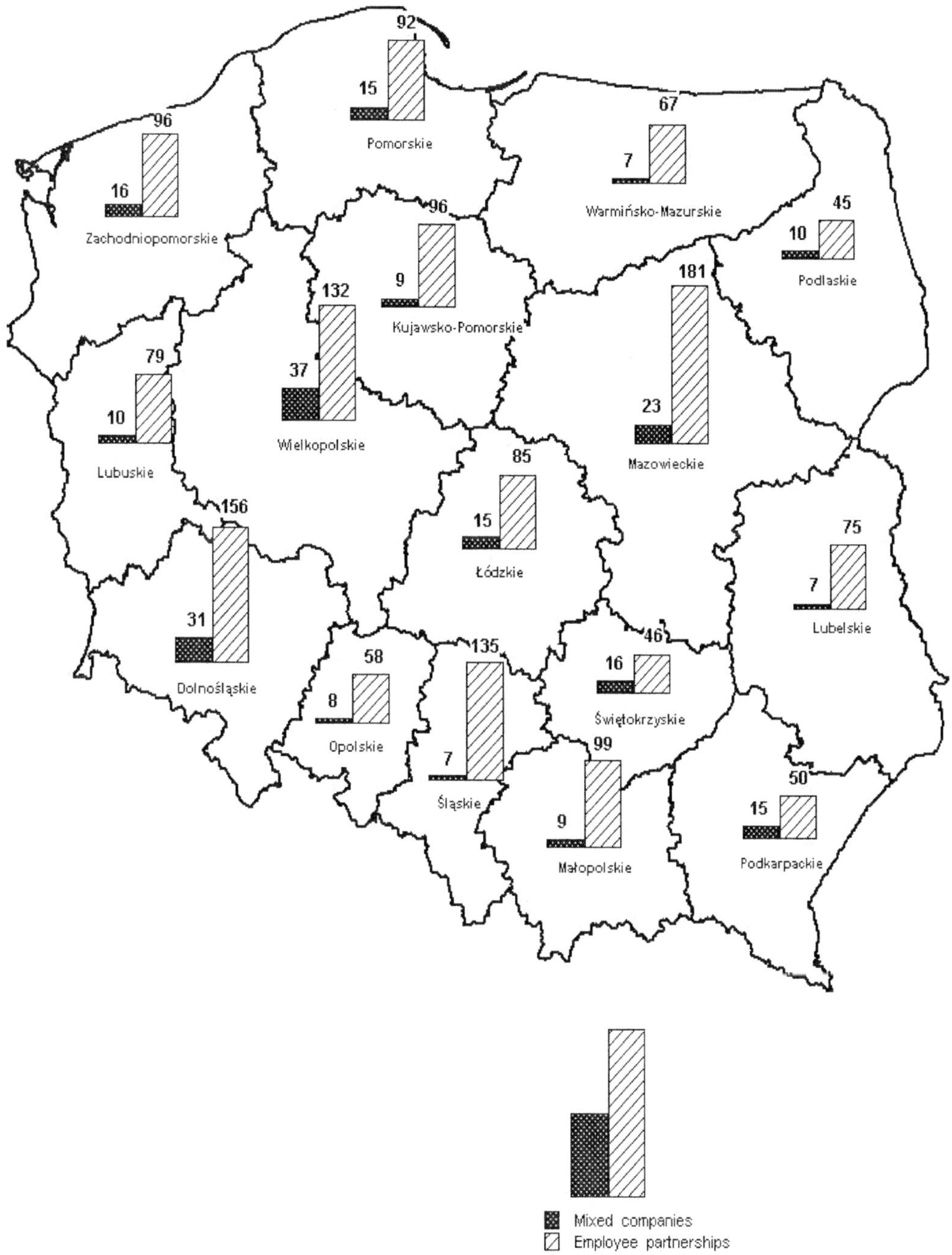

Figure 8. Companies established by 31. December 2002 using the assets of directly privatised and liquidated state enterprises, by voivodeship.

It should be noted, however, that the poor economic performance of state enterprises results from the fact that those chosen for sale to investors under the privatisation programme were profitable ones, while the state has been left with those for which a buyer is hard to find due to their very difficult situation.

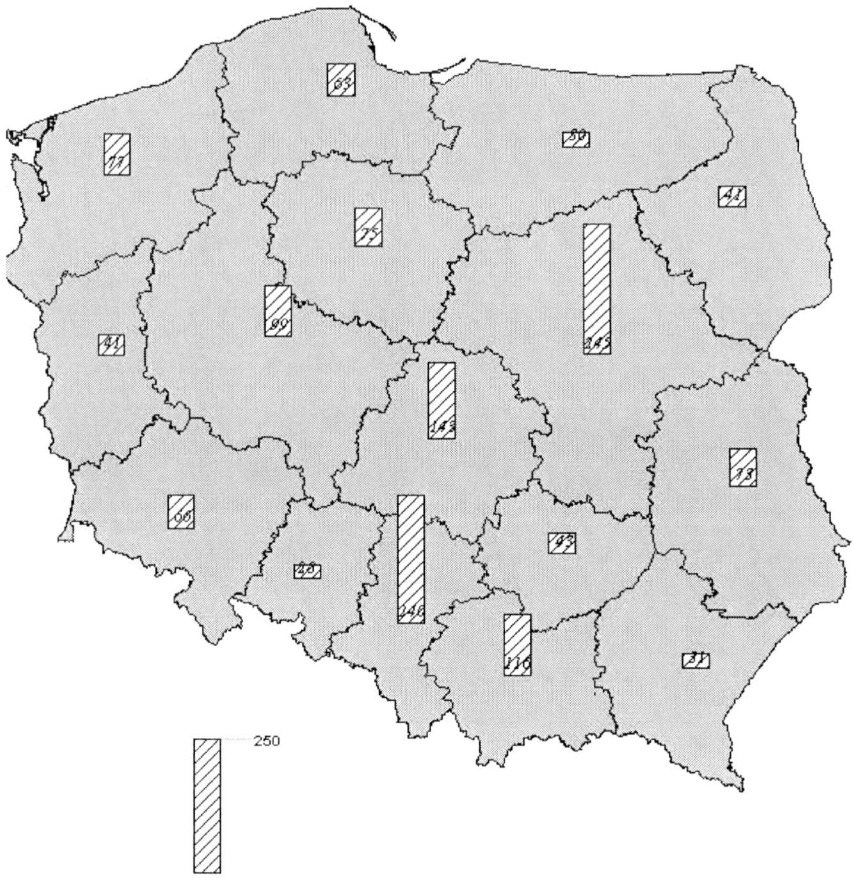

Figure 9. Number of state enterprises by voivodeship (as of 31 December 2002).

Privatisation of the Economy of a Big City: The Case of Poznań

The process of privatisation in the Polish economy has followed different regional patterns. Its rate has been affected by a number of factors, not only the state's macroeconomic policy and its legal regulations, but also the socio-economic situation of the individual regions or towns (cf. Matykowski, Szulc 1994). Creativity and the spirit of entrepreneurship, or readiness to risk a new activity, are often conditioned by historical and cultural tradition as well as the operation of various special institutions (cf. Czyż 1993). The differences in the adaptive ability of the regional industrial and economic subsystems in the period of transition to a market economy have been studied, among others, by Kukliński and Szul (1990) as well as Matykowski and Stryjakiewicz (1992). In the opinion of Czyż, Matykowski and Rogacki (1992), the region in which advantageous changes in the socio-economic structure even preceded those occurring at the national scale was the then Poznań voivodeship with Poznań itself as its chief urban-industrial centre. Poznań has nearly 600,000 inhabitants, 85,451 economic entities were based there in June 2003, and its industrial employment alone exceeds 60,000. In the initial stage of the economic transformation, the city boasted a faster rate of private sector development than the other regions of Poland. In June 2003, this sector included 83,576 economic entities, which constituted 97.8% of all entities registered in the city. Only four other, the largest, cities in Poland surpassed Poznań in this respect: Warsaw (264,534), Cracow (98,581), Wrocław (89,222), and Łódź (88,191). In terms of employment, however, Poznań ranked third, after Warsaw and Cracow: in June 2003 the city's private businesses employed a total of 122,400 people, as against 502,600 in Warsaw and 133,700 in Cracow.

Ownership changes in state enterprises, winding-up, mergers and splits, as well as the establishment of brand new firms have made the statistics of economic entities registered in the city change from year to year. There has been a general decline in the number of state enterprises and an increase in all kinds of commercial companies, both in the private and public sectors.

Table 3. Changes in the number of economic entities in Poznań by sector and ownership, 1991-2003

Number of entities	1991	1992	1993	1994	1995	2000	June 2003
Total	15,987	23,903	63,602	64,531	62,984	80,526	85,451
Public sector,of which:	884	1,064	1,077	1,078	1,065	2,044	1,875
State enterprises	236	-	156	150	124	64	61
Private sector,of which:	15,103	22,839	62,525	63,453	61,919	78,482	83,576
Companies with participation of foreign capital	240	427	589	749	1,102	1,887	2,104
Natural persons engaged in economic activity	14	22,412	61,936	52,277	48,137	58,481	63,534

Source: Own compilation on the basis of data from the Poznań Voivodeship Statistical Office.

The number of economic entities registered in Poznań in June 2003 was up 69,464 from 1991, i.e. it increased more than fivefold. The biggest increase (almost fourfold) took place in the initial stage of the transformation, between 1991 and 1993. The changes in the number of economic entities in Poznań are presented in Table 3.

The net balance of the number of economic entities in the study period was due primarily to the sharp increase in private businesses from 15,103 in 1991 to 83,576 in June 2003. In the public sector, the number of state enterprises dropped from 236 in 1991 to 61 in June 2003. The bulk of private businesses are those owned by natural persons; their number was rising steeply until 1993 to a peak of 61,936, later to fluctuate widely due to people registering a business but failing to undertake any activity, or due to winding-up because of the inability to face the hard rules of the market and too stiff competition. As a result, the number of firms owned by natural persons dwindled to 48,137 in 1995, to increase again to 63,534 in June 2003. The most numerous among them are trading establishments and estate agencies. In turn, the private sector registered an increase in the number of commercial companies and private partnership, including those with the participation of foreign capital. The most numerous among manufacturing companies with the participation of foreign capital are those with German capital (34.8% in 1998), followed by those with Dutch, French, Swedish, Belgian, US, and British capital (cf. Table 4).

Table 4. Commercial companies with the participation of foreign capital in Poznań's manufacturing

	1995		1996		1997		1998	
	number	%	number	%	number	%	number	%
Totalof which with:	272	100	300	100	324	100	336	100
German capital	93	34.2	93	31.0	111	34.3	117	34.8
Dutch capital	16	5.9	20	6.7	21	6.5	24	7.1
French capital	16	5.9	16	5.3	20	6.2	20	6.0
Swedish capital	13	4.8	14	4.7	16	4.9	14	4.2
Belgian capital	15	5.5	15	5.0	16	4.9	14	4.2
US capital	11	4.0	13	4.3	13	4.0	14	4.2
British capital	6	2.2	7	2.3	9	2.8	11	3.3

Source: *Sytuacja społeczno-gospodarcza Poznania w IV kwartale 1966, 1997, 1998 roku.*

Most foreign investment consists in the buying of shares in manufacturing enterprises. That is how well-known industrial brands representing a variety of lines have appeared in Poznań, e.g.: Corn Product Corporation, EXIDE, Nestle, Reemtsma, Beiersdorf, Bridgestone-Firestone, Volkswagen, the Swedish concern SKF, or Glaxo Wellcome, later after a merger, GlaxoSmithKline.

When analysing ownership changes in Poznań's biggest industrial plants, one can notice that they have chosen widely differing privatisation paths and as a result, after the first decade of the transformation, their advancement in this matter varies. Privatisation is least advanced in Poznań's largest manufacturing enterprise, H. Cegielski-Poznań PLC (known as the HCP), formerly the H. Cegielski Metal-Processing Enterprise. It is still at the commercialisation stage and keeps looking for a strategic investor, which is no easy task considering its size (in 1990, a workforce of over 7,000) and a very unwieldy organisation (in 1990 it consisted of nine separate factories, four other subsidiary service shops, several branches outside the city, and a huge social benefit system including a hospital, a transport base, residential buildings, holiday resort homes, etc.). It should be noted, however, that after the Cegielski had been transformed into a joint-stock company, attempts have been made to adjust the firm's manufacturing and organisation to the new economic rules: eight companies have been set up with the HCP having a 100% stake in them. The factories that have remained are those of key importance to the firm: Marine Engines, Mechanical Equipment, Precision Industrial Products, Rolling Stock, and Diesel Engines and Generating Sets. The firm has also disposed of its transport base and social benefit system, starting with the school, hospital, kindergartens and cruches, residential buildings, and holiday resorts. As a result, by the end of 1996 the HCP workforce dropped to 4,254, and after further restructuring measures, to 2,500 in 2002. This strategy was intended not only to simplify the organisational structure of the firm, but also to allow the disposal of those objects that could be sold or leased. As early as 1997 the building that used to house the liquidated Machine Tool Factory was hired to Volkswagen Poznań for the manufacture of car spares. Besides, by focusing on production in engine factories, it was easier to undertake steps towards their privatisation. The firm's latest moves have been establishing co-operation with the Rostock shipyard, which is supposed to enhance the production of engines and the transport of their parts to the coast, and negotiations to transfer the management of the Rolling Stock Factory to the Municipal Transport Company.

The situation is a bit different for the 11 Poznań-based enterprises qualified to take part in the National Investment Funds (NIF) programme; their list is presented in Table 5. Until 1995, transformed into Treasury's sole-shareholder companies, they awaited a further government programme, and when the NIF programme had been launched, majority shareholdings in each of them were transferred to the Funds. One of the assumptions of the NIF programme was the restructuring of the enterprises taken over by the Funds and facilitating access to domestic and foreign sources of capital. However, the only change registered so far among the manufacturing enterprises of this group has been the change of the owner of the Pollena-Lechia Cosmetics Plant and the sale of a majority shareholding in this company to the German concern Beiersdorf in September 1997. In the Modena Clothing Works, whose controlling interest had been transferred to NIF 6, it was only in November 1998 that a new strategy was worked out, and its main points were an increase in the manufacture of own-label clothes, an increase in the number of factory outlets, the introduction of new collections, and a reduction in operating costs by, among other things, a reduction in employment. As a result of this strategy, the factory has been closed down in Poznań and transferred to a branch at Środa Wielkopolska, while its Poznań premises, the factory's property since the 1920s, have been sold.

Table 5. Poznań-based enterprises taking part in the National Investment Funds (NIF) programme (1995 data)

Enterprise	NIF no.
1. Pollena-Lechia Cosmetics Plant	8
2. Poznań-Północ Building Corporation	13
3. POZBAC Fodder Plant	8
4. Pe-Ka-BEX Poznań Building Corporation	11
5. Poznań Roadwork Enterprise	8
6. ELBUD Electrical Power Building Enterprise	5
7. Communication Work Enterprise in Poznań	9
8. POMET Metallurgical Plant	8
9. Rolling-Stock Repair Shop	8
10. Modena Clothing Works	5
11. POLON Research and Industrial Equipment Works in Poznań	5

Source: Materials of the Poznań Representation of the Ministry of Privatisation.

When analysing ownership changes in Poznań's biggest industrial plants, the most effective path seems to have been individual privatisation by the sale of shares to a strategic investor (cf. Tobolska A., 1997, Matykowski R., Tobolska A., 2000). This is how the Amino Concentrated Food Plant was privatised, with the sale of 80% of its shares to the Corn Product Corporation in 1992; as a result of further mergers and takeovers, since 2001 it has belonged to the Unilever concern. In May 1993, the Polmo Agricultural Vehicle Factory at Antoninek signed an investment contract and entered into a joint venture with Germany's Volkswagen; since 2003, as a result of the concern's substantial investment, e.g. the construction of a modern paint shop, the company has been the biggest industrial plants in Poznań with a workforce of more than 4,000. In May 1994, a 75% stake in Poznań's Centra Accumulator Plant was bought by the French firm CEAC - Compagne Europeenne d'Accumulateurs, which in turn was taken over together with Centra by the EXIDE concern in 1996. In 1994 the Swiss concern Nestle acquired a majority shareholding in the Goplana Chocolate Works, while in 1996 the German Reemtsma bought one in the Tobacco Products Plant. One of the last big privatisation acts with the participation of a foreign strategic investor was the sale of 80% of shares in Polfa, the Poznań pharmaceutical factory, to Glaxo Wellcome (later GlaxoSmithKline after a merger) in January 1998. For the Pozmeat Meat Works and LECH Wielkopolska Breweries, the strategic investor has been Polish capital. 60% of Pozmeat shares were bought in 1993 by a capital group consisting of the plant's management, workers, and local investors, and it was only in 1996 that a joint venture with the American concern Hormel Foods Corporation was formed. Its capital served to modernise the machinery, but primarily to build a new plant at Robakowo near Poznań. As to the LECH Breweries, its shares were bought in August 1993 by the Euro Agro Centrum, a company owned by J. Kulczyk, who sold a part of them to the African concern SAB in 1996 thus forming the Kompania Piwna (Beer Company). By purchasing a 75% stake in the Tyskie Breweries, the Beer Company has acquired one-third of the beer market share in Poland.

The advantage of privatisation through the sale of a controlling interest in a company to a strategic investor is undoubtedly the influx of substantial capital to it. This means new investments for the company in the form of modernisation of the machinery, modern manufacturing technologies, and the liquidation of unprofitable departments. An example is the former Amino Concentrated Food Plant, in which after the sale of its shares to the CPC corporation the Pasta Department had been wound up while expanding the ready-to-eat food division and introducing new brands, like Knorr and Hellmann's. Other examples of investment by new owners of old Poznań state enterprises include greenfield investment and the construction of completely new buildings at new locations. As soon as the late 1998, the new owner of the cigarette plant, the Reemtsma corporation, moved the entire factory from Wojskowa Street in the centre of Poznań to the suburban commune of Tarnowo Podgórne and sold the downtown premises to a housing-estate co-operative. The new owners of the Pozmeat plant have built a modern factory at Robakowo near Poznań, while the old downtown buildings of historic merit have been turned into a recreational-shopping centre. Another greenfield investment has been the new factory constructed at Janikowo near Poznań by Bridgestone Firestone, the new owner of the old, pre-war Poznań tyre and rubber goods plant, Stomil. Major new greenfield investments by foreign entrepreneurs also include the building of a fish-processing plant by the German firm Liesner, a US chewing-gum works by Wrigley, and a German chocolate works, Stollwerck, taken over by the Kraft corporation in the late 1990s.

The Polish Rural Areas: A Field of Consolidation and Privatisation

The systemic transformation in Poland has brought about a total disappearance of state farming, which used to be a permanent feature of the Polish countryside for almost 40 years since the change of regime after the Second World War and collectivisation. The introduction of free prices for agricultural produce in 1989 and of a market economy in 1990 revealed all the organisational and social weaknesses of state farms: too heavily subsidised production, inefficient systems of organisation and central management, overemployment, over-investment (mainly a large number of buildings), and too heavy a load of social functions.

The transformation in state agriculture started with the introduction of a new act of 19 October 1991, On the Management of Treasury's Agricultural Property, and the setting up of the Treasury's Agricultural Property Agency (TAPA) on 1 January 1992. It is a trust institution endowed by the Treasury with rights to state agricultural property in order to improve the size structure of farms and take over all state land for further development. The first stage in the restructuring and ownership transformation was the taking over of state property by the Treasury's Agricultural Property Reserve (TAP Reserve). From the start of the Agency's operation to the end of December 2002, the TAP Reserve amassed a total of 4,705,000 ha, including 3,759,400 ha of land from liquidated state farms and 608,100 ha of land belonging to the State Land Fund (which had been set up in the times of the Polish People's Republic from unwanted land that farmers handed over to the state in return for state pensions). Out of this total acreage, 84.2% was farmland, 3.6% woodland and tree-covered land, and 7.3% lakes and ponds.

The land takeover was the most extensive in North-Western Poland, in the voivodeships of Warmia-Mazuria (815,800 ha) and West Pomerania (811,000 ha), i.e. areas incorporated into Poland after the Second World War and settled by people expatriated from the eastern regions that Poland had lost then. A detailed spatial distribution of land taken over by the Agency is presented in Figure 10.

Together with land, the Agency came into possession of other assets of former state farms: workers' flats, farm buildings, agricultural-industrial plants, shops and service units, as well as mansions, palaces and parks of historic value. The total worth of the property was estimated in 1997 at $4.7 billion (after Zgliński 1999). The land and assets taken over by the Agency have been restructured and privatised in a variety of ways. The most popular has been obtaining new owners for the property, i.e. its sale, gratuitous transference, or bringing into an Agency company. By the end of 2002, a total of 1,559,500 ha had been disposed of in this way, of which 1,272,000 ha had been sold; 243,900 ha had been transferred gratuitously; 15,00 ha had been brought into companies; and the title to 10,700 ha had been changed from perpetual usufruct to property rights. Most land was sold in Warmia-Mazuria (238,700 ha) and West Pomerania (191,400 ha) (cf. Figure 10). The buyers were largely private farmers a majority of whom purchased less than 1 ha of land. Only a mere 1% bought more than 100 ha; among them were artificial persons, including banks, which had bought state farms for their liabilities (cf. Zgliński 1999).

At the end of 2002, the Reserve still possessed 3,145,500 ha, or 66.9% of all land transferred to it. The basic form of its disposal was tenancy - 2,407,500 ha, or 76.5% of all Reserve land. Perpetual usufruct accounted for 74,500 ha, permanent management for 37,100 ha, and administration for 4,800 ha. The principal forms of disposal of the land included in the TAP Reserve are presented in the diagram in Figure 11.

The basic form of the TAP Reserve land disposal has been tenancy. As has been established by Zgliński (1999), a vast majority (about 90%) of tenancy contracts involve plots up to 10 ha, but in terms of acreage they constitute only a slight percentage of all land leased. 80% of its total area has become part of very big farms, of more than 500 ha. The tenants are private farmers, employee co-operatives usually belonging to the former state-farm management staff, and other enterprises, such as banks and ventures with the participation of foreign capital (mainly German, Dutch, Danish, British, and French). Tenancy is also the dominant form of management of Reserve-owned assets other than land, like distilleries, wineries, breweries, forage driers, fodder mixers, slaughterhouses, as well as sports and cultural facilities, mansions, and palace and park complexes. 80% of lakes and nearly 50% of ponds of former state fish farms are under lease. Since the mid-1990s, however, there has been a growing tendency to return the leased land. At the close of 2002, 2,407,500 ha were still under lease, down 520,000 ha from 1996.

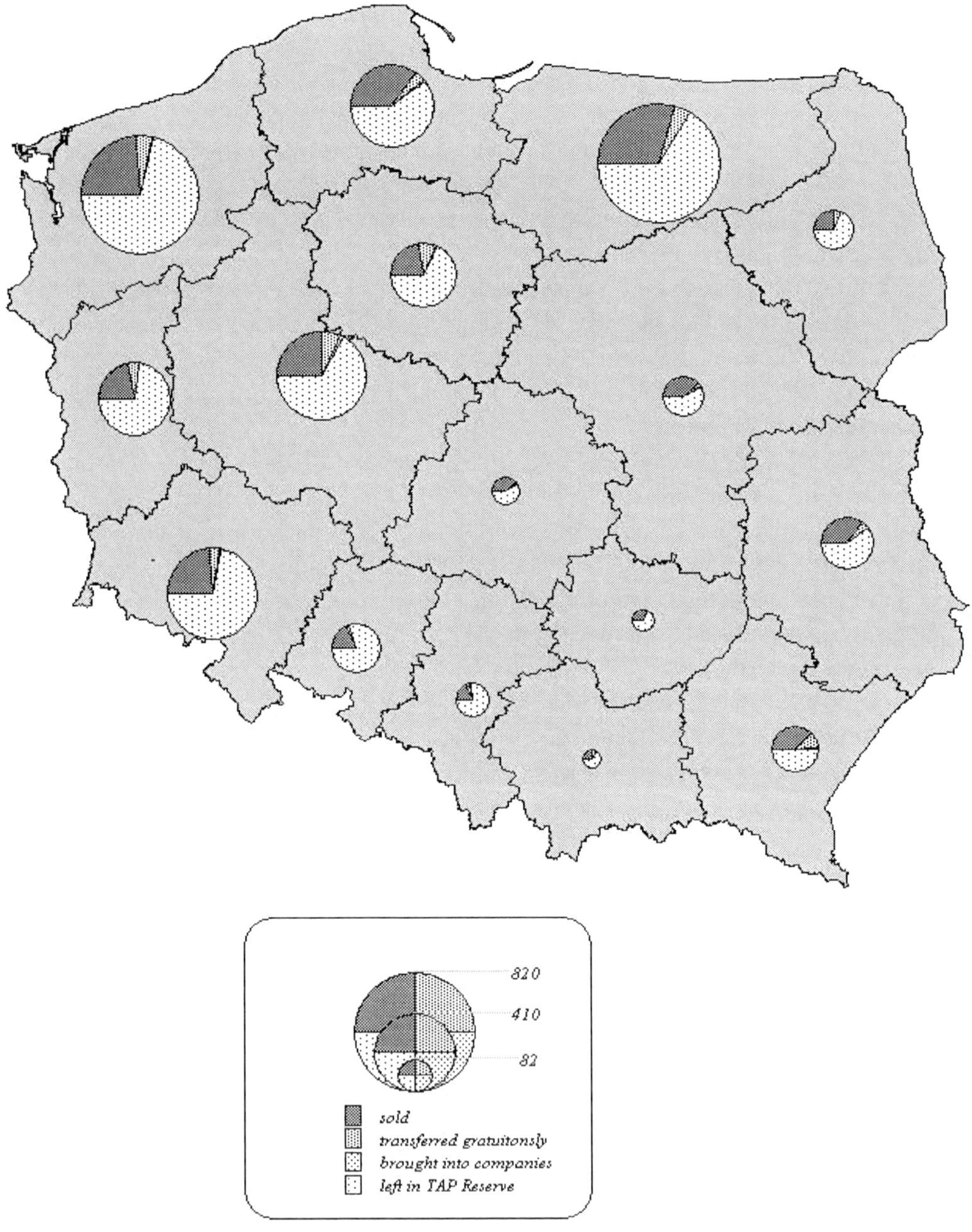

Figure 10. Land taken over by the Treasur's Agricultural Property Reserve, as of 31 December 2002 (thous. ha).

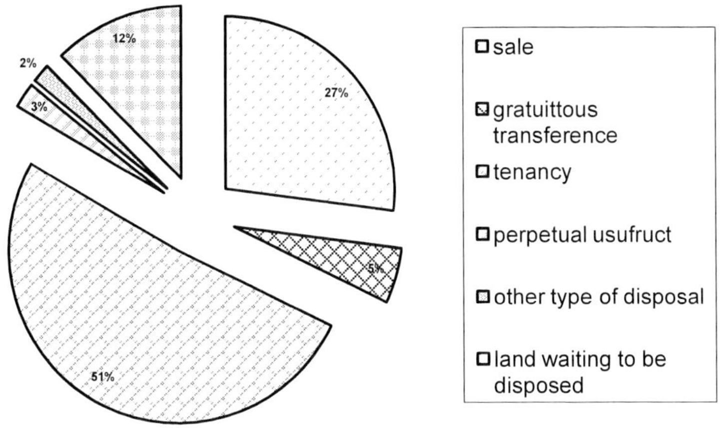

Figure 11. Forms of disposal of land included in the Treasury" Agricultural Property Reserve in 2002.

As a result of the privatisation of state farming, the structure of Polish agriculture has changed: the total area of state farms dwindled from 5,326,000 ha in 1987 to 2,842,000 in 2001, while the average size of a private farm grew from 5.8 ha to 8.0 ha between 1987 and 2001. The liquidation of state farms has produced a substantial drop in employment, especially in north-western Poland where most of them were located. The 260,000 people or so who had lost their jobs in this way were treated with complete indifference: they were neither offered shares in the privatised entities they had worked for, nor were compensated, as was the case when other sectors of the economy were being privatised, e.g. industry or telecommunications. The rural unemployment resulting from the liquidation of state farms has been a serious social and economic problem, because apart from their strictly agricultural functions they performed a lot of other important roles: in many areas they set up rural settlement and infrastructural networks, developed social and cultural functions, and ensured employment to 440,000 workers, thus providing subsistence to 2 million people (the workers plus their families). With attention focused on privatisation and improvement in performance, the scale of the social effects of the transformation has been underestimated. The dramatic decline in the standards of living of the former state-farm labourers as a result of the ensuing structural unemployment has been accompanied by the frittering away and liquidation of the social infrastructure and the socio-economic marginalisation of state-farm settlements.

PRIVATISATION PLANS: INVESTORS ARE WELCOME

Privatisation has been the fundamental element of economic reforms designed to build a whole new political and socio-economic system in Poland. An important aim has also been an increase in budgetary revenues as a result of sale of shares in companies, so far state-owned. Since 2001 there has been a slackening in the privatisation rate, and therefore a slump in the anticipated receipts. In 1999 the proceeds from privatisation amounted to 13 billion zlotys, as against 26.7 billion in 2000, a mere 6.5 billion in 2001, and 2.2 billion in 2002 (after Łakoma A., 2003a). By November 2003, the proceeds equalled 1.7 billion zlotys and came largely from the sale of shares in two Polmos liquor plants, in Siedlce and Zielona Góra, the Limestone Works at Trzuskawica, and the Silesian Sugar Company, among newly privatised enterprises. However, most of the 2003 proceeds came from the privatisation programme continued from the previous years: the sale of successive blocks of shares in the Upper Silesian Power Plant, the thermal-power plants at Toruń and Połaniec, and the rest of shares in the Rybnik Power Plant to E.D.F. International and EnBW Energie Würtemberg (after Łakoma, 2003b). This year's privatisation plans announced by the Treasury also include the sale of shares in Telekomunikacja Polska (among others, to France Tйlйcom, the co-owner of the company) and an 85% stake in the so-called G-8, a group of eight power plants. There are also plans to sell the remaining 4% of shares in Orbis, the company running hotels in Poland, to the French hotel-keepers, Accor. There is also a privatisation procedure in progress involving seven PKS companies, the largest transport firms in Poland, in which the Treasury has majority shareholdings. The plans include the sale of three pharmaceutical firms from Warsaw, Tarchomin and Pabianice, which are planning to form a pharmaceutical holding in order to float their stock on the exchange later on. But an equally probable variant of their privatisation is sale to strategic investors. In 2004, making their dйbut on the Warsaw Stock Exchange will be the PKO BP bank, the Southern Power Engineering Concern with the Bytom, Zabrze, Tychy and Stalowa Wola thermal-power plants, and Polish Oil Mining and Gas Engineering, which chiefly expects to find financial investors. Shares in PZU, the biggest Polish insurance company, and the Enea Group of five power plants (from Poznań, Gorzów, Szczecin, Bydgoszcz, and Zielona Góra) are being prepared for public trading. The Ministry is planning to complete privatisation procedures in the spirits industry by the end of 2004; it is going to seek investors for the Polmos plants at Józefów, Bielsko-Biała, and Toruń. The 2004 plans also include the start of privatisation of the Polish Press Agency and the Polski Cukier Domestic Sugar Company with the participation of sugar-beet planters. Awaiting their turn are fuel firms, nitrogen works, and the Polish Airlines LOT.

References

Balicki A., 1994. Postępy i efekty prywatyzacji. [w:] *Wiadomości Statystyczne nr* 1/94, s.9-13.

Czyż T., 1993. Procesy prywatyzacji w miastach województwa poznańskiego. [w:] *Ruch Prawniczy, Ekonomiczny i Socjologiczny*, rok LV, z.3., s.73- 84.

Czyż T., Matykowski R., Rogacki H., 1992. Przejawy ożywienia społeczno- gospodarczego w województwie poznańskim. [w:] *Biuletyn PAN KPZK nr* 159, Warszawa.

Domański B., 2001. *Kapitał zagraniczny w przemyśle Polski.UJ,* Instytut Geografii i Gospodarki Przestrzennej, Kraków.

Domaszewicz Z., 1998. Porządki w portfelu. *Gazeta Wyborcza z* 26.06.1998, s.32.

Jałowiecki B., Mync A. (red.), 1994. *Przedsiebiorczość i prywatyzacja*. Biulety PAN KPZK, 168.

Kostecka D., Grzeszczak R., 2001. *Prywatyzacji wciąż pod górkę*. Nowe Życie Gospodarcze nr 14/306

Kostrz – Kostrzewska A., 1995. Jak NFI *wpłynie na rynek kapitałowy.* Rzeczpospolita nr 152/95.

Karwowska M.A., Krause A., 1997. Prywatyzacja bezpośrednia czyli sprzedaż przedsiębiorstwa. *Rzeczpospolita* z 8.01.1997.

Kukliński A., Szul R., 1990. Powstawanie nowej przestrzeni przemysłowej w Polsce.[w:] *Gospodarka Narodowa*, 2-3, s.24-27.

Łakoma A., 2003a. Lepiej będzie w grudniu. *Rzeczpospolita* z 31.07.03.

Łakoma A., 2003b. Państwowe firmy na giełdę. *Rzeczpospolita* z 1.09.03.

Matykowski R., Szulc R., 1994. Przekształcenia własnościowe przedsiębiorstw państwowych w województwie poznańskim. [w:] Z.Zioło (red.), *Funkcjonowanie przedsiębiorstw przemysłowych w zmieniających się warunkach gospodarowania*. Kraków – Warszawa, s.76-86.

Matykowski R., Stryjakiewicz T., 1992. Adaptacja przemysłu w nowych warunkach ekonomicznych Polski. [w:] Z.Zioło (red.). *Geografia przemysłu w warunkach nowego systemu gospodarowania*. Krakyw –Warszawa, s.62-76.

Matykowski R., Tobolska A., 2000. Tendencje lokalizacyjne i funkcjonowanie przedsiębiorstw przemysłowych w Poznaniu i jego strefie podmiejskiej w warunkach transformacji. [w:] J.J.Parysek, H.Rogacki (red.), *Procesy społeczno- gospodarcze w Polsce w końcu XX wieku*. Bogucki Wydawnictwo Naukowe, Poznań, s.183-199.

Misztal S., 1993. *Regionalne zróżnicowanie procesu prywatyzacji przemysłu w Polsce*. [w:] Przegląd Geograficzny, t.LXV, z.3-4.

Mojkowski J., 1996. NFI. *Ty zarobisz najmniej*. Raport. Polityka nr 21 (2038).

Pakiet Informacyjny 1-6, *Departament Narodowych Funduszy Inwestycyjnych*, 20.04.1995, Warszawa

Program Narodowych Funduszy Inwestycyjnych. *Konferencja prasowa Ministerstwa Przekształceń Własnościowych w Radio "Merkury"S.A.*, 9.11.1995, Poznań (opracowanie pisemne)

Prywatyzacja przedsiębiorstw państwowych. GUS, Warszawa 1994.

Prywatyzacja przedsiębiorstw państwowych w 2002. Informacje i opracowania statystyczne. GUS, Warszawa, 2003.

Stryjakiewicz T., 1999. Adaptacja przestrzenna przemysłu w Polsce w warunkach transformacji. Wydawnictwo Naukowe UAM, *Seria Geografia* 61, Poznań.

Surdykowska S.T., 1997. *Prywatyzacja*. Wydawnictwo Naukowe PWN, Warszawa.

Suwalski A., 1996. *Ekonomiczno- społeczne uwarunkowania przekształceń własnościowych przedsiębiorstw państwowych w Polsce w latach 1990 – 1995*. Maszynopis rozprawy doktorskiej, napisanej pod kierunkiem prof. H.Januszka, Akademia Ekonomiczna w Poznaniu.

Sytuacja społeczno- gospodarcza Poznania w IV kwartale 1996, 1997, 1998 roku. Wojewódzki Urząd Statystyczny w Poznaniu.

Szczęsny R., 1999. *Rolnictwo polskie w okresie transformacji 1988-1996*. Biuletyn PAN KPZK, z.188, s.71.

Szulc R., 1994. *Szanse i zagrożenia NFI*. Przegląd Ekonomiczny PTE.

Tobolska A., 1997.Przejawy transformacji w przemyśle województwa poznańskiego. [w:] Z.Zioło (red.), *Problemy transformacji struktur przemysłowych w procesie przechodzenia do gospodarki rynkowej*. Warszawa - Kraków.

Wilczyński W., 1994. Transformacja gospodarki polskiej 1989-1994. [w:] Ruch Prawniczy, *Ekonomiczny i Socjologiczny* nr 3/94, s.65.

Zgliński W., 1999. *Przekształcenia restrukturyzacyjno- własnościowe rolnictwa państwowego i ich wpływ na zagospodarowanie wsi i przestrzeni rolniczej*. Biuletyn PAN KPZK, z.188, s.91-115.

Zioło Z. (red.),1994. *Funkcjonowanie przedsiębiorstw przemysłowych w zmieniających się warunkach gospodarowania.* Kraków – Warszawa, s.76-86.

Z.Zioło (red.), 1997. *Problemy transformacji struktur przemysłowych w procesie przechodzenia do gospodarki rynkowej.* Materiały z Ogólnopolskiej Konferencji Naukowej, Warszawa- Krakyw.

In: Economic and Political Developments in Poland
Editor: Maureen P. Larsen
ISBN 978-1-61209-951-4

Chapter 2

POLISH INDUSTRY IN THE TRANSFORMATION PERIOD

Henryk Rogacki
Institute of Socio-Economic Geography and Spatial Management, Adam Mickiewicz University, Poznań, Poland

ABSTRACT

The article presents changes that have occurred in the industry of Poland during the economic transformation which started in 1989. The changes described concern the branch and spatial structure of industry as divided into the extractive and processing sectors. Special attention is paid to factors accounting for the processes taking place.

DEVELOPMENT AND STRUCTURAL CHANGES

The industrial revolution on the Polish lands started in the mid-19th century. Poland as a state did not exist then, because its territory had been seized by Russia, Prussia and Austria in 1795. Each of the partitioning powers pursued a different economic and social policy. 200 years after the event, the effects of a given Polish land having belonged to the particular country are still noticeable in space, in the form of differences in development, social behaviour, susceptibility to transformation processes, and level of entrepreneurship.

After Poland had regained independence in 1918, industry found itself in a difficult situation. It had suffered losses as a result of military operations while new state borders had cut it off from the markets in Russia and Germany. The difficulties were compounded by the world economic crisis of 1929-1933. A substantial jump in industrialisation was recorded in the final years before the Second World War. A serious investment effort launched in 1937 was the Central Industrial District, in which the dozen-odd plants set up before the outbreak of the war provided a basis for new manufacturing centres. The Second World War inflicted heavy losses; an estimated 65% of industrial plants suffered damage (table 1).

Table 1. War damage in industrial plants registered in 1945 in selected industries

Industries	Number of plants		Average % of damage	
	total	damaged	buil-dings	technical equip-ment
Mining	476	301	41	51
Mineral	2,296	1,802	39	47
Metals	3,355	2,420	33	52
Electrical	290	188	34	58
Chemical	819	520	36	50
Textile	1,142	553	29	39
Wood-processing	3,667	2,604	36	47
Food-processing	13,601	8,710	34	41
Power stations, gas works, water pipes	888	565	26	40
Total	30,017	19,592	35	45

Source: Industrial Yearbook, 1945-1965.

The postwar systemic changes turned Poland into a centrally planned economy controlled largely by Soviet policy. As early as 1945, obligatory state control was introduced in major plants, and after the Nationalisation Act of 1946 almost the entire economy, especially industry, passed into the hands of the state. Under the successive economic plans, principal emphasis was put on the development of the heavy industry (mining, iron and steel, power, electromechanical engineering, cement plants), while investment in consumer industries kept being postponed. This pattern of industrial development was also maintained in the 1970s, when the economy received a big injection of foreign credit. As a result, the amount of money flowing into the market, especially that earned in the heavy industry, could not be balanced against goods manufactured for the individual customer. The emptying shop shelves prompted the authorities to earmark a part of the foreign credit, not for investment, but imports in order to fill the gap in the consumer market.

Admittedly, Poland's industrial potential increased enormously between 1945 and 1980. Over the years 1950-1980, employment grew from 2.1 million to 5.2 million, and the contribution of industry to national income, from 32% to 54% (table 2). What failed to be implemented was the declared principle of a uniform distribution of industry. Some progress in this respect had been achieved, although initially the industrialisation rate was the fastest in areas with long manufacturing traditions.

Taking into consideration industry as a whole in various periods, one can state that it underwent a steady, though ever slower, dispersal. The process was the fastest in the periods 1946-1949 and 1971-1975, but it was a result of the appearance of new places of industry concentration and an increase in the industrialisation of a big number of towns. It was accompanied by relative stagnation or a regression of those that had previously achieved a very high level of industrialisation. Over the two decades from 1960 to 1980, the number of towns with industrial employment in excess of 1,000 grew from 301 to 464. It was associated with an extensive growth model, which required the expansion of manufacturing into ever new areas. In this way Polish space filled with industrial activity. Special cases include the formation of new districts or centres engaged in the extraction and processing of mineral raw materials: Konin (brown coal), Rybnik (hard coal), Tarnobrzeg (sulphur), and Legnica-Głogów (copper).

Table 2. Industrial employment, 1950-2002

Year	Employment (in thous.)
1950	2,109
1960	3,158
1970	4,453
1980	5,245
1990	4,503
1991	4,143
1992	3,784
1993	3,671
1994	3,641
1995	3,757
1996	3,730
1997	3,740
1998	3,701
1999	3,430
2000	3,223
2001	3,169
2002	2,939

Source: GUS Statistical Yearbooks.

In the 1980s Polish industry first slowed down and then slid into a recession. This was the tendency when, with its obsolete structure and technology, it was brought face to face with the market economy and its foundation, competition, in 1989. The resultant collapse of industrial production was caused by a reduced demand for means of production, competitive imports, disintegration of the COMECON, a decline in the society's purchasing power, and rapid demilitarisation of the economy.

In the years 1989-1991, industrial employment dwindled by 13%, output by 31%, and contribution to the GDP by 3.9%. These were the highest figures among all the sectors of the economy. The decline also sprang from difficulties with adapting to realistic cost accounting and self-reliant operation of plants without subsidies from the state budget (under the centrally planned economy, in some industries the subsidies exceeded the value of their output). Many factories failed and collapsed. The industries where the system of subsidies has been kept (e.g., hard-coal mining, ferrous metallurgy, the Polish Railways) have been generating big losses and require huge means (from the budget) for restructuring.

After 1991, tendencies in employment and production output changed. Since 1992, output (measured at constant prices) has been growing steadily to exceed the 1990 level by 75% in 2002. As to employment, after the slump of 1989-1992, it has been showing a slow downward tendency as a result of a faster decline in the heavy (especially extractive) industry than the increase in most of the other industries (table 3).

The share of industry in the GDP dropped from 34% to 21% over the years 1992-2002 (table 4). This indicates that structural changes in Poland have been very fast and involve a decline in the importance of manufacturing, although accompanied by an increase in industrial output. Hence the conclusion that the growth dynamics of other components of the country's economic life exceeds that of industry. This refers especially to broadly understood services.

In the recent years, industry in Poland has been steadily losing importance as a place of gainful employment. The time has come for a rational treatment of this sector of the economy and for its development to be attuned to the possibility of selling its products on the markets at home and abroad. Accordingly, many plants have closed down while others have totally changed their lines. The effect has been a gradual disappearance of industrial functions from some heretofore industrial towns and areas which in a few years' time may hardly deserve the epithet (e.g., the Tarnobrzeg sulphur district). There are also areas where the decline of industry will follow the depletion of mineral resources. Thus, the prospects facing industrial districts developed for brown coal extraction look dim (e.g., Konin and Turoszów, but also Bełchatów in the long run).

An important manifestation of change in industry has been privatisation. In 1989 almost entire production took place in public-sector plants. The proportion of this sector has been declining yearly, but it is still too big for optimum productivity.

Table 3. Employment and output dynamics in industry, 1990-2002

Years	Employment dynamics 1990 = 100	Output dynamics (constant prices, 1990 = 100
1990	100	100
1991	92	92
1992	84	95
1993	82	101
1994	81	113
1995	83	124
1996	83	134
1997	83	149
1998	82	155
1999	76	160
2000	72	171
2001	70	172
2002	66	175

Source: GUS Statistical Yearbooks.

The aim of an industrial plant, as of any economic entity, is to obtain profit. This requires low production costs or high prices of the product, or both. In a market economy with its strong competition, practically the only measures to generate profit include efforts to constantly modernise the product and lower the cost of its manufacture. These are the conditions to which Polish factories have been trying to adapt, but they face competition not only from domestic manufacturers but also foreign ones seeking a market in Poland. This international milieu has been exerting an ever stronger influence on domestic industry. Production in the most advanced countries tends to be more and more efficient, which means that the productivity of each worker increases while the consumption of materials and energy decreases. This development has radically changed the demand for Polish minerals, the more so as the process has been going on in Poland too.

Table 4. Changes in the share of industry in the Gross Domestic Product, 1992-2002

Years	Share in GDP (%)			
	Total industry	Mining and extraction	Manufacturing[a]	Power, gas and water supply[a]
1992	34.0	3.4	26.8	3.8
1993	32.9	3.7	25.2	4.0
1994	32.2	4.2	24.3	3.7
1995	28.9	4.2	21.0	3.5
1996	27.1	3.5	20.1	3.5
1997	25.8	3.1	19.7	3.0
1998	24.3	2.5	18.9	2.9
1999	23.6	2.3	18.4	2.9
2000	23.4	2.4	18.1	2.9
2001	22.3	2.2	16.9	3.2
2002	20.9	2.0	15.4	3.5

[a] Manufacturing together with power, gas and water supply are termed 'processing industry'.
Source: GUS Industrial Yearbooks.

The necessity to respond to the quickly changing patterns of demand has made the average plant size to dwindle. They are more flexible and can switch to a new line of production at lower costs. Smaller objects also have greater location freedom, hence it has become possible to locate more and more plants in villages. Some 25% of industrial workers find employment in rural areas. Entities set up in the recent years often utilise buildings vacated by liquidated enterprises. In 2002 there were 243 industrial plants in Poland with employment in excess of 1,000, down by 217 from seven years before. Equally declining was the number of plants with 500 to 1,000 workers, while those employing under 20 people were fast on the increase (table 5).

Over the transformation period, there have also been shifts in industrial branches. An analysis of the years 1989-1993 shows it to have been a period of structural regression of industry manifesting itself in a 10% increase in the share of the fuel and power industry in output. It was the result of a jump in the prices of fuels and the state's protective policy towards this industry, thanks to which the slump in its output was not as big as in the other industries. For the light industry, electromechanical engineering, and metallurgy, it was a contraction period. The downturn was especially dramatic in high-technology industry. The structural changes taking place after 1993 indicate, however, that Polish industry has been striving to become more and more modern, even though not all the unfavourable tendencies have yet been curbed.

To give a more precise description of changes, use is made of a synthetic indicator of structural transformations ranging over the interval of 0 to 1. This means that when it assumes the value 0, the structure of industry of the two periods compared has not changed at all, whereas 1 means that it has changed completely. The indicator for the years 1993-2002 equals 0.23, which shows that rather marked changes took place in that period.

The development and structural changes in Poland's industrial potential are largely connected with the transformation of large enterprises. The process includes:

- the setting up of new enterprises,
- degradation or disappearance of previously established objects,
- changes in the ownership and organisational structure of enterprises,
- changes in the line of production of enterprises,
- changes in size relations in the group of large enterprises,
- changes in relations between the volume of output and employment, and
- changes in the distribution of large enterprises.

Table 5. Industrial entities by employment

Employment	1995	2002
100-199	1,990	2,349
200-499	1,628	1,537
500-999	588	431
1,000 and over	460	243

Source: GUS 1996 Statistical Yearbook and 2003 Industrial Yearbook.

The research was carried out for two years, 1990 and 2002. The former shows the situation at the start of the systemic transformation while the latter provides the latest picture of its outcome. A comparison of these two states allowed the scale and directions of change to be determined.

The statistical basis was provided by published lists of figures characterising the 500 biggest industrial enterprises in Poland. To ensure comparability of the two time sets, only processing plants were selected (omitting, however, section 41 - collection, purification and distribution of water), adding some remarks about mining and extractive enterprises that could be formulated on the basis of other information and data concerning those objects in 2002.

The spatial analysis was carried out at two territorial scales: of the voivodeships and of localities. Changes in the number of big industrial plants[1] by voivodeship are presented in table 6. The increase in the concentration of big enterprises was most significant in Mazovia, and the decrease, in Silesia. The increase in Mazovia followed two paths: one was a growing economic strength of many firms that had not initially been included in the 500 group, and the other was the establishment of new enterprises that soon found themselves on the list. There were comparatively few enterprises in that region that had collapsed or markedly diminished their output. In Silesia, the situation was the opposite. Only occasionally were big new

[1] In the present article the term 'big enterprise' or simply 'enterprise' is taken to mean one of the list of the 500 biggest industrial enterprises in Poland.

enterprises set up, while a substantial number of existing ones showed a strong downward tendency, though few went bankrupt thanks to the system of state protection. Wielkopolska maintained its third position, with a slight increase in the number of big enterprises.

Table 6. Large industrial enterprises by voivodeship in 1990 and 2002

Voivodeship	1990		2002	
	Number of enterprises	Proportion of total number of enterprises	Number of enterprises	Proportion of total number of enterprises
Lower Silesia	39	7.8	32	6.4
Kujawy-Pomerania	35	7.0	30	6.0
Lublin	18	3.6	20	4.0
Lubuska Land	10	2.0	10	2.0
Łódź	32	6.4	25	5.0
Małopolska	41	8.2	38	7.6
Mazovia	64	12.8	103	20.6
Opole	15	3.0	14	2.8
Podkarpacie	27	5.4	28	5.6
Podlasie	9	1.8	14	2.8
Pomerania	22	4.4	24	4.8
Silesia	93	18.6	66	13.2
Świętokrzyska Land	16	3.2	13	2.6
Warmia-Mazuria	12	2.4	12	2.4
Wielkopolska	48	9.6	54	10.8
	19	3.8	17	3.4
Total	500	100.0	500	100.0

Source: own calculations on the basis of The 1990 List of 500 Enterprises of the Processing Industry, Zarządzanie, 6-7, 1991 and Polish Enterprises, The 500 List, Rzeczpospolita, 9 October 2003.

Table 7. Localities with large industrial enterprises

Type of locality	Number of localities	
	1990	2002
Towns with population over 100,000	40	40
Towns with population of 50,000-100,000	36	34
Towns with population under 50,000	112	113
Villages	18	41
Total	205	228
Localities repeating themselves in 1990 and 2002	141	

Source: as in table 6.

Generally, the level of concentration of the enterprises under study as measured by the diversification index (the number of voivodeships accounting for at least 75% of big enterprises) dropped slightly.

The 1990 and 2002 sets of localities with big industrial enterprises differ in the number of elements and their composition (table 7). The 2002 set contains more localities: 228. Both sets share 141 localities, though the number of enterprises located in them changed, of course. In the group of 41 biggest cities (over 100 thous. population), in each year there was only one city with no industrial plant (in 1990 Jastrzębie Zdrój, and in 2002, Bytom). Out of the 49 towns with a population between 50 and 100 thousand, 11 had no big enterprise in either 1990 or 2002. They included three towns of Upper Silesia as well as Przemyśl and Tarnobrzeg.

A comparison of towns that had at least five big plants in either of the years analysed (table 8) shows great shifts. There was a marked increase in Warsaw, from 38 to 64 of such plants, while their number dropped in Szczecin and Bydgoszcz (from 14 to 8) as well as Łódź and Katowice. In Poznań, Wrocław and Cracow their number had kept steady. It should be added, however, that in each case this is a balance of the development and degradation of enterprises in those cities. Out of the remaining 16 towns, 11 registered a downward tendency especially pronounced in Gliwice, Zabrze, and Gdynia. A marked increase took place only in Lublin and Bielsko-Biała.

Significant conclusions emerge when attempting to determine the relationship between the administrative function of a town and its number of industrial plants. An analysis was made of the set of 49 towns that are, or used to be until the 1998 reform, the capitals of voivodeships. Out of the 18 towns that are capitals at present, 15 met the criteria underlying the compilation of table 8. The list did not include Opole, Zielona Góra and Gorzów Wielkopolski, nor 25 of the former voivodeship seats. They all have no more than three enterprises, and moreover in most of them the number of enterprises have diminished. Six had no big plant at all (Przemyśl, Tarnobrzeg, Suwałki, Biała Podlaska, Sieradz, and Skierniewice). This goes to show that, apart from Warsaw, the administrative function had been of much less significance for the location and development of industrial plants than might have seemed from various statements suggesting a priori that institutions situated in voivodeship capitals attracted industry, which fully appreciated the weight of this factor in its hope for faster, more effective decision-making paths. This issue, however, has turned out to be much more complicated and requires a separate study that should be based on a survey research carried out among the management of big enterprises. The directions of change presented above rather indicate that the administrative function has been losing its importance, and even earlier (in 1990) it could not have been the principal factor of development of industrial plants. These conclusions are corroborated by a research conducted by Śleszyński (2003: 208-210), who observed, when analysing incomes of enterprises from various sections, that "the lowest centralisation index is characteristic of manufacturing" (61.7% of incomes in section D). The conclusions are reinforced by a steep increase in the number of villages where big industrial enterprises are located. In 1990 there were 18 of them as against 41 twelve years later, of which 34 were the headquarters of new enterprises.

Table 8. Changes in the number of large industrial enterprises in towns[a] over the period 1990-2002

Town	Number of large industrial enterprises	
	1990	2002
Warsaw	38	64
Poznań	18	18
Wrocław	15	15
Cracow	11	13
Lublin	5	10
Gdańsk	10	9
Szczecin	14	8
Bydgoszcz	14	8
Łódź	12	8
Katowice	12	7
Bielsko-Biała	4	7
Białystok	5	6
Olsztyn	5	6
Toruń	7	5
Częstochowa	6	5
Kalisz	4	5
Rzeszów	5	4
Włocławek	5	4
Gliwice	8	3J
Tarnów	6	3
Kielce	6	3
Elbląg	5	3
Gdynia	5	2
Zabrze	8	1

[a] Those towns were considered that had at least 5 enterprises in 1990 or 2002.
Source: as in table 6.

Table 9. Share of the largest industrial enterprises in total output and employment in 1990 and 2002

Position in hierarchy of firms	Share in output sold (%)		Share in employment (%)	
	1990	2002	1990	2002
1-10	12.3	16.5	4.5	3.9
11-20	3.2	5.0	2.0	1.5
21 -30	2.6	3.4	1.5	1.1
31 - 40	2.2	2.8	1.3	1.0
41 -50	2.0	2.4	1.2	0.9
51 - 100	7.0	9.2	4.7	3.3
101 - 200	8.1	10.0	6.2	4.3
201 - 300	5.5	5.7	4.2	2.6
301 - 400	4.2	3.9	2.9	1.5
1 - 400	47.1	58.9	28.5	20.1

Source: As in table 6 and 1991 and 2003 GUS Industrial Yearbooks.

So far, the analysis of rank of the particular units depended on the number of plants located in them, which was treated as a substitute of their economic importance. A deeper characterisation of the set of enterprises under study can be given using two measures: volume of output and employment. The weaknesses of both measures are well known, but at this stage they can be useful in determining changes in the concentration of economic potential of Poland's biggest enterprises. When analysing the volume of output in the conditions of variable inflation and the denomination of the zloty, a comparison could only be made of relations holding among enterprises occupying a given position on the biggest-enterprise lists in 1990 and 2002. However, it was also possible to determine the direction of change in the relation between output and employment, albeit to a limited extent. The calculations presented in the tables were restricted to 400 enterprises.

A comparison of 1990 and 2002 incomes indicates an increase in financial concentration in big enterprises (table 9). The contribution of the 400 biggest of them to Poland's industrial output grew from 47.1% to 58.9%. This refers especially to the top ten on the list, but also to those from the next hierarchical intervals up to the 200th. Below this level (in the third and fourth hundreds) the contribution in both years were similar. The tendency is reversed in employment, where the proportion of big enterprises declined from 28.5% to 20.1% of total industrial employment. As a result, the rate of the share in output to the share in employment, which was only 1.65 in 1990, grew to 2.93 in 2002. This figure can be treated as an indirect measure of the increase in performance of the set of the 400 biggest enterprises.

An important manifestation of the transformation in industry is the different employment figures for enterprises that occupied the same position on the list in both years (table 10). In 2002 they were two or three times lower than in 1990 (with the exception of the enterprises heading the lists).

Table 10. Employment in industrial enterprises of various ranks in 1990 and 2002

Rank in the set of enterprises	Employment	
	1990	2002
1	28,676	32,252
10	12,465	5,256
20	8,149	3,630
30	6,604	3,105
40	5,861	2,735
50	5,227	2,400
100	3,649	1,643
200	2,249	957
300	1,603	543
400	1,043	350

Source: As in table 6.

The level of financial concentration in industry can be presented in more detail by analysing the importance of the ten largest cities (table 11). Their share in output grew from 17.2% to 24.6%, even though their proportion of the total population remained at 15%.

Especially pronounced was the increase in the economic performance of Warsaw and Katowice, and to a lesser extent, of Poznań and Gdańsk. Szczecin and Bydgoszcz declined. An attempt was also made to determine the specificity of a city by calculating the extent to which the output of the entire industrial centre depended on the single biggest plant located in it. In 1990 this type of concentration was the highest in Cracow (60%), Gdańsk (54.1%), and Lublin (47.6%). This high contribution of a single plant to the output of its city continued in 2002, or even grew to 66.8%. The tendency was registered in six of the cities.

Table 11. Output in large industrial enterprises in towns[a] in 1990 and 2002

Town	Share in industrial output in Poland (%)		Share in industrial output of 500 largest industrial enterprises in Poland (%)		Share of town's largest enterprise in output of town's[b] industry (%)	
	1990	2002	1990	2002	1990	2002
Warsaw	6.3	11.7	12.4	19.0	40.3	25.1
Poznań	1.4	2.2	2.8	3.6	17.4	20.5
Wrocław	1.1	1.1	2.1	1.7	19.6	16.4
Cracow	2.4	2.5	4.8	4.1	60.0	32.4
Lublin	0.4	0.4	0.8	0.6	47.6	15.7
Gdańsk	1.5	1.8	3.0	3.0	54.1	66.8
Szczecin	1.1	0.6	2.2	1.0	21.1	34.2
Bydgoszcz	0.9	0.4	1.8	0.7	19.5	31.7
Łódź	0.7	0.9	1.4	1.5	19.9	21.2
Katowice	1.4	3.0	2.7	4.8	22.5	44.1
Total	17.2	24.6	34.0	40.0	x	x

[a] the list includes 10 towns which had the largest number of industrial plants in 2002.
[b] with all large plants in the given town (belonging to the 500 largest industrial enterprises in Poland) taken as 100%.
Source: as in table 9.

A complementary picture of the concentration of industrial potential was obtained using the other measure, employment (table 12). The results show that in 1990 the total contribution of the cities under analysis to employment was about half of that to output, and was on a decline. As a result, in 2002 their share in employment was one third of that in output, and the disproportion was especially pronounced in Lublin, Gdańsk, and Cracow. Generally, in this approach the dominance of Warsaw over the other cities was not so overwhelming.

In 1990, the importance of a single enterprise (in terms of employment) was the highest in Lublin and Cracow and the lowest in Łódź. In 2002, the dominance of a single enterprise was the most conspicuous in Katowice. An increase in the importance of their single enterprise was recorded in six cities.

At this point some remarks are in order about extractive enterprises. There were 28 of them on the biggest-enterprise list in 2002, including 14 in Silesia engaged, naturally, in hard-coal mining. The other enterprises extract (and sometimes process) brown coal, copper, salt, sulphur, petroleum, and natural gas. They are distributed over seven voivodeships. Much has changed in the extractive industry in terms of organisational concentration, but no new enterprises have been set up to extract minerals.

An important role in closing the technological gap between Poland and the advanced economies is played by foreign capital. While 45% of it (or about $29 billion) had been invested in industry by mid-2003, only a small proportion had gone to high-technology industry. However, the food and transport equipment industries had been highly modernised, and recently the building materials industry has been receiving substantial means. Foreign capital tends to be located largely in industries offering quicker returns on investment. It has to be stated that, generally, foreign capital is not interested in the growth of the domestic research and development sector, therefore yielding to this tendency may delay the modernisation of Polish industry and make some fields of the economy dependent on the import of ready-made technologies. A study of firms with foreign capital participation showed them to be less alarmed about competitive imports than Polish firms; instead, they were more worried about insufficient export possibilities. This may indicate that their offer is attractive to the Polish market, but not attractive enough to the foreign markets, where it is well known. Firms with foreign capital participation also tend to have more modern machines and equipment, which allows them to respond to a developing demand more flexibly.

A research into the economic performance of industrial plants (carried out in the first quarter of 2000) permitted the manufacturers to indicate several barriers to their operation. What they rated as the most serious were an insufficient domestic demand (76% of respondents), an insufficient demand on the foreign markets (54%), and competitive imports (42%). A substantial obstacle was also unclear and inconsistent law (22%). Worth noting is the fact that a barrier to 5% of respondents was a shortage of skilled workers. The insufficient domestic demand was the most serious barrier in the production of textiles, clothes, footwear, and electromechanical devices; another was competitive imports. The shortage of skilled labour was rated high by representatives of the wood-processing (about 20%), leather, and electromechanical industries (about 10%).

Polish commodity exports and imports can practically be seen as consisting almost exclusively of industrial goods, and their proportion keeps growing (98% of the 2002 exports as against 97% in 1994). However, there is still too low a proportion in exported goods of highly processed and technologically advanced ones. While the share of the electromechanical engineering in the exports has grown (41% in 2002), it must be kept in mind that it is made up of as many as five industries (machine-building, metal-processing, transport equipment, electrical and electronic, and precision equipment), and their exports is equivalent to the combined exports of the light, wood-and-paper, and food industries. The share of the fuel and energy industry has declined markedly, and this downward tendency seems to be permanent (5.1% in 2002 as against 22.7% in 1960). The metallurgical industry displays a similar tendency, with a remarkably big slump in the export of ferrous-metals goods. A cause for worry is too small a share of the chemical industry and, even worse, lack of any noticeable progress in this matter. While its share in exports is a bit larger than in the pre-transformation period, the goods exported are still those from the initial stages of chemical processing. That is why, despite the fact that 30% of its products are exported and the industry itself is counted among those heavily involved in exports, its share in the export proceeds is a mere 8%.

Table 12. Employment in large industrial plants in towns[a)] in 1990 and 2002

Town	Share in industrial employment in Poland (%)		Share in employment of 500 largest industrial enterprises in Poland (%)		Share of town's largest enterprise in town's industrial employment[b)] (%)	
	1990	2002	1990	2002	1990	2002
Warsaw	3.1	3.4	10.2	16.1	17.1	32.4
Poznań	1.0	0.6	3.2	3.0	24.3	18.9
Wrocław	0.7	0.5	2.3	2.3	21.8	13.8
Cracow	1.1	0.9	3.7	4.3	56.2	33.9
Lublin	0.3	0.1	1.0	0.6	59.9	23.3
Gdańsk	0.6	0.4	2.0	1.8	26.6	36.8
Szczecin	0.6	0.5	1.9	2.2	22.1	35.2
Bydgoszcz	0.8	0.3	2.6	1.6	17.8	20.4
Łódź	0.6	0.4	2.1	1.8	14.5	25.5
Katowice	0.9	1.1	3.0	5.1	31.8	50.7
Total	9.7	8.2	32.0	38.8	x	x

[a, b] As in table 11. Source: as in table 9.

An analysis of the export involvement of industries (the proportion of exports in their output) leads to the conclusion that it is the heaviest in the wood-and-paper and metals industries. Over the recent years it has stopped growing, and in the metals industry it has even declined markedly from the early 1990s. The lowest level of export involvement is recorded in the food industry. Generally, one can note an increase in the importance of exports in industries processing raw materials that employ simple, labour-intensive technologies (wood-and-paper, mineral, and chemical). This corroborates the opinion that the main sources of the competitive edge of Polish exports on the West European markets are relatively low labour costs and availability of many raw materials. The competition we find hard to face concerns goods heavily involving capital, advanced technologies, and skilled labour.

The Extractive Industry

The extractive industry is in a peculiar situation because its operation is controlled by both, the domestic transformation and a simultaneous globalisation of economic processes. These processes have extended the criteria of extraction profitability. The profitability cannot be measured exclusively in terms of the domestic market, but has to take into consideration the prices and current stage of the trade cycle on the world market. Technological changes also reinforce the global nature of the economy. These are the factors that made facing the operation of the world market more of a shock for the Polish extractive industry than for manufacturing. The industry is still at a stage of adapting to changes that have been taking place in its surroundings.

Economic growth, whether in the world or at home, is not proportionately dependent on an increased consumption of raw materials. For instance, over the years 1980-2001 the global population grew by 38.5%, gross world product by 107%, industrial output by 63%, and the per capita consumption of fuels by a mere 1%. Taking into consideration the entire world mining output, it turns out to have increased by 3% in that period. This means that the rate of economic growth is much faster than that of materials consumption. In the case of some of them (notably sulphur, iron, hard coal, brown coal, and tin), the world product increases as their extraction declines. As a result, advanced countries are less and less absorptive markets for producers of raw materials, and more and more demanding. This situation crucially restricts the extractive and exporting potential of Polish mining.

Table 13. Extraction of selected minerals in Poland in the years 1970-2002

Mineral	Unit	1970	1980	1985	1990	1995	2002
Hard coal	million t	140	193	192	148	137	104
Brown coal	million t	33	37	58	68	64	58
Petroleum	thous. t	424	329	194	163	292	728
Natural gas	hm^3	5,200	6,300	6,390	3,867	4,803	5,207
Copper ores	million t	7	27	29	24	27	7
Zinc and lead ores	million t	3.6	5.5	5.3	4.9	5.0	
Iron ores	million t	2.6	0.1	–	–	–	–
Sulphur[a)]	thous. t	431	5164	4876	4660	2427	940
Salt	thous. t	2,904	4,533	4,865	4,055	4,214	4,473

[a] pure (100%) mineral.
Source: GUS Statistical Yearbooks and Industrial Yearbooks.

An important change in the extractive industry is an increase in uncertainty as to the economic worth of a given deposit. Several factors are involved, the most important including technological changes that produce a change in demand in industries using the mineral, as well as the discovery and exploitation of the mineral in new places. The result is stiff competition in the world market that brings about a decline in the prices of an increasing range of raw materials. As a consequence, some deposits have become unprofitable to mine. One can trace this process by observing fluctuations in the prices of iron ores in the world and their effects manifesting themselves in abandoning the extraction of those ores in Poland and a decline in the extraction of sulphur and hard coal table 13).

The heightened uncertainty as to the profitability of extracting a mineral from a given site affects the behaviour of investors, who prefer to engage their capital in ventures where the quality of a deposit, its reserves, and the economic and political situation of the place minimise investment risk. This is connected with the fact that today the level of capital investment in developing a mine is as a rule much higher than it used to be, and exceeds the outlays necessary to establish a processing plant. As a result, it now takes longer for a newly opened mine to return the development costs. This means that there is an ever-growing probability of sustaining losses in mining due to changes in external conditions. Among those external conditions that enhance the risk of any investment in the Polish extractive industry is the possibility of a discovery in another country of deposits with better parameters, better geological conditions offering cheaper exploitation and better access to the market. Another risk to the workability of minerals is their growing substitutability, or the possibility of obtaining artificial ones through a chemical technology. This makes investors prefer deposits that will face competition more readily, which is important in that the competition keeps expanding its spatial range. It manifests itself in the growing distance between the place of extraction of a mineral and the market where it is sold. Thus, more and more common minerals from ever farther countries have recently been flowing to the Polish market. This is associated with the declining proportion of transport costs among the elements of economic calculation.

Employment in mining and extraction as well as its proportion in total industrial employment are on the decline in Poland, and so is the industry's share in total output. Worth noting is the fact that its share in employment is higher than in output (7.2% and 5.3% in 2002, respectively), which indicates that its workers have lower productivity than those employed in the processing industry (table 14). Small extractive firms belong largely to the private sector, while predominant among big ones is still the public sector, which accounts for 82% of mining employment.

Poland is numbered among countries rich in minerals. It accounts for 2.3% of the world extraction (the 12th place in the world, table 15). The minerals found in Poland can be grouped into four categories:

- those satisfying the country's own needs and being exported: hard coal, ores of copper, silver, zinc, lead, sulphur, and rock salt;
- those satisfying the country's own needs: brown coal, rock minerals (sandstones, limestones, granites, basalts, etc.);
- those partially covering the country's own needs: natural gas, petroleum, potash salt, nickel; and
- proved deposits not extracted because of their low quality or too small reserves: iron ores, phosphorites, arsenic, uranium.

Table 14. Employment and output in mining and extraction in the years 1993-2002

Years	Employment		Percentage of output
	Thousands.	Percentage of industrial employment	
1993	398.8	11.0	8.3
1994	376.8	10.1	8.7
1995	357.7	9.6	8.0
1996	339.1	9.0	7.6
1997	325.9	8.7	7.3
1998	297.0	8.1	6.2
1999	256.7	7.5	5.9
2000	223.2	7.1	5.6
2001	216.6	7.2	5.2
2002	209.0	7.2	5.3

Source: GUS Industrial Yearbooks and own calculations.

Hard coal has been Poland's top-ranking mineral for many decades. Until recently, the economy has been too dependent on its extraction, especially the power industry and exports. For instance, in 1956 the proceeds from the export of coal and coke equalled 43.2% of total export value. Over the next years this proportion kept declining to reach 2.8% in 2002 (table 16).

Table 15. Poland's place in the extraction of selected minerals, 2002

Mineral	World	Europe
hard coal	7	2
brown coal	6	3
copper	8	3
silver	7	2
native sulphur	3	2

Source: GUS Statistical Yearbooks; The World in Figures, Wyd. Szkolne i Pedagogiczne.

Table 16. Changes in Polish coal and coke exports, 1980-2002

Year	Exports in million metric tons	Share in Poland's exports
1980	32.8	10.0
1985	37.8	13.8
1990	31.7	8.3
1995	35.2	6.8
2000	26.9	3.2
2002	26.8	2.8

Source: GUS Industrial Yearbooks and own calculations.

Characteristically enough, the drop in the proportion of exports did not match the drop in the amount of Polish coal sold abroad, and at times this amount even tended to increase (1980, 32.8 million tonnes; 1985, 37.8 m t; 1995, 35.2 m t). On the one hand, the declining share of coal in exports is due to a growing proportion of other goods, and on the other, it is also the result of a comparative fall in its prices, which makes 1 tonne of exported coal bring ever lower returns.

Over the years 1995-2002 coal exports dwindled from 32 to 23 million tonnes, but even this amount was possible to be sold abroad thanks to substantial state subsidies. Polish mines are unable to face the competition of cheaper coal from Australia, South Africa, the USA and Canada, where this mineral is largely surface-mined.

Export destinations are scattered widely. Polish coal is sold to 31 countries, including 29% to Germany, 9% to Austria, 11% to Finland, and 8% to Denmark. Poland also buys coal; in 2002 its import (chiefly from Russia and Kazakhstan) was nearly 3 million tonnes.

The restructuring programme for hard-coal mining is still in progress. Its aim is to leave in operation only those mines that are profitable. This requires substantial cuts in employment and the liquidation of some 20 mines in which the conditions preclude profits. Between 1995 and 2002 almost 150,000 people left mining. By the end of 2002 hard- and brown-coal mines employed a total of 167,000 workers.

Out of metallic minerals, the one most important for the Polish economy is copper. The 2002 proceeds from the export of copper and its products amounted to 63% of those of coal and its products; being fully profitable, the export of copper needs no subsidies.

At present copper is mined and processed by the Polish Copper Mining-Metallurgical Combine. Minerals also found in the copper deposits include silver, nickel, cobalt, molybdenum, vanadium, germanium, arsenic, zinc, and lead. Only silver, nickel and lead are recovered.

Poland's deposits of native sulphur are among the most abundant in the world. Its reserves have been estimated to last at least 300 years. They were discovered in 1953. Because sulphur can be recovered not only from deposits (native sulphur) but also, and cheaper, from the desulphurisation of natural gas, petroleum, hard coal, or nonferrous metal ores, the demand for native sulphur is on the decline in the world. This limits its export possibilities. As a result, by 2002 sulphur extraction in Poland had dwindled 5.5 times in comparison with its 1980 level. Hence the drop in its export, which in 2002 amounted to 0.05% of total Polish exports. Sulphur is largely sold to Morocco and the Czech Republic.

THE PROCESSING INDUSTRY

The Polish power system is now sufficient to ensure the country's needs. The biggest customer, viz. industry (60% of domestic power consumption), strives to cut its costs by, among other things, reducing power consumption. Also households (15%) try to reduce power consumption by buying energy-saving appliances. In this situation no plans are made to build new large power stations, especially atomic.

The largest percentage of electric power is produced by plants fuelled by hard coal (57%) and brown coal (40%); and the smallest, by hydroelectric power plants (3%). This supply structure has a detrimental effect on the economy because the high prices of power boost the manufacturing cost of other goods, thus making them less competitive. Besides, it is impossible for coal-fuelled power plants to respond to a daily or weekly pattern of change in demand. Another weakness is the high level of environmental damage they cause. That is why even coal-rich countries, especially the advanced ones, are switching from the traditional power generating technology to one based primarily on petroleum products (e.g., mazout) and natural gas. In Poland, the tendency is to replace hard coal with brown coal.

Changes in the Polish metals industry include a drop in employment over the years 1995-2000 by 75,000 people and of its contribution to output from 6.6% to 3.7% (table 17). They largely resulted from restructuring and a slump in the iron and steel industry. Taking into consideration the fact that steel production in the world has been kept at roughly the same level for the last ten years while forecasts anticipate a decline in the economy's steel intensiveness, the Polish metals industry will soon be going through a very difficult period. The hard task of meeting the requirements of a market economy, for which the industry was completely unprepared, has been made even more daunting by a rapid and deep transformation in more advanced economies that has resulted in falling prices in the world markets.

The very poor quality of Polish iron ores has caused all mines to close down because cheap ores are in abundance in the world. Poland imports them from Ukraine (66%), Russia

(19%), and Brazil (13%). What it exports are steel and steel goods. Unfortunately, the export structure enhances the economy's energy-intensive character because the goods sold abroad are products of the initial stages of processing which consume the greatest amounts of energy. Besides, they are of poor quality, hence their export, though exceeding imports four times in terms of weight, does not even cover its costs.

Table 17. Output of the metals industry, 1970-2002

Product	Unit	1970	1980	1990	1995	2002
Steel	mT	11.8	19.5	13.6	11.9	8.4
Electrolytic copper	thous. T	72	357	346	407	509
Zinc	thous. T	209	217	132	166	146
Lead	thous. T	55	82	65	66	60.7
Aluminium	thous. T	99	95	46	56	43.0
Silver	T	231	766	832	1,001	1,227

Source: GUS Statistical Yearbooks and Industrial Yearbooks.

As to refined copper, Poland occupies the eighth place in the world accounting for 3.3% of its production.

The industry manufacturing machinery and transport equipment, electrical and electronic appliances, bearings, casts, and other metal products is treated as a measure of technological progress and advancement of the economy of fundamental importance for the development of the entire economy. Its distribution in Poland shows a strong relation with that of skilled labour and is dependent on easy access to the transport network and the location of the demand. These factors are not of equal strength in all the cases. The more complicated the technology a plant employs, the greater the probability that it will be situated in a large city. It is there that it can find secondary and higher schools, generally well-developed communications links, and other factories to co-operate with. Co-operation is a crucial condition for the operation of this industry (table 18).

The growth dynamics of plants of the transport equipment industry varied after 1990. Until 1998, the tonnage of ships built in Poland kept increasing to drop in 1999 by 20%, and this is the tendency it has shown since. After 1990 there was a steep increase in the manufacture of cars, but between 1999 and 2002 the production of automobiles slumped from 650,000 to 288,000 and of trucks, from 63,000 to 21,000. The manufacture of buses and bikes was stable with only slight fluctuations. Throughout the transformation period the production of farm tractors was falling steeply, while electric locomotives and passenger carriages had practically stopped being produced.

The increase in the production of automobiles is connected with marked economic growth whose effects manifest themselves in the demand for particular goods, including cars. The demand for cars in Poland is to an extent compensatory, i.e., it strives to make up for limitations of those times when only a very narrow group of people could purchase one. Another reason why automakers have become interested in the Polish market has been easy credit conditions generating an additional demand. The result has been the enlargement of the existing factories, establishment of new ones with a large proportion of, or exclusively, foreign capital, stiff competition among the producers, and an ever improving ratio of car prices to average wages. A characteristic feature of the Polish car industry has been a large proportion of plants assembling cars from imported parts. This is not a desirable development for the Polish labour market and Polish makers of car parts. However, the proportion of Polish-made parts in the cars produced can be observed to be rising slowly. The leading foreign concerns include Fiat, Daewoo, General Motors, and Volkswagen.

Table 18. Output of selected electromechanical devices, 1970-2000

Product	Unit	1970	1980	1990	1995	1998	2002
Automobiles	thous.	64	351	266	366	592	288
Trucks	thous.	41	54	39	31	56	21.0
Buses	thous.	9,0	13.1	3.9	1.4	1.9	1.7
Tractors	thous.	39	58	35	22	15	5.1
Seagoing ships	thous. DWT	518	392	134	603	915	542
Bicycles	thous.	903	1,637	1,339	1,090	1,114	1,491
Telephones	thous.	635	1,520	1,589	409	691	724
Radio sets	thous.	987	2,695	1,433	225	154	10.4
TV sets (colour)	thous.	–	147	338	1,136	4,436	7,795
Automatic washing machines	thous.	–	360	144	249	293	847
Bearings	million	51	125	96	86	79	153

Source: GUS Statistical Yearbooks and Industrial Yearbooks.

The economic condition of automakers in Poland has deteriorated substantially over the last two years because they find it hard to face the competitive import of cars. For instance, in 2001 about 210,000 home-made cars were purchased as against almost 410,000 imported ones. Moreover, the increase in car imports exceeded that of exports, with the result that in 2001 the entire domestic car output was lower than car imports. The number of jobs in the industry has dwindled by 30,000. Fiat has closed its factory in Bielsko-Biała, Daewoo in Lublin, FSO-Daewoo in Warsaw is facing bankruptcy, and Opel in Gliwice has noticeably reduced employment.

The Polish shipbuilding industry has generally successfully overcome the difficulties of adjusting to a market economy, in which it has been aided by an upturn in the ships market. At present, however, all shipyards are going through a difficult period as a result of strong in-house opposition against restructuring and a temporary slump in the world demand. The output of Polish shipyards is exported almost in its entirety.

The rolling-stock industry has been the one worst hit by the effects of the economic change. Economic entities have been striving to reduce shipping to cut production costs, hence they seek co-operating firms located closer; the transport-consuming export of coal and sulphur has dwindled, making it necessary to close many railway connections; and for the ever longer distances road transport has become cheaper. This situation has got the Polish Railways into serious financial trouble making it impossible for the enterprise to buy new rolling stock. Also, Polish goods of this line are not competitive enough in the foreign markets. As a result, their output has fallen and now amounts to less than 1% of the peak production of the 1960s and '70s.

Changes in agriculture and its present difficult situation have brought about a fall in the demand for farm tractors and some of the machinery. Especially hard hit by the downturn were the Ursus Enterprise in Warsaw and its branches. The firm's restructuring has caused a big reduction in employment. Today, the Warsaw plant, which is now exclusively an assembly unit, employs 900 people as against 12,000 a few years ago (some of them now work in companies that have separated from the enterprise).

The opening of the Polish economy to outside markets has revealed a huge technological gap dividing the domestic electrical and electronic industries from those of other countries that is impossible to bridge fast unaided, the more so as new-generation goods are produced every few years. However, Poland has been assessed by foreign capital as a very absorptive market where inputs will produce returns very quickly. The inflow of capital has helped to establish new plants and modernise those that have survived despite dramatic hardships. Foreign concerns have mainly invested in the manufacture of telephone exchanges (Siemens of Germany, Alcatel of France), lighting (Philips of The Netherlands, Matsushita of Japan), and TV sets (Philips again, Daewoo of South Korea). The output of computers and electronic data processing devices has increased 4.6 times since 1990. It should be emphasised, however, that they are largely assembled from imported parts. The biggest, and seemingly permanent, slump has been recorded in the production of radio equipment; in 2000 its output fell to 7% of the 1990 figure.

The chemical industry, like the electronic and machine-building industries, is treated as a progress-carrying and -stimulating factor in the economy. In Poland, the organic industry that is dominant in the chemical engineering of advanced countries is too poorly developed. Its basic raw materials are hard coal (though the role of this highly capital- and energy-intensive mineral is on the decline), petroleum, and natural gas. The processing is done in coking and petrochemical plants and other combines manufacturing intermediate products.

The demand for fertilisers is closely dependent on the situation in farming, hence their production displays fluctuations.

The modernisation of the chemical industry is associated with a heavy involvement of foreign capital. However, it flows mainly to the branches of chemistry more immediately connected with the market rather than to that needing investment the most, viz. mineral processing. For instance, Dutch capital has invested in the dye and varnish industry; British, Dutch, German and US capital, in household chemicals; British, in pharmaceuticals; and French, in tyres.

Poland's chemicals exchange has for years been in deficit, and the exports/imports ratio has deteriorated even further over the last few years. In 2002 the exports amounted to less than one-third of the imports. The imbalance is especially conspicuous in the case of medicines and other pharmaceuticals. The imports are ten times the export figures and pose a serious threat to domestic producers and the possibility of conducting research in the field of pharmacy.

Polish cement plants have greatly modernised their technology and now nearly all employ the so-called dry method which takes half the energy required by the wet method commonly in use a few years ago. The modernisation has involved the privatisation of the plants with a substantial participation of foreign investors (Germany, France, Belgium). However, some cement plants with the highest production costs are planned to be liquidated.

The wood industry starts in sawmills. Their distribution is connected with that of woodland, but timber production does not correspond to the woodiness index of the particular regions of Poland.

Most timber is used by factories of pulp and paper, boards, and plywood. Paper mills are large objects situated on rivers. They can be divided into two groups. The older ones (established mostly in the early 1900s) are located in the south of Poland, chiefly in Silesia and Lower Silesia. The largest plants were built in the 1960s and '70s (in Ostrołęka, 1960; Świecie, 1967; Kwidzyń, 1975) in the northern half of the country. The capital that has a substantial share in the ownership of this industry is American, Swedish, and British. Over the years 1990-2002 the output of pulp increased by 50% and of paper, by 135%. This has made Poland come closer to the world's mean per capita paper output, though it is still several times lower than that in the advanced economies.

The furniture industry has grown very dynamically, satiating the domestic market. What has greatly contributed to its modernisation was foreign capital, largely German. Other big investors have been furniture firms from the US and Sweden. However, the changes were mainly intended to ensure fuller use of the productive capacities of existing plants or their enlargement; no new large units have been built over the last years. More than 60% of furniture output is sold abroad, mainly to Germany, Belgium, and Great Britain. The export of furniture is six times greater than its import.

The textile industry, like the remaining light industries, shows a decline in output in all the basic branches, especially woollen and cotton yarn. Big, antiquated plants still predominate in it; those employing in excess of 500 people account for 32% of the industry's employment. Apart from some branches of the chemical industry and the metals industry, no other processing sector displays such a concentration of production in big enterprises. To this must be added a hugely delayed process of privatisation, which only started to assume any major proportions in this industry in 1997. The textile industry is also characterised by technological obsolescence. Its machines show a depreciation of 67%, which is among the highest figures in entire industry. Owing to very stiff competition in the world market, foreign capital has deemed investment in this industry to be of little attraction and too much risk.

A characteristic feature of the clothing industry is its great dispersion. It is almost totally privatised. A substantial proportion of clothes are exported, but they are largely made of foreign textiles and sold under foreign brand names. Recently one can observe foreign entrepreneurs to be shifting production to countries with even cheaper labour.

It did not take the food industry long to overcome the difficulties of adapting to a market economy. What was important was its attractiveness to foreign capital owing to comparatively quick returns on the inputs and a large domestic market. It is in this industry that the largest proportion of foreign capital has been invested.

The industry's biggest plants are sugar factories. Their location in beet-growing areas is determined by the fact that a metric tonne of sugar beets yields about 130 kg of sugar. The remaining 870 kg are waste products that are partly used as animal feed. An average cost of sugar production in Poland is higher than its world prices, which precludes profitable imports, and the domestic market does not need such quantities of sugar. As a result, the number of sugar factories will have to be reduced. Foreign capital has not been inclined to invest in them.

The situation of the other divisions of the food-processing industry is much better. They have accomplished considerable technological progress, especially the dairy, brewing, confectionery, and concentrated food industries. The tobacco industry has started to experience difficulties. It has been greatly modernised, largely owing to foreign investment, but met a demand barrier. When investing in the industry, tobacco firms expected the demand for cigarettes in Poland to make up for the losses they were incurring in the West. However, also in Poland the sale of tobacco goods turned out to be on the decline. Relevant for the growth of the particular food-processing industries are changing consumption patterns, including a fall in the consumption of meat and animal fats in favour of vegetable fats, and a drop in the consumption of spirits in favour of beer. The share of the food industry in the Polish exports has been a steady 10% for the last few years.

THE SPATIAL STRUCTURE OF INDUSTRY

Until 1989, the spatial structure of industry, in a regional approach, was highly stable. While the level of industrialisation grew, the hierarchy of regions changed little. In a matter of a few years, the transformation of the economic system has produced some clear shifts. The present industrialisation ranking of the regions is not a repetition of the spatial pattern obtaining under the centrally planned economy. The old, prewar traditions of entrepreneurship in some regions and their higher educational level turned out to be stronger development factors than the heritage of socialist investment.

Polish industry displays ever smaller spatial disparities. When comparing extreme values from the year 1970 (when the administrative division was very similar to the present one), the highest figure for voivodeship employment was 14 times the lowest one, while in 2002, only 8 times. A significant change of the recent years has been a clear decrease in the importance of Silesia, in absolute terms as measured by its employment figure and in relative terms as measured by the voivodeship's share in Poland's industrial potential (table 19). While it still retains the top position in terms of its fixed assets (18.9%) and employment (17%), in terms of output it has been overtaken by Mazovia (20.6%). Predominating in Polish industry are three voivodeships: Mazovia, Silesia, and Wielkopolska. Together they account for 48% of total output and 40% of the employment figure.

Only in two voivodeships (Mazovia and Pomerania) is their share in output greater than that in employment. In the remaining 14 voivodeships the relation is reversed, i.e., the productivity of their industry is lower than the national average. However, the regional pattern of industry is still in a state of flux because in some regions the adaptation processes started later and only now have they begun to produce effects. Among them are Silesia, Łódź and Lublin, which at first concentrated on preserving the old structure, waiting out threats, and protection from a downfall. The regions where the advancement of adaptation processes and growth dynamics are the highest are Mazovia and Wielkopolska. These two differ as to the level of their intra-regional disparities, however: in Wielkopolska the transformation has occurred dynamically almost throughout the entire voivodeship, while in Mazovia the disproportions between the core and the peripheries are still great.

The information about the spatial structure of industry and its changes can be made more precise when analysing basic forms of its concentration, viz. industrial centres and districts. An industrial centre is taken to mean a locality with an industrial potential, as measured by the volume of output or employment, which is significant at a regional or national scale, while an industrial district is a set of such centres located in close proximity to one another, bound by mutual links, and with a joint potential significant at the national scale. The concentration of industry is a result of seeking economic advantages offered by a large scale of production, the opportunity to use existing infrastructure, and co-operation with other plants. A comparison of changes occurring in the individual centres leads to the conclusion that the processes of restructuring and adaptation of industry seem to have been more smooth in towns with a diversified industrial structure and plants of various sizes. The most acute crisis tended to hit those centres whose entire industry was actually a single large enterprise on which the town depended for its existence.

Table 19. Industry in voivodeships in 2002

Voivodeship	Share in employment (%)	Share in output (%)
Lower Silesia	8.0	7.3
Kujawy-Pomerania	5.5	4.9
Lublin	3.7	2.7
Lubuska Land	2.5	2.1
Łódź	7.9	6.2
Małopolska	7.4	7.1
Mazovia	12.3	20.6
Opole	2.5	2.4
Podkarpacie	5.2	3.8
Podlasie	2.1	1.8
Pomerania	5.5	6.1
Silesia	17.0	16.9
Świętokrzyska Land	2.7	2.2
Warmia-Mazuria	3.1	2.6
Wielkopolska	10.8	10.3
West Pomerania	3.7	3.0
Poland	100.0	100.0

Source: calculated on the basis of GUS Statistical Yearbooks.

Poland's largest industrial centre (in terms of employment) is Warsaw; next come Cracow, Łódź, and Poznań. The ranking of the particular centres have changed since 1980. A comparison of the set of 50 largest centres in 1980, the time of peak industrial employment for most of them, with such a set from 2002 shows them to have 42 towns in common. Almost all of them had registered a fall in employment, but its scale differed widely. With an average slump of about 30%, the Upper Silesian centres had lost 50%, Wałbrzych 70%, and Łódź 65%. In absolute terms, employment in Łódź fell the most steeply, from 200,000 to 57,000. The positions of the top ten centres had changed only slightly with the exception of Lublin, which had moved up from the 20th to the 11th place. Outside this group, the most dramatic shifts were recorded by Olsztyn (35 positions up), Konin (34), and Nowy Sącz (23). The fall was the sharpest for Wałbrzych, the Upper Silesian centres, and Radom.

Industrial districts differ in genesis, size, pattern of centre distribution, and branch structure. These characteristics were taken into consideration when drawing up a list of the 12 most important districts (table 20, figure 1). Those with much industrial potential also include the Lublin, Legnica-Głogów, and Tarnobrzeg ones. It should be emphasised that there are no uniform criteria for delineating the districts, hence their number varies from study to study. As a rule, about 20 districts are distinguished.

The transformation of the industrial districts is at various stages of advancement. It is the most advanced in the Warsaw and Poznań ones. They are characterised by highly diversified industries, a strong spirit of entrepreneurship, and well-developed institutions and infrastructure.

The second group is made up of the Łódź, Gdańsk, Wrocław, Podkarpacie, Rzeszów, Bydgoszcz-Toruń, and Szczecin districts. Their industries turned out to be very sensitive to the change in the economic system. Initially, it caused a dramatic slump in output and employment, but also the elimination of inefficient enterprises. This provided a basis for structural changes intended to improve competitiveness. Today, the districts are at the stage of evident growth, though its rate is not the same everywhere; Gdańsk, Bydgoszcz-Toruń, and Szczecin are more advanced than the remaining districts, especially Łódź.

The third group includes the Silesian-Cracow, Legnica-Głogów, and Konin districts. Using the protection it has forced the state to give it, the heavy industry predominant in them keeps postponing its full adaptation to the new system. That is why structural changes are slow in them and the threat of a major breakdown is still looming.

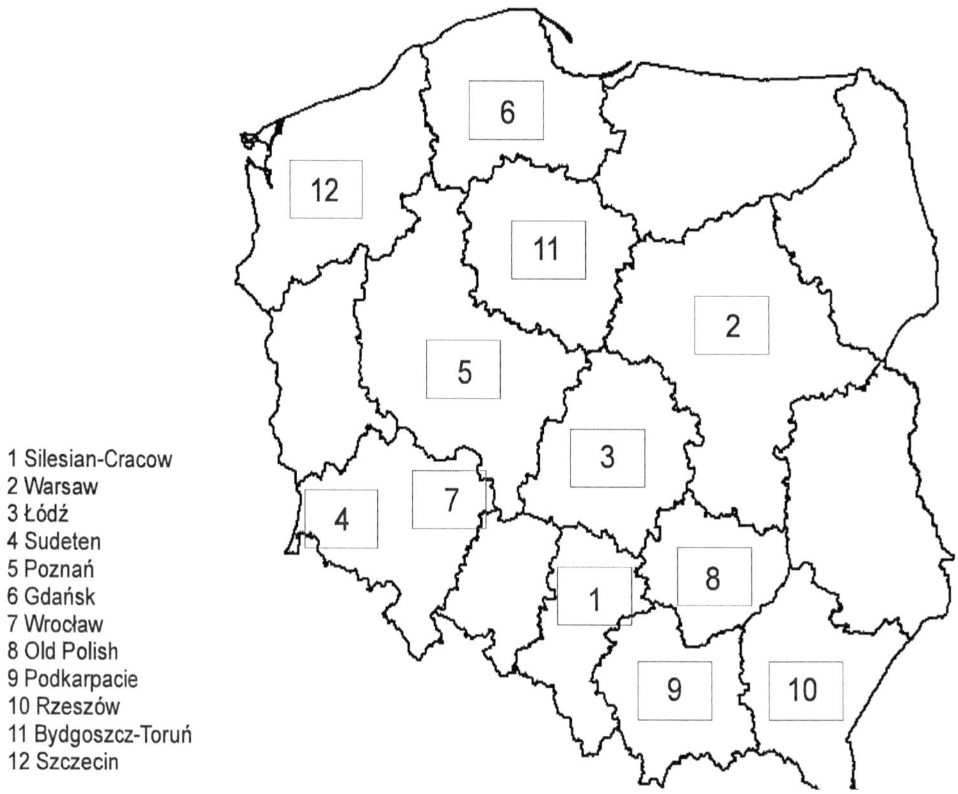

Figure 1. Major industrial districts of Poland.

The most difficult situation is that of the final group embracing the Sudeten, Tarnobrzeg and Old Polish districts. It is believed that what they have been going through is the process of de-industrialisation. The stage of the collapse of production was not followed by a growth stage, but by a further decline in the importance of industry.

In all the districts and large centres, industry has been moving to the peripheries, including rural areas. The process manifests itself in moving old plants from the city centre to the suburban zone and in the location of new objects in this zone. In this way they can avoid the inconvenience involved in running an industry in a crowded metropolitan area. What facilitates such spatial shifts are lower land prices and encouraging conditions offered by local authorities.

Table 20. Major industrial districts in Poland

Name of district	Principal industrial centres	Main factors of establishment and development	Distribution of centres and size relations	Major industries
Silesian-Cracow	Katowice, Bytom, Gliwice, Zabrze, Tychy, Dąbrowa Górnicza, Chorzów, Rybnik, Cracow, Olkusz, Bielsko-Biała, Oświęcim, Cieszyn, Częstochowa	minerals, water resources labour market political considerations	dispersed with a few areas of concentration no clearly dominating centre	extracting hard coal and zinclead ores, power engineering, iron and steel, machines, cars and power devices
Warsaw	Warsaw, Pruszków, Skierniewice, Żyrardów, Nowy Dwór Maz., Piaseczno	location in terms of communications, labour market, political considerations	concentrated, decidedly Warsaw-dominated	machine tools, cars and tractors, construction machines, semiconductors, TV sets, plastics, chemicals, steel, food
Łódź	Łódź, Pabianice, Zgierz, Zduńska Wola, Łask, Aleksandrów, Konstantynów	water resources labour, location	concentrated, decidedly Łódź-dominated	textiles, clothing, food, rubber goods
Sudeten	Wałbrzych, Jelenia Góra, Świdnica, Bielawa, Nowa Ruda, Bolesławiec, Kłodzko, Bogatynia	minerals, water resources, communications, market	dispersed, no clearly dominating centre	power engineering, ceramics, glassware, textiles, machines, clothing, chemicals
Poznań	Poznań, Swarzędz, Luboń, Mosina, Oborniki	location in terms of communications, labour	concentrated, decidedly Poznań-dominated	food, transport equipment, machine tools, chemicals, furniture
Gdańsk	Gdańsk, Gdynia, Pruszcz Gd., Wejherowo, Rumia, Sopot	location in terms of communications, labour	concentrated, decidedly Tri-City-dominated	shipbuilding, refining, chemical, electromechanical, food
Wrocław	Wrocław, Oława, Jelcz, Brzeg Dolny, Oleśnica	location in terms of communications, labour	concentrated, decidedly Wrocław-dominated	machines, power devices, transport equipment, chemicals, food

Table 20. (Continued)

Name of district	Principal industrial centres	Main factors of establishment and development	Distribution of centres and size relations	Major industries
Old Polish	Kielce, Radom, Starachowice, Skarżysko-Kamienna, Ostrowiec Św., Kozienice, Pionki	minerals, water resources	dispersed, no clearly dominating centre	transportequipment, machines, minerals, food, power engineering
Podkarpacie	Nowy Sącz, Gorlice, Krosno, Jasło, Sanok	minerals, water resources, labour	dispersed, no clearly dominating centre	glassware, chemicals, electronic, transport equipment
Name of district	Principal industrial centres	Main factors of establishment and development	Distribution of centres and size relations	Major industries
Rzeszów	Rzeszów, Mielec, Dębica, Jarosław, Łańcut, Przeworsk	location in terms of communications, labour, political considerations	dispersed, no clearly dominating centre	transport equipment, machines, food, rubber goods, glassware
Bydgoszcz-Toruń	Bydgoszcz, Toruń, Barcin, Inowrocław, Janikowo	water resources, location in terms of communications, labour	dispersed, clear domination of Bydgoszcz and Toruń	electromechanical, chemical, food
Szczecin	Szczecin, Stargard Szcz., Police, Gryfino, Goleniów	location in terms of communications, water resources, labour	dispersed, decidedly Szczecin-dominated	shipbuilding and other electromechanical industries, power engineering, food

REFERENCES

Lista 500 przedsiębiorstw przemysłu przetwórczego za 1990 (The 1990 list of 500 enterprises of the processing industry), 1991. *Zarządzanie*, 6-7.

Polskie przedsiębiorstwa, Lista 500 (Polish enterprises, the 500 list). *Rzeczpospolita*, 9 October 2003.

Śleszyński P., 2003. Struktura i rozmieszczenie ośrodków zarządzania w polskiej gospodarce w 2002 r. (The structure and distribution of management centres in the Polish economy in 2002). *Przegląd Geograficzny* 74/2: 199-226.

In: Economic and Political Developments in Poland
Editor: Maureen P. Larsen
ISBN 978-1-61209-951-4

Chapter 3

THE ECONOMIC BASE OF THE MAJOR CITIES IN POLAND IN THE POLITICAL AND ECONOMIC RESTRUCTURING PERIOD

Dariusz Sokołowski
Institute of Geography, Nicolas Copernicus University,
Toruń, Poland

ABSTRACT

The article refers to the classical conception of economic base, which determines theoretical and methodological basement for research on functions of major cities in Poland. Beside updating on empiric knowledge about size and structure of the cities' economic base, there were attempts on defining direction of its rearrangement during system transformation, as well as on the cities' functional types.

INTRODUCTION

The political transformations at the end of the 20th century induced deep changes in the economy of cities in Poland. That is why it is necessary to define their economic base under the new conditions. The object of the present study are cities with a population of at least 100 thousand. This is a group of 42 units widely differing in size and in administrative status, which should be reflected in their functional diversity.

The theoretical foundation of the study is the classical conception of the economic base, in the framework of which the city's development is considered to consist of two factors (Dziewoński 1971, Jerczyński 1971). One of them includes territorially open activities, directed to the extra-urban market. Those exogenous functions are considered to be the basic factor of the city's development and existence, defining its identity or its position in the social or spatial division of labour (Jerczyński 1973). The other factor encompasses locally enclosed, endogenous activities, meeting the demands needs of the residents and the commuters.

The theory of economic base was gradually developed and formulated until W. Sombart (1907), who was first to use the division of urban employment into the endogenous and the exogenous group (cf inter alia Alexander 1954, Blumenfeld 1955, Alexandersson 1956, Dziewoński 1971). That theory regards the city as an integrated system of interacting elements. The impulses generated by the development of the exogenous sector initiate growth of other elements of the urban system. The development of that sector initiates the multiplier mechanism of the economic base, meaning that increased income from export beyond the city boundary is partly used for the city's development but it also increases the demand for endogenously produced goods.

The method used to investigate the cities' economic base was that of indirect measurement, viz. index of surplus workers, comparing labour surplus in a given section in a particular city with that in the whole country[1].

This article refers to the previous, partially not up-to –date research on economic base and functional structure of cities made on the territory of the whole Poland by M. Jerczyński (1973, 1977) and A. Matczak (1992), for example. The research has been conducted on the data from the 1970s and the 1980s, e.g. the time before system transformation.

Information on the size of employment allowed comparative analyses casting light on the present state of economy of the major cities in Poland and the trends in their transformations in the years 1993-2001 (it was the most intense period of proprietoral transformations in polish economy). The object of the study is the definition of the following characteristics of the economic base of the particular cities: 1) size, 2) structure, 3) degree of diversity, 4) trends in restructuring, 5) types of the cities.

The measurement of employment surplus was carried out in the system of sections distinguished according to the European Activity Classification[2]. It distinguishes 17 sections marked with symbols from A to Q: A – agriculture, hunting and silviculture, B – fishery and fishing, C – mining, D – manufacturing activity, E – producing and delivering electric energy, gas, water, F – construction, G – wholesale and retail trade; repairs of motor vehicles etc., H – hotels and restaurants, I – transport, storing economy and communication, J – finance agency, K – property service, leasing and business activity, L – public administration and national defence; legally guaranteed social welfare, M – education, N – health care and social welfare, O – other communal, social and individual services, P – households employing workers, Q – international organizations and teams.

In the present study the extreme sections: A, B and P, Q have been disregarded, as A and B do not play any significant role in the economy of large cities and do not generate employment surpluses, in P and Q the complete employment in the national scale was insignificant.

---

[1] The exogenous employment has been calculated by classical Hoyt's method (1944, cf Jerczyński 1971). $Eegz_iC_j = E_iC_j - \left(PC_j \frac{E_iCo}{PCo}\right)$. Denotations: $Eegz_iC_j$ – exogenous employment in section i in city C_j, (i=1,2,...,m; j=1,2,...,n), E_iC_j – employment in section i in city C_j, E_iCo – employment in section i in the whole country, PC_j – number of inhabitants of a given city, PCo – number of inhabitants of the country.

[2] *Nomenclatures des Activites de Communite Europeene – NACE rev. 1.*, Official Journal of the European Communities (OJ) No. L 293, 1990.10.24.

Size of the Economic Base

The degree of predominance of Warsaw over the other cities is disproportionately high relatively to population[3] (Figure 1). Considering that, the national capital can be distinguished as a separate category, a cen ter leaving behind all the remaining cities (functional macrocephaly). The disproportions among the remaining big cities (with populations from 300 to 800 thou) are much smaller and the size of the economic base is not always proportionate to the population. The highest position in that group of city centres is held by Katowice, which is the working place for the residents of many neighbouring towns and cities and performs numerous functions for the Upper Silesian conurbation. High positions are also held by Cracow and Poznań, which results from their favourable development conditions (cf among others B. Domański et al. 2000, R. Domański 2000) as well as from their winning the competition for investments against other centres. The situation of Łódź, one of the largest cities in Poland, is comparatively unfavourable – it is less successful than other centres of similar size in resisting functional degradation.

Besides the capital also Katowice, Cracow, Poznań, Wrocław and possibly Łódź (all of them with employment surplus exceeding 100 thou) can be defined as dominant centres, but the border line between them and the following cities is not clear.

The following positions are held by Szczecin, Gdańsk, Bydgoszcz, Jastrzębie-Zdrój, Bielsko-Biała, Rzeszów, Gliwice, Kielce, Lublin, Opole, Toruń, Olsztyn, Częstochowa, Dąbrowa Górnicza, Białystok, Tychy. Each of them has an employment surplus exceeding 25 thou people. The surprisingly high position of Jastrzębie-Zdrój with its population of only 101 thou in 2001 can be explained by the structure of its economic base – it is a monofunctional centre, where nearly the entire employment surplus (98%) is related to the mining industry. A similar structure is found in several other cities of the Upper Silesian Industrial District.

Centres in the eastern part of the country, Lublin and Białystok, rank lower than could be expected judging from the size of their population and their administrative rank. The worst situation is found in Grudziądz and Wałbrzych, which are nearly completely devoid of economic base. The economic crisis of the former two cities is to a large extent the result of the collapse of our export to the eastern markets, the latter two have suffered mainly as a result of the decline of traditional, obsolete industries.

As far as the relation of the employment surplus to the number of inhabitants is concerned, the leading position is held by Warsaw and Katowice. At the beginning of the system transformation period (beginning of the 1990s) high positions in that respect were also held by some smaller cities in the group (100-200 thou inhabitants), situated mostly in the densely populated south of the country: Dąbrowa Górnicza, Tychy, Jastrzębie-Zdrój, Gliwice, Rzeszów, Opole, Bielsko-Biała. The first four are parts of an urban-industrial conurbation, which implies a division of functions among complementary centres. The remaining ones are centres of urban agglomerations performing definite functions for the surrounding areas, or else they are situated in the midst of densely populated, fairly urbanized rural areas with high labour supply. However, a well developed economic base in cities of the first group is not a rule, examples of which are such cities as Zabrze, Chorzów and Sosnowiec. Until 2001

[3] Appropriate data for Warsaw are extended because of measuring an employment according to an enterprise head office method.

Warsaw was one of the few cities that strengthened their position and became the only large centre, in which the size of employment surplus exceeded the number of inhabitants.

Figure 1. Size of economic base of the major cities in Poland (1993-2001).

The changes in size of the economic base of many cities in the years 1993-2001 were deep enough to result in considerable rank shifts. Rises in employment surpluses were noted in only five cities: Warsaw, Cracow, Poznań, Jastrzębie-Zdrój and Chorzów, stabilization – in Płock and Kielce. In the remaining cities a higher or lower drop in employment surpluses was observed, the lowest in Łódź, Toruń, Gorzów Wielkopolski and Zabrze, the highest in Wałbrzych, Ruda Śląska, Dąbrowa Górnicza, Tychy, Bytom, Gliwice, Radom, Lublin and Bydgoszcz. The total of employment surpluses in the whole group of cities under study decreased from 3635 to 3462 thousand, while the entire employment in the sectors under discussion increased nationwide from 13 198 to 14 775 thousand. That is the result of two coinciding phenomena: 1) a drop in total employment in most large cities, 2) an increase in endogenous employment. The decrease in total employment in many cities shows that they did not overcome the unfavourable economic as well as social effects of the system transformation. The increase in endogenous employment is explained by Hoyt (1954) both by an increase in social affluence and by a rise in unemployment (usually the unemployed are conventionally rated as belonging to the endogenous group). Both phenomena were observed in Polish cities in the system transformation period; increased unemployment and greater affluence of a considerable part of society resulted in substantial social polarization.

The crisis affected particularly the cities of Upper Silesia and Wałbrzych, whose economy was based until recently (and in some of them still is) on heavy and mining industry, which is characterized by low efficiency and high liability to economic fluctuations. The roots of the difficulties of the remaining cities can be to some extent elucidated by an analysis of the structure of their economic base.

Structure of the Economic Base, Predominant Functions

In analysing the structure of the economic base absolute numbers should be taken into account, since in the case of very low employment surpluses even their high diversification may not be a significant development factor.

A characteristic feature of the economy of Upper Silesian cities is its low diversity; it is usually dominated by one section, mostly C or D. On the other hand, the provincial capitals have a favourable structure – most of them can be defined as multifunctional centres (Figs 2-4). In 1993 employment in section C prevailed in Jastrzębie-Zdrój, Tychy, Rybnik, Ruda Śląska, Bytom and Sosnowiec (>50% employment surpluses) as well as in Gliwice and Wałbrzych (30-50%). Until 2001 the situation remained basically unchanged in the first five cities, while in the remaining cities employment in section C decreased considerably – in Wałbrzych down to zero (closing of coalmines).

In most cities under study, the predominant kind of economic base has been and still is the manufacturing activity (section D). In 1993 it generated more than one half of employment surpluses in Dąbrowa Górnicza and Bielsko-Biała, and in 2001 in Dąbrowa Górnicza, Częstochowa, Tarnów and Kalisz. A preponderance of the manufacturing activity over other sections (less than 50%) in 2001 was noted in eleven more cities, Włocławek, Płock, Bielsko-Biała, Toruń, Łódź, Gdynia, Elbląg, Bydgoszcz, Gorzów Wielkopolski, Słupsk and Szczecin, and in several others it held significant, second or third positions. Section E (production and delivery of electric energy, gas and water) does not play any important role except in Zabrze and Wałbrzych, where it is the predominant activity (50-80 per cent). A more even distribution characterizes construction (section F), which shows from several to twenty per cent surpluses in most cities under study, and the situation did not change significantly in the years 1993-2001. That kind of activity is of greatest importance in Płock, Kielce and several cities in Upper Silesia.

Trade (section G) plays an important role in a large number of cities; its maximum employment surplus exceeds 40% (Radom), while its mean percentage is about 20%. In several cities of Upper Silesia and in Elbląg employment in trade shows deficit (negative index value). Section H (hotels and restaurants) does not hold a high position in any city, while section I is concentrated in several cities (Warsaw, Katowice, Gdynia), where its share reaches 20-30%.

Figure 2. Economic base of the major cities in Poland in 2001 according to the kind of the dominant function.

In 1993 the situation was different: at that time activities in transport, storage economy and communication constituted important parts in the economic base of nearly two thirds of the cities under study. Section J (finance agency), too, shows progressing concentration in several centres, particularly in Warsaw and Wrocław (shares of the order of 10%), also in Cracow, Łódź, Katowice and Poznań.

At the beginning of the transformation period that activity was fairly evenly distributed, and did not exceed 5% share in any city. Section K (broadly understood activity associated with business) is among the most widespread activities; it shows surpluses in most cities under study. In recent years it has developed particularly well in Legnica (over 50% surplus employment), Chorzów (over 40%), Zielona Góra, Gliwice and several largest cities.

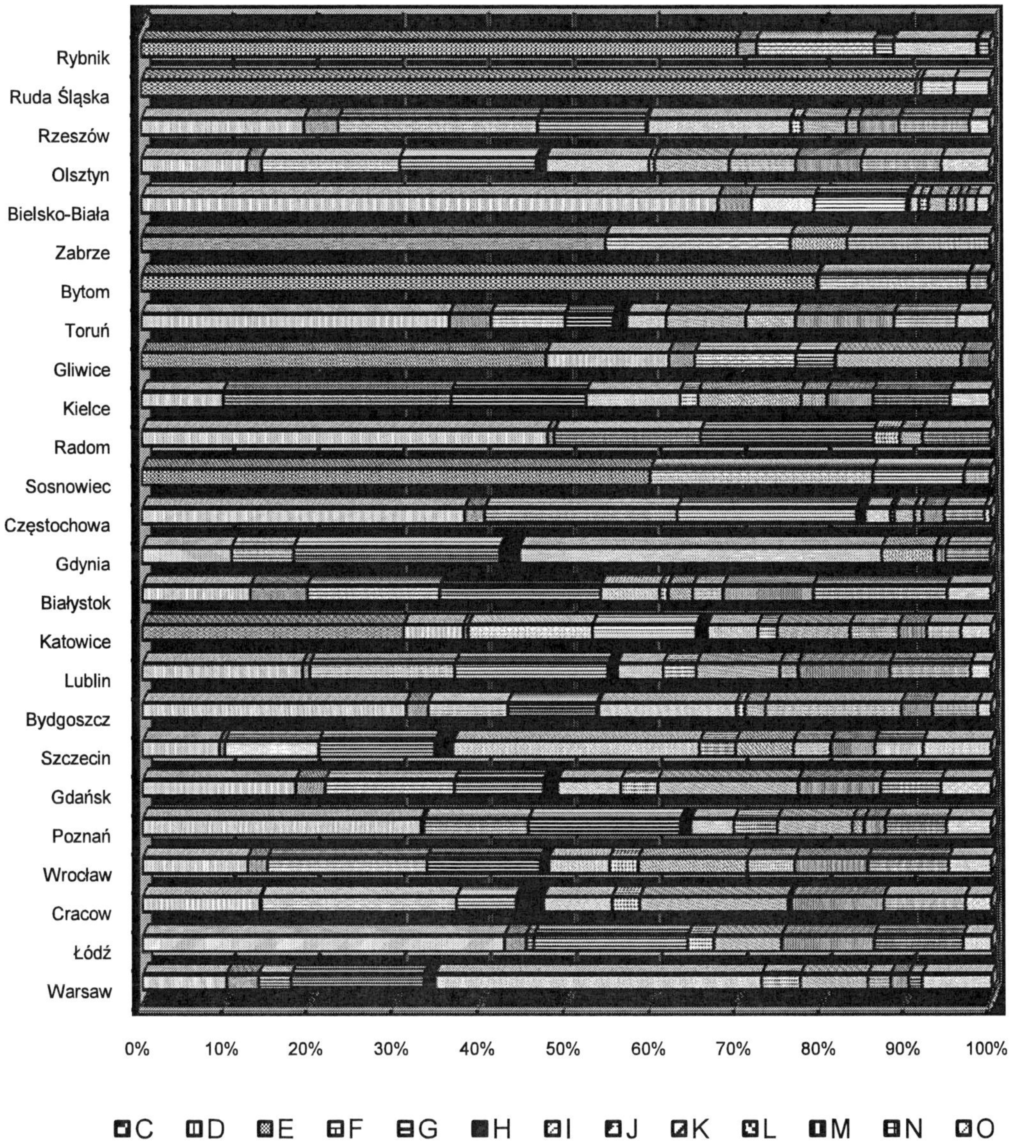

Figure 3. Structure of the economic base of 25 major cities in Poland in 1993 (according to sections).

Section L (mainly public administration and national defence) constitutes a particularly high percentage in the activities of provincial centres, which evidently follows from their rank in the territorial and administrative structure of the country. Elbląg, Koszalin and Grudziądz are exceptions – in their case high percentages do not translate into adequately high absolute values. The only present-day provincial capital with no surplus in that activity has been and still is Gdańsk. Section M (education) is among stable activities, i.e. it is subject to but little change, and it is evenly spread over most cities. Exceptions from the rule are most cities of Upper Silesia, Płock Włocławek, Gdynia, Elbląg, Gorzów Wielkopolski, Kalisz and Legnica, which have no surpluses in that section.

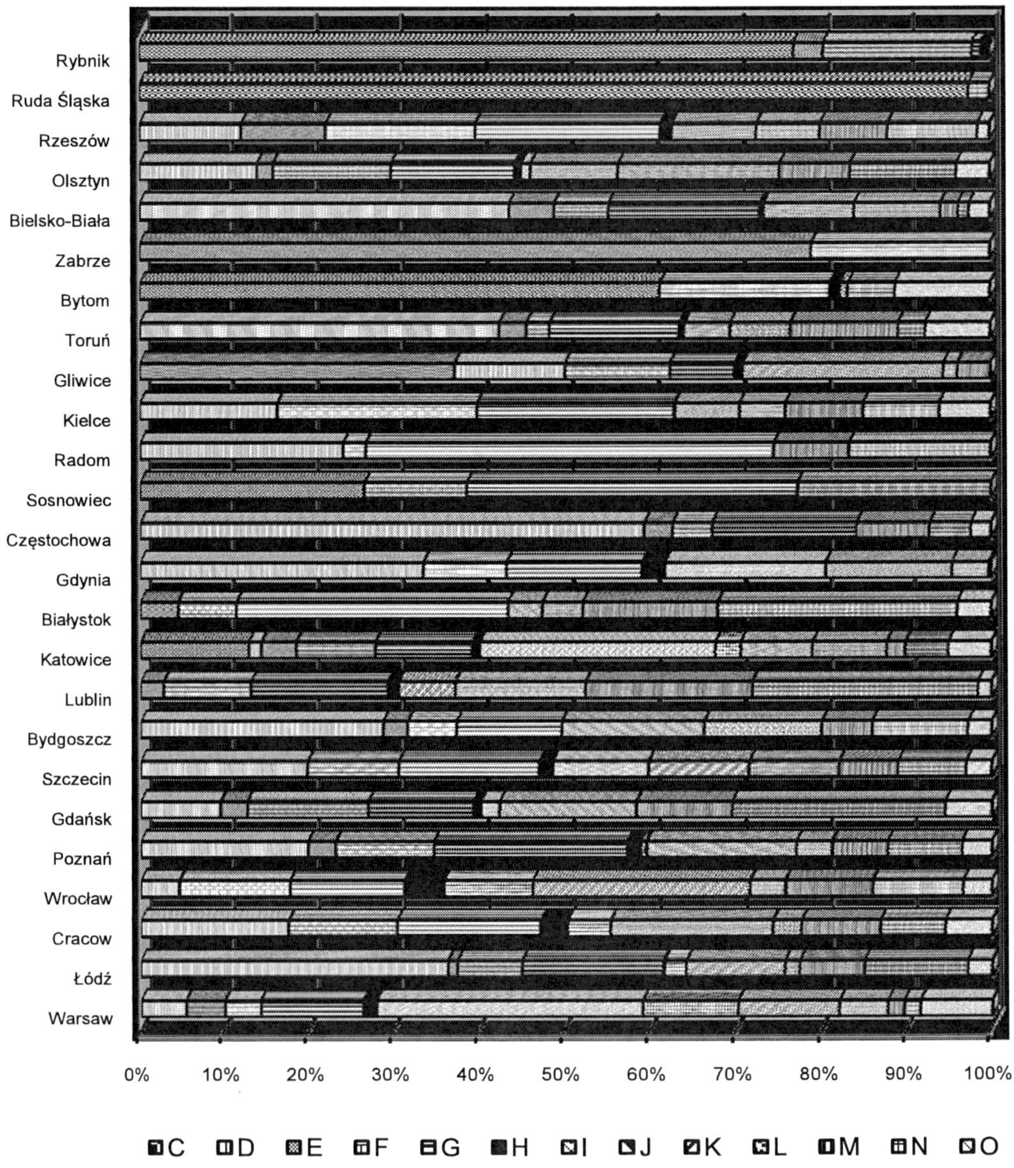

Figure 4. Structure of the economic base of 25 major cities in Poland in 2001 (according to sections).

A certain growth in the part of education has been noted in Lublin and Białystok but that results mainly from a considerable drop in employment in other kinds of activities. Section N (health care and social welfare) shows a somewhat lower stability. In 1993 it showed several up to twenty per cent employment surpluses in 39 out of 42 cities under study (except Gliwice, Dąbrowa Górnicza and Ruda Śląska). Until 2001 the list of cities without section N in the structure of their economic base increased by three: Rybnik, Zabrze and Gdynia, while a significant increase was noted in Grudziądz, Lublin and Gdańsk. Like in the case of education, it is often reletive in character.

DIVERSITY

The structure diversity degree can be measured by means of the synthetic index known in literature as Amemiya's index[4] (Jerczyński 1973). The index values (η) are comprised in the range from 0 to 1, and their interpretation is that lower values denote higher diversity of structure. The index reaches its maximum value when the structure is homogeneous, i.e. when the total employment surplus is concentrated in one section.

At this stage it seems possible to put forward and verify the thesis on the growth of the diversification degree of the cities' economic base. The confirmation of that tendency would point at a favourable trend in the development of urban economies, from the point of view of both increasing their immunity to transitory disturbances in the economic situation and of improving the accessibility of certain goods and services to consumers. A comparison of the corresponding values from 1993 and 2001 (Figure 5) does not confirm the validity of that thesis. The mean value of the index grew between the years 1993 and 2001 from 0.228 to 0.276, which even points to a drop in the structure diversification degree.

Table 1. Classification of cities according to size and diversity of the economic base in 1993

Diversity degrees	Size (globally)		
	low (<10% of the city's inhabitants)	medium (10-25% of the city's inhabitants)	high (>25% of the city's inhabitants)
Very low (η≥0,600)		Ruda Śląska, Bytom	Dąbrowa Górnicza, Tychy, Jastrzębie-Zdrój
Low (0,600>η≥0,300)	Sosnowiec, Zabrze		Bielsko-Biała, Rybnik
Medium (0,300>η≥0,150)	Chorzów, Grudziądz	Częstochowa, Łódź, Kalisz, Gdynia, Płock, Włocławek, Tarnów, Radom	Gliwice
High (η<0,150)		Wrocław, Gdańsk, Koszalin, Słupsk, Białystok, Legnica, Cracow, Kielce, Gorzów Wielkopolski, Bydgoszcz, Wałbrzych, Toruń, Elbląg	Opole, Olsztyn, Zielona Góra, Lublin, Szczecin, Rzeszów, Katowice, Poznań, Warsaw

The comparative evenness of distribution of surpluses in the cities under study declines gradually in favour of their concentration in selected centres. There follows an increase in index dispersion, which is associated with an increase in specialization of cities in some domaines. An increase in diversification of the economic base has been noted in 10 cities (Warsaw, Łódź, Szczecin, Gdynia, Sosnowiec, Bytom, Bielsko-Biała, Tychy, Dąbrowa

[4] $\eta = \sum_{i=1}^{m} \frac{m}{m-1}\left(\frac{Eegz_iC_j}{EegzC_j} - \frac{1}{m}\right)^2$. Denotations: m - number of sections (13), $Eegz_iC_j$ – exogenous employment in section i in city C_j, $EegzC_j$ – total exogenous employment in city C_j.

Górnicza, Grudziądz), decrease – in 32. In some smaller cities (Legnica, Elbląg, Wałbrzych, Zielona Góra, Zabrze) the degree of reduction in diversity in employment surpluses was very considerable. It is noteworthy that the first three of the cities mentioned are former provincial capitals degraded in 1999, which clearly demonstrates the relationship between the administrative function and the economy.

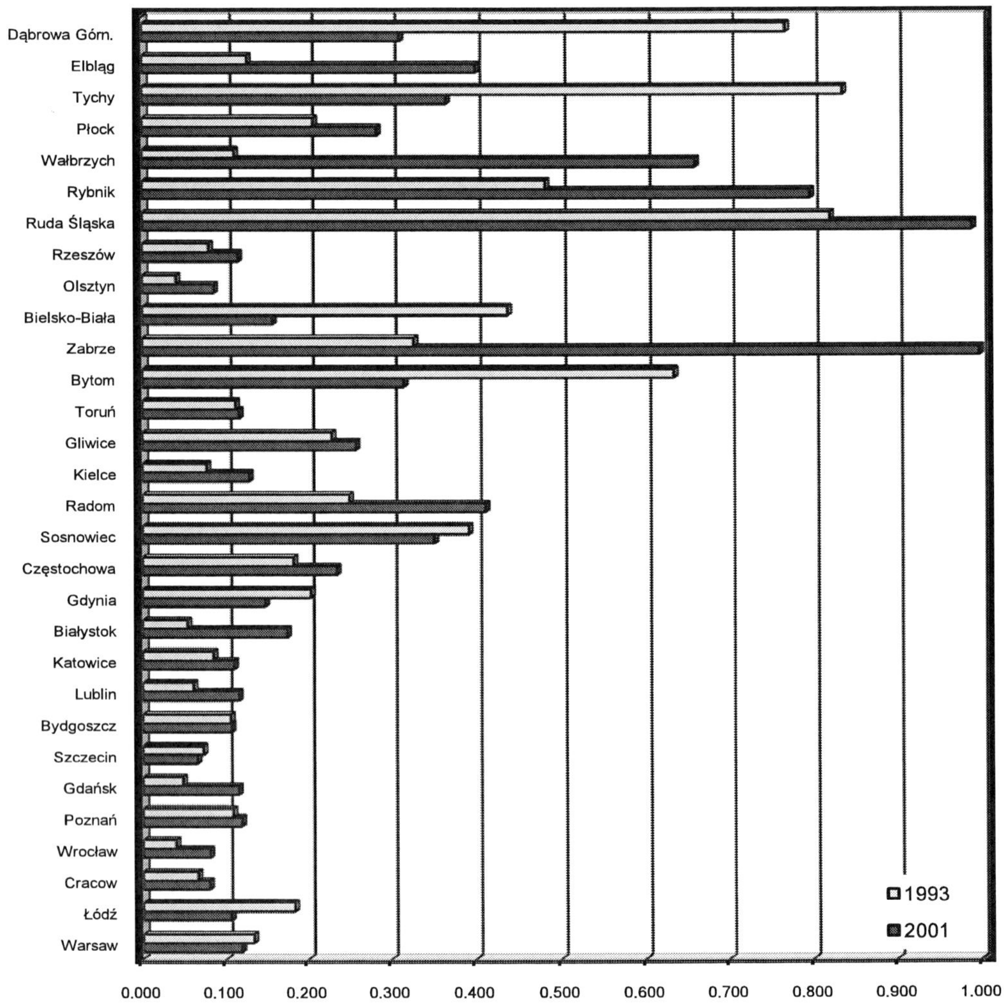

Figure 5. Changes in diversity degree of the cities' economic base in the years 1993-2001 (index η; 30 major cities in Poland).

On the ground of the structure diversity index and of the absolute value of the economic base a classification based on two characteristics has been constructed, allowing to classify each city to one of 12 categories (Table 1, 2). Shaded areas indicate cities with the most favourable (lower right-hand corner) and the most unfavourable (upper left-hand corner) situation in point of the size and diversity of the economic base.

Table 2. Classification of cities according to size and diversity of the economic base in 2001

Diversity degrees	Size (globally)		
	low (<10% of the city's inhabitants)	medium (10-25% of the city's inhabitants)	high (>25% of the city's inhabitants)
Very low (η≥0,600)	Wałbrzych, Zabrze	Rybnik, Ruda Śląska	Jastrzębie-Zdrój
Low (0,600>η≥0,300)	Legnica, Bytom, Elbląg, Radom, Sosnowiec	Dąbrowa Górnicza, Tychy, Tarnów, Chorzów	
Medium (0,300>η≥0,150)	Białystok, Grudziądz	Włocławek, Częstochowa, Kalisz, Gliwice, Płock	Bielsko-Biała
High (η<0,150)	Gdynia	Szczecin, Wrocław, Olsztyn, Koszalin, Łódź, Bydgoszcz, Gorzów Wielkopolski, Gdańsk, Lublin, Toruń, Słupsk, Kielce, Zielona Góra	Cracow, Opole, Katowice, Rzeszów, Warsaw, Poznań

In general terms, in the system transformation period the situation of the cities deteriorated. In the first place, the number of units with a high (favourable) level of both characteristics dropped from nine to six and that of units with low or very low level increased from two to seven; that with combined levels: medium/low (very low) increased from four to eight. As far as individual cities are concerned, the greatest shift was found in Wałbrzych: from the high/medium type in the extreme upper left-hand corner it fell to the low/very low area.

TYPES OF THE CITIES

In order to define the cities' types with reference to the character of their economic base as well as to the trends and degree of transformations, the Ossan triangle method was used (Figure 6). Its construction imposes a tripartite structure; that is why a division of urban economies into three sectors has been adopted: production activity (P), which is a sum of sections C-F, material services (M) – a sum of sections G-I, non-material services (N) – sum of sections J-O.

Types P, N and M include cities with a clear predominance of one sector (at least 50%) and low percentages of the remaining sectors (less than 25% each); type R is of mixed character with comparable percentages of the particular sectors (centre of triangle). The remaining types consist of two significant sectors with a dominance of one sector and a high percentage of the other one (denoted by the second letter), fluctuating between 25 and 50%.

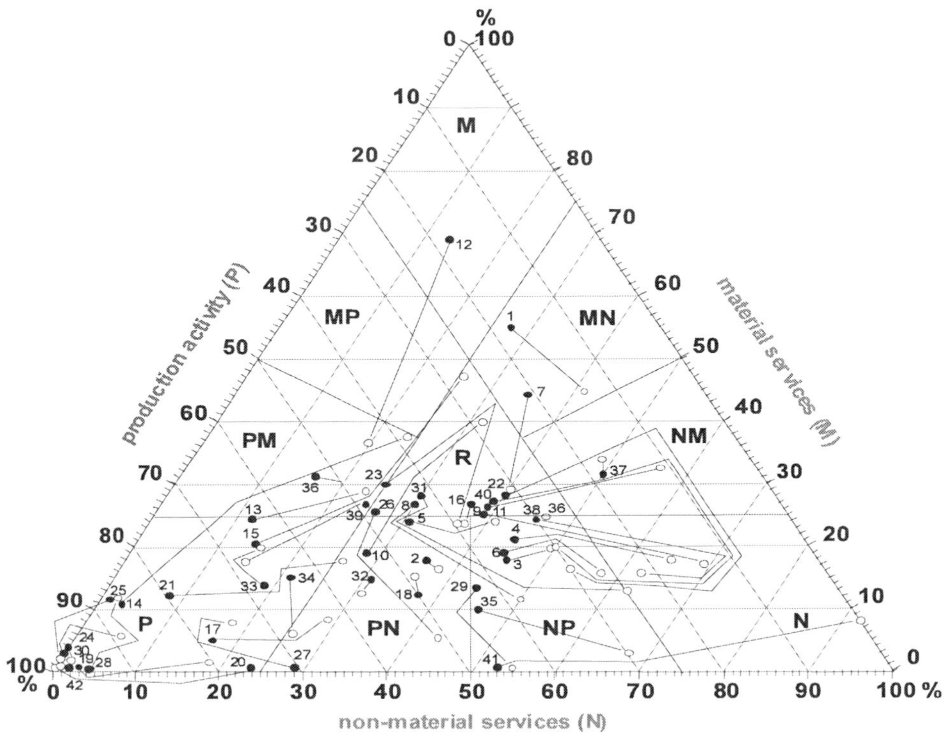

Figure 6. Structure of the economic base of Poland's major cities in the sector perspective; account has been taken of the shifts in the years 1993-2001 (numbering of cities in descending order of population size in accordance with Table 3).

In the group under study it is type P that predominates (Figure 6, list of cities in Table 3).

The transformations of the large cities' types in the transformation period show characteristics typical of the whole economy. The most distinctive of them is the decrease in the number of cities with a preponderance of manufacturing activities (P) from 14 to 10 and of cities of mixed character (R) from 8 to 3. The predominant transformation trend was the shift towards non-material services (towards the right-hand corner in the diagram), which resulted in an increase in the number of cities of type N (from 0 to 5) as well as of other types of cities with a considerable percentage of component N (NP, PN).

The restructuring of the economic base towards an increased percentage of non-manufacturing services is characteristic of highly developed countries. For that reason, in spite of the high costs of social transformation (unemployment, poverty) and the unfavourable property structure, particularly in the key areas of the economy, such as banking, it should be regarded as a positive phenomenon.

Individual shifts were not always in line with the dominant trend. Thus Płock, Kalisz, Gdynia and several other cities showed an increase in the importance of the manufacturing activities (P). In the diagram they shifted towards the left-hand corner. A shift up the diagram indicating an increase in importance of material services was observed in the first place in Katowice, Częstochowa, Sosnowiec and Radom.

The longest shift trajectory, and therefore the deepest restructuring was noted in Grudziądz (NP→N), Opole (R→N), Sosnowiec (P→PN), Radom (P→R) and Gdynia (M→PM). The least shifts, indicating practically stabilization of the structure of the economic base were found in the following cities: Łódź, Toruń and Gorzów Wielkopolski (all represent type PN), Ruda Śląska, Dąbrowa Górnicza, Jastrzębie-Zdrój and Włocławek (all – type P), Cracow (type NP), Koszalin (NM), Kielce (minimal shift from R to PN).

Table 3. Cities according to the types of economic base in particular years

Type of economic base	1993	2001
P	13-Częstochowa, 14-Sosnowiec, 15-Radom, 17-Gliwice, 19-Bytom, 20-Zabrze, 21-Bielsko-Biała, 24-Ruda Śląska, 25-Rybnik, 28-Tychy, 30-Dąbrowa Górnicza, 33-Włocławek, 34-Tarnów, 42-Jastrzębie-Zdrój	19-Bytom, 20-Zabrze, 24-Ruda Śląska, 25-Rybnik, 27-Płock, 28-Tychy, 30-Dąbrowa Górnicza, 33-Włocławek, 39-Kalisz, 42-Jastrzębie-Zdrój
N	-	4-Wrocław, 9-Lublin, 31-Opole, 38-Legnica, 41-Grudziądz
M	12-Gdynia	-
R	8-Bydgoszcz, 9-Lublin, 11-Białystok, 16-Kielce, 22-Olsztyn, 26-Wałbrzych, 31-Opole, 40-Słupsk	7-Szczecin, 10-Katowice, 15-Radom
PM	23-Rzeszów, 36-Zielona Góra, 39-Kalisz	12-Gdynia, 13-Częstochowa, 14-Sosnowiec
MP	-	-
MN	1-Warsaw, 7-Szczecin	1-Warsaw
NM	37-Koszalin	11-Białystok, 37-Koszalin
NP	3-Cracow, 4-Wrocław, 6-Gdańsk, 29-Elbląg, 35-Chorzów, 38-Legnica, 41-Grudziądz	3-Cracow, 5-Poznań, 6-Gdańsk, 8-Bydgoszcz, 22-Olsztyn, 29-Elbląg, 35-Chorzów, 36-Zielona Góra, 40-Słupsk
PN	2-Łódź, 5-Poznań, 10-Katowice, 18-Toruń, 27-Płock, 32-Gorzów Wielkopolski	2-Łódź, 16-Kielce, 17-Gliwice, 18-Toruń, 21-Bielsko-Biała, 23-Rzeszów, 26-Wałbrzych, 32-Gorzów Wielkopolski, 34-Tarnów

Conclusion

The dominance of the state capital becomes reinforced, often at the cost of a certain functional degradation of other cities.

In most cities the economic base weakened, particularly in those which lost their rank of provincial centres in 1999 and in the industrial centres of the Upper Silesian conurbation. In the latter and in Wałbrzych the crisis in the urban economy is due to a large extent to the fact that it is based on the low-yield heavy and mining industry. An essential feature of the cities under study is the prevailing drop in diversification of the economic base, observed in as many as 32 cities. A concentration of employment surpluses is observed in select cities, which results in increased specialization of ci ties, especially in the realm of finance agency (Section J). That refers to a lesser extent to the traditional, more stable sections of economy, including education and health care.

The leading role in most cities is still played by the production activity (Section D). The effect of the restructuring processes in economy is changes in the types of cities, observed in the division into sectors. Except for a few cases, the dominance of the production activities in the cities' economic base has been on the decrease in favour of an increase in the part of non-material services. As a result of those transformations, the character of the economic base of the major cities in Poland makes them closer to West-European cities.

References

Alexander J.W., 1954, *The basic–nonbasic concept of urban economic functions*, Economic Geography, 30, 246-261.

Alexandersson G., 1956, *The industrial structure of American cities*, Lincoln, University of Nebraska Press.

Blumenfeld H., 1955, *The economic base of the metropolis*, Journal of the American Institute of Planners, 21, s. 114-132.

Domański B., Guzik R., Gwosdz K., 2000, *Konkurencyjność i ranga wielkich miast Polski w świetle inwestycji zagranicznych firm produkcyjnych*, [in:] R. Domański (ed.), *Nowe problemy rozwoju wielkich miast i regionów*, Biuletyn KPZK PAN, 192, 99-124.

Domański R., 2000, *Poznań jako ośrodek przyciągania na trajektorii Berlin–Warszawa. Możliwości pośrednie*, [in:] R. Domański (ed.), *Nowe problemy rozwoju wielkich miast i regionów*, Biuletyn KPZK PAN, 192, 213-219.

Dziewoński K., 1971, *Baza ekonomiczna i struktura funkcjonalna miast. Studium rozwoju pojęć, metod i ich zastosowań*, Prace Geograficzne IG PAN, 87, 9-110.

Hoyt H., 1944, *The economic status of the New York Metropolitan Region in 1944*, New York.

Hoyt H., 1954, *Homer Hoyt on development of economic base concept*, Land Economics, 30, 182-186.

Jerczyński M., 1971, *Metody pośrednie identyfikacji i pomiaru bazy ekonomicznej miast*, Prace Geograficzne IG PAN, 87, 111-141.

Jerczyński M., 1973, *Zagadnienia specjalizacji bazy ekonomicznej większych miast w Polsce*, [in:] *Studia nad strukturą funkcjonalną miast*, Prace Geograficzne IG PAN, 97, 9-134.

Jerczyński M., 1977, *Funkcje i typy funkcjonalne polskich miast*, [in:] *Statystyczna charakterystyka miast.*

Matczak A., 1992, *Zmiany w strukturze funkcjonalnej miast Polski w latach 1973-1983*, [in:] *Funkcja administracyjna miast*, Acta Universitatis Lodziensis, Folia Geographica, 17, Łódź, s. 9-25.

Sombart W., 1907, *Der Begriff Stadt und das Wesen der Städtebildung*, Archiv für Sozialwissenschaft und Sozialpolitik, 225, 1-9.

In: Economic and Political Developments in Poland
Editor: Maureen P. Larsen
ISBN 978-1-61209-951-4

Chapter 4

Regions and Regionalism in Poland

Roman Matykowski
Institute of Socio-Economic Geography and Spatial Management,
Adam Mickiewicz University, Poznań, Poland

Abstract

The aim of the article is to characterize selected components of contemporary regionalism in Poland. Manifestations of regionalism are analysed against the backcloth of historical processes, changes in the administrative structure, and ethnic issues.

Introduction

The concept of regionalism is closely connected with that of a region, and the latter has kept changing over the last century, not only in geography but also in other sciences employing this term, like sociology, history, or anthropology. The region has been among the most widely used terms in geography for over a hundred years, but it has also been one of the most imprecise and ambiguous ones. The concepts of a region developed in Poland under the influence of French, German and Anglo-Saxon geographers now regarded as classics, and in the 1950s and 1960s, also under the influence of Soviet geographers. The works by Hartshorne (1959, 1961) and Whittlesey (1954) became beacons to Polish regional studies from 1960s on, and the region was often treated as a tool for analysis or a basis for a specific research method in geography. Hence, in the works by Polish geographers of that time, the discussion about the notion of a region was combined with a discussion about the subject matter of geography. Polish geography of the later half of the 20th century, making use also of the external inspiration of world science, has worked out its own specific approaches to the region: classical, dogmatic, positivistic, dialectic, and realistic (Rykiel 2001).

In West European and American geography, regionalism has usually been understood as organised collective political or cultural action whose aim is gaining autonomy for a region or even supporting its secession (cf. Knight 1984). Such action, also intended to raise regional consciousness, is what Bahrenberg (1993) calls political regionalism. He distinguishes its two forms, 'hard' (associated with autonomist and separatist movements, e.g. Corsican, Breton, or Friesian) and 'soft' (connected with changing the decision-making arrangement in hierarchised administrative structures). Apart from political regional movements relying on cultural differences, there have appeared new forms clearly referring to the specific nature of economic or planning practices of regional strategy (cf. Deas, Ward 2000; Cooke 2002). However, these new forms of regionalism also have their critics (Lovering 1999). An interesting example of the new activity is the political regionalism of the Northern League in Italy advocating the regional separateness and secession of the wealthiest, northern part of Italy, 'Padania' (cf. Giordano 2000).

In the Polish studies devoted to regionalism, one can observe several approaches to the definition of the subject matter. In many cases the authors make no attempt to give the term a precise meaning. Others, while failing to come up with an unequivocal operational definition of regionalism, suggest the notional scope of the term indirectly through the description of their research object. It is only rarely that one can find any operational definitions which provide a starting point for a further analysis of the phenomenon. Still, there are three interpretations of regionalism currently in use in Polish science (cf. Chojnicki, Czyż 1992; Skorowski 1993; Matykowski 2003a).

On one interpretation, regionalism is understood as a kind of social awareness present among the inhabitants of a specified territory which is a fragment of the internal spatial structure of a state.

A second approach sees regionalism as economic, cultural and political activities of a territorial community that are intended to defend its interests (including the modernisation of the economy) and to preserve its distinctiveness (values threatened, among others, by the central authorities of the state).

The two forms of regionalism are generally thought to be its complementary constituents (cf. Chojnicki, Czyż 1992; Szczepański 1995). However, in the world literature one can often find a different opinion according to which studies of people's emotional ties with the territory they inhabit are not identical with studies of regionalism, but are a segment of social or cultural geography. This type of research is concerned with, e.g., regional identity and regional images, regional-cultural distinctiveness (e.g. in the shape of Oklahomaness, Englishness, etc.), or vernacular regions. In the other kind of regionalism, in turn, there are serious difficulties with establishing the scope of pro-regional activities. Included among the manifestations of this kind of regionalism are not only artistic activity based on regional motifs but also a regional policy devised by organs of the highest-order administrative units and other regional institutions.

A third approach to regionalism can be found in the world literature of the 1990s, where the term is meant to denote a form of supra-state integration based on a search for a common cultural identity or on the pursuit of common economic goals (Hine 1992; Gibb, Michalak 1994). This kind of regionalism refers to a totally different spatial scale than the traditional one, and its syndromes are sometimes treated as complementary, and sometimes as contrary, to globalisation. Similarly, in the political scientific literature the term regionalism is used to denote 'states lying close together geographically' seeking the most effective forms of international co-operation in the form of various integration alliances and associations (cf. Haliżak 2000). It seems to the present author that, given its spatial range and character and to distinguish it from the two aforementioned types, this kind of regionalism should be termed economic, political or cultural pan-regionalism.

Region as a Source of Regionalism

Since the 1960s, the conviction has gained ground in the Polish geographical literature that there are three basic concepts (and forms) of the region: (1) as a tool of analysis, (2) as a tool for action (i.e., an administrative-political unit), and (3) as an object of knowledge (Dziewoński 1967). In the 1990s, Chojnicki (1996) modified this view by distinguishing two forms of region, analytical and substantive. In the analytical approach, a region is a homogeneous area of occurrence of a property (or a set of properties) significant in terms of the adopted research assumptions. In the substantive approach, a region is understood as a real social object, or a component of social reality. It can therefore be treated as a special type of social-territorial formation (cf. Murphy 1991).

Regionalist studies have been developing at the crossroads of several disciplines, including geography, sociology, history, and cultural anthropology, and the notion of a region they employ tends to be ambiguous. In anthropology, a region usually denotes an ethnic territory, i.e. an area inhabited by a group of people sharing a distinct culture (e.g., folk/ethnic or denominational) which is part of general national culture. Thus, it is endowed with a set of cultural characteristics and phenomena different from those in any other place within the same society. In sociology, a region is understood as a correlate of a territorial community sharing an awareness of separateness. Its essence, apart from the sense of separateness, is the presence of links based on an emotional attitude towards the area inhabited, regarded as an 'ideological fatherland'. Jałowiecki (1996: 42) is of the opinion that a region in the sociological approach is "an area whose residents' awareness is so well developed that it is experienced daily". In social science a region is often treated as a product of social interactions (cf. Lefebvre 1974; Giddens 1984). Historic regions, in turn, as Rykiel (2001) observes, are treated as 'naturally' given and immutable, and what interests scholars is at most their genesis, not development. Hence, one can often encounter the opinion in Poland that historic regions also exist today and exhibit socio-cultural peculiarities resulting from their traditions (cf. Kiełczewska-Zaleska 1980; Piskozub 1987).

In this multitude of region definitions, one should note their spatial aspect, characteristic of geography, and their constitutive aspect, peculiar to the individual disciplines.

The spatial dimension of an object inhabited by a community can assume the form of, e.g., a region, a territory, a natural (or social) area, and a place. The notion of regionalism seems to be inalienably connected with that of a region, although it is sometimes also transferred to links of a community with a natural area or territory. However, a region is an object which is extremely flexible spatially in geography and can assume the size of a playing field or a small housing estate (hence sometimes called a *microregion*), or it can be a superstructure of continental dimensions (*megaregions*). Therefore, a crucial issue in regional study is the size of the region in which the links between the territory and its inhabitants have developed. The Polish sociologist S. Ossowski (1967) distinguished between 'a private fatherland' and 'land' when writing about man's emotional ties with a territory. An individual is connected with 'a private fatherland' through direct, personal experiences with this territory.

This concept is similar to that of place developed by Yi-Fu Tuan (1977), although less extensive in the spatial dimension. A place assumes a concrete reality for an individual through the experiences and impressions it offers him. Häkli (1994) suggests that while a region is clearly collective in nature, a place is an expression of an individual's practice and experience. Like regions, places can exist in a variety of scales. In turn, an individual is connected with Ossowski's 'land' through his membership of the community which is assigned to this area in a sense. Thus, the lower limit to the size of a region that can be a source of regionalism is what Ossowski calls a 'land' and geographers, a *subregion* (the size of a US county). In turn, Chojnicki (1996) claims that an important factor in the formation of regional links is the region's institutional development. This development is associated with the institutionalisation of the region as a unit of a country's administrative division. Therefore, one can take Chojnicki to suggest that the territory being the source of regionalist feeling is determined historically and culturally, and in modern times it should be connected with the highest-order administrative unit in terms of size (in Poland, a voivodeship). It seems that a study of a community at a scale smaller than a subregion in the European tradition can be regarded as a study of locality.

The other basic component of a region is a human community inhabiting a territory. The community (often termed regional or territorial) is sometimes treated as a collectivity of residents with a complex social structure. At times it is assumed that the community is comparatively homogeneous, having experienced advanced processes of cultural and social integration. If it stands out for its ethnic characteristics, it is termed an ethnic regional group. Yiftachel (1997) point out that ethnic regionalism can also develop in areas of ethnic tension (e.g., in Israel). Regional interests and the tendency for the ethnic minority and majority to seek benefits protect and preserve regional-ethnic identity. Thus, the community inhabiting a region can be seen as:

a) a homogeneous group,
b) as a dichotomous collectivity in which one group stimulates the whole to region-forming actions and attitudes; or
c) as a community with a complex social structure in which some groups can display authentic regionalist attitudes while others imitate them.

German geographers (e.g., Hard 1987; Kerscher 1992) draw attention to the manipulation of the phenomenon of regionalism leading to 'spatial abstraction'. Kerscher (1992) even carries out an identification of actors propagating this abstraction. It seems that also in Poland there are interest groups within territorial communities which by propagating 'spatial abstraction' change into 'quasi-regional players'. Still, even this group of actors can aim at the social formation of a region, as well as at the appropriation of social space.

MANIFESTATIONS OF REGIONALISM

Regionalism manifests itself in the identification and emotional ties of a community of residents with the territory they inhabit, in differences between this community and other collectivities of this kind, and in the community recognising the values, standards and patterns of behaviour typical of the region. The components (or syndromes) of regionalism understood in this way are usually taken to include regional awareness, regional mentality, regional identity, and a regionalist attitude.

Regional awareness is considered a part of social consciousness referring to the sense of a separateness or peculiarity of one's own region or regional group. Various constructs (mental images) of a region and its boundaries tend to form in the social consciousness, depending on people's system of values and experiences. While regional awareness is treated by researchers as a separate segment of social consciousness, one should keep in mind its connection with historical awareness and cultural identity. The most frequently analysed components of regional awareness are regional identity, spatial representations of a region, and stereotypes, symbols and characteristics attributed to the region as a whole (cf. Shamai, Kellerman 1985; Rykiel 1989b; Budner, Matykowski 1993). Stereotypes provide a basis for the formation of opinion about certain objects (e.g., regions, elements of the natural or economic environment of a region, etc.), events, or people, and are used to motivate or rationalise one's course of action towards these objects (cf. Belcher 1973). Stereotypes emerge as a result of a repeated association between some symbols and a category of phenomena (cf. Fishman 1956).

Regional mentality is made up of a set of psycho-social features characteristic of the residents of the given territory (cf. Kwaśniewski 1986; Domański 1990). It can be expected, however, that basic sets of such regional features undergo deformations during social assessment (and self-evaluation), and acquire evaluative colour (e.g., the thrift and prudence of people in Wielkopolska, according to Domański). Hence, like stereotypes, they hardly yield to verification.

Regional identity, in turn, is a special case of social and cultural identity. It is based on regional tradition referring to a clearly defined territory with its unique social, cultural, economic and natural traits (cf. Szczepański 1999).

A *regionalist attitude* is characterised by a set of such features as: (a) attachment to one's own 'land' (territory); (b) a conviction that this territory displays appreciated properties that differentiate it from other areas of this type; (c) a conviction that the community inhabiting this land generates, or generated in the past, specified values that are part of one's own, original culture; (d) a sense of identity with this community and its culture; and (e) a wish to manifest this attachment to the land, the appreciation of its properties, and the identification with the community through various actions, social and institutional (cf. Kwiatkowski 1984).

Regionalism is also connected with broadly understood action for a region and struggle to preserve its values threatened by the central power. Today such action has an explicit or hidden political dimension, although it generally relies on cultural activities (a defence of the cultural heritage) or economic ones (including the moulding of regional policy). The totality of organisations and institutions supporting such action is termed regional institutional actors. A *regional movement* is a type of social movement whose aims (and ideology) are to cultivate the heritage of the region and ensure its socio-economic development. Regional movements are on the one hand a response to excessive centrality as well as cultural and economic uniformity, and on the other, they are moulded by the existing regional differences (cultural, economic, etc.). Some Polish researchers (e.g., Kwaśniewski 1993) believe that in pursuing their goals these movements preserve their identity without jeopardising national interests, i.e. they are not separatist in nature.

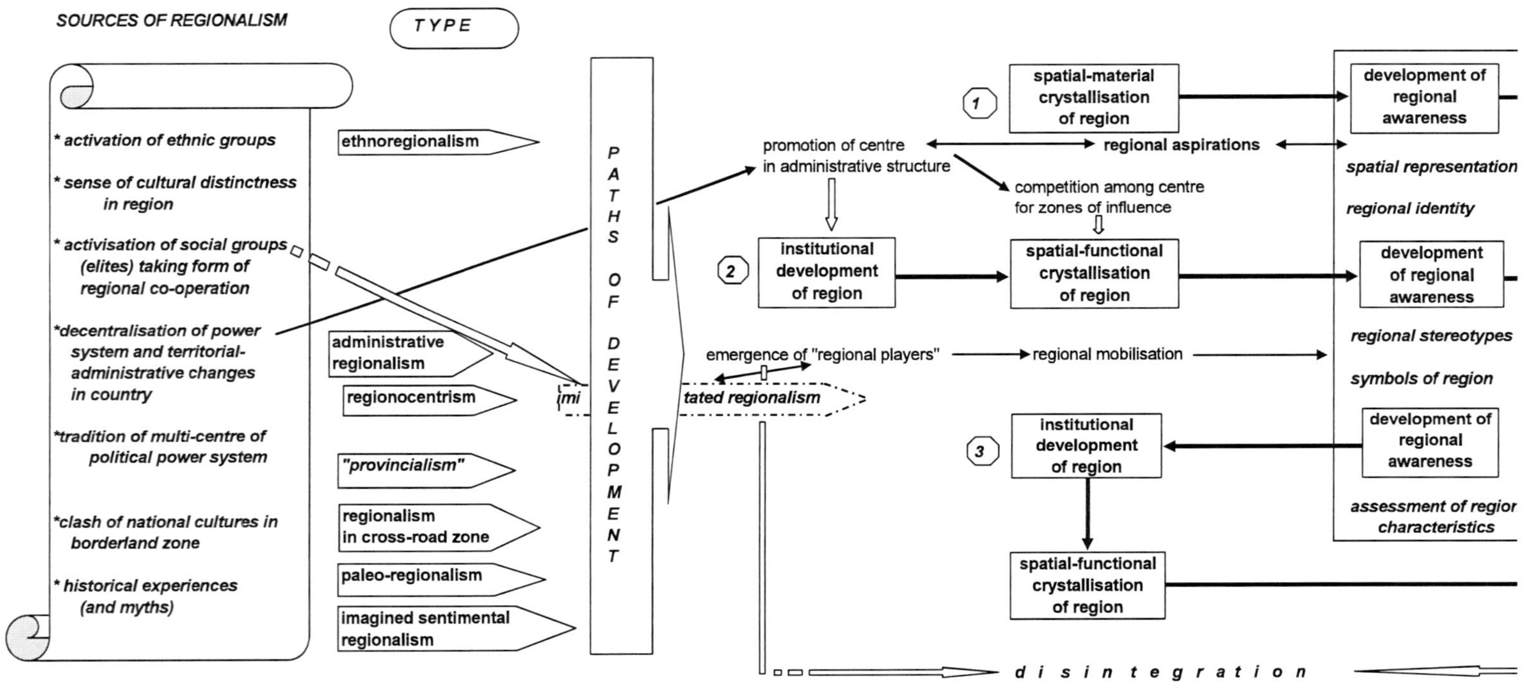

Figure 1. Model of the formation of regionalism.

SOURCES AND MECHANISMS OF REGIONALISM

According to Paasi (1986), a region is a territorial unit that has been formed institutionally in the course of social development. Thus, it is a social product of a community, and its basic constituent elements are human groups and a territory. It is also a spatial construct going through a variety of stages, and may disintegrate or disappear. Hence, regionalism and changes in societal attitudes towards a region can spring from various territorial structures and activities of a human community. When carrying out a typology of the kinds of regionalism observed in Poland, Rykiel (1993) tried to establish their source. He distinguished political, cultural, economic and folk types of regionalism, but he also identified quasi-regionalisms where there were a hazy regional awareness, an unformed regional community, and activities of a limited scope invoking regional interests. Mentioned among the factors shaping and enhancing the awareness of regional inhabitants of Europe are: (1) activation of ethnic movements (minorities), (2) changes in the administrative structure and decentralisation of the power system, (3) the tradition of a multi-centre political power system and historical (and mythical) experiences, (4) a clash of national cultures in the borderland zone and a sense of cultural distinctness in regions, and (5) activation of social groups (élites) taking the form of regional co-operation (cf. Dobrowolski 2000; Sowa 2000).

Inspired by Paasi's (1986) approach to the region, the Polish geographer Z. Chojnicki (1996) modified the model of region formation. According to him, this process goes through a number of stages: (1) spatial-material crystallisation of a region; (2) development of regional awareness; (3) institutional development; and (4) stabilisation of the region. As can be seen, each of these stages marks not only the development of a region, but can also be used to characterise the development of regionalism.

The spatial-material crystallisation of a region occurs as a result of both, differentiation and integration of the community inhabiting an area. These processes lead to the development of a sense of separateness based on different historical experiences, conservation of elements of the folk culture, or the attitude towards socio-economic processes. In Poland, a frequent source of regionalism has been shifts of the political boundaries and changes in the country's administrative division. In such cases the character of a territorial community may change as a result of the emergence of a new system of functional links, rather than owing to changes in the material substance of the territory. That is why in such a case it is better to describe this stage as one of the spatial-functional crystallisation of the region. It is also the case when the model sequence of stages of region formation is reversed: its institutional development precedes the other stages. An important element of regional awareness building is the appearance of the region's common or colloquial name, apart from the official one (cf. Paasi 1986). Its appearance is a manifestation of the sense of separateness; in consequence, it moulds the inhabitants' regional identity and awareness. Stabilisation is practically the final stage in the formation of a region and the development of regionalism; at this stage social and administrative institutions actively reproduce regional awareness and work towards greater cohesion of the region. Sometimes heightened activity of regional movements can be a factor fuelling separatist tendencies in an otherwise administratively stable unit, and can lead to the disintegration of a state. Sometimes also a long period of stabilisation of a region can bring about an increase in regional awareness at a lower spatial level, in an area corresponding to that of the Polish poviat. A model of the formation of a region and regionalism in the Polish conditions is presented in Figure 1.

Geographical-historical Regions and Sentimental Paleo-regionalism

Traditional concepts of a geographical-historical region in Poland have always assumed a co-occurrence of physical-geographic (natural) and socio-economic phenomena, and social-cultural differences appearing within them have been thought to result from historical tradition. Rykiel (2001) points out that although a geographical region is usually considered a form of natural region (uniform in terms of natural features) and a historical region is 'artificial' in a sense (being a tool of management), some Polish scholars disregarded the discrepancy and tried to employ the concept of a geographical-historical region to carry out a regionalisation of Poland. Therefore, attempts were made to show there to be a great similarity between natural and historical regions (cf. Szczepkowski 1977; Kiełczewska-Zaleska 1979). Janiszewski (1959) carried out a geographical regionalisation of Poland by the criterion of the transport cohesion of waterways (important for the economy in the late Middle Ages) as manifested by the basins of principal rivers. He accounted for some deviations of historical boundaries from water divides in terms of 'geographical capture' (regional disturbances).

New divisions of Poland into geographical (or historical-geographical) regions appeared in the postwar period in response to external (extra-scientific) factors. They included a significant change in Poland's borders (and the necessity for the classification to take the new Western Territories into account) and the need to justify this change and to support the idea of a uniform state (cf. Piskozub 1987; Otremba 1997). Hence references to the Piast dynasty period in the history of Poland when state borders (at the start of the 12th century) resembled the ones of today (they also enclosed the Western Territories of Silesia and West Pomerania), and Poland appeared to be an ethnically uniform country. The paradox of this reference to history consisted in the fact that these regional divisions usually corresponded in broad outlines to the principalities into which Poland had been fragmented in the 12th and 13th centuries, i.e., those divisions indirectly reflected the state's political weakness of that period.

The proponents of this conception of Poland's regionalisation assume as a rule that the number of regions and their territorial extent are immutable, although individual scholars differ significantly in this matter. Janiszewski (1959) distinguished seven regions (West Pomerania, Pomerania, Silesia, Wielkopolska, Mazovia, and Małopolska); the same number was established by Kiełczewska-Zaleska (1980), but their territorial structure was different (Pomerania, Silesia, Wielkopolska, Mazuria, Mazovia, Małopolska, and Podlasie). Rykiel (2001) lists several historical inconsistencies in those divisions, but it seems that for their authors the cores are more important than the boundaries (e.g., Kiełczewska-Zaleska 1980 does not bother with inter-regional boundaries at all).

Divisions into geographical-historical regions were used in geographical education at primary and secondary schools in Poland in the second half of the 20th century, and the school along with the family played an important role at that time in the formation of young people's regional identity and awareness. Sometimes in school education the historical names of regions were replaced by physical-geographic ones (e.g., Wielkopolska - the Wielkopolska Lowland, Mazovia - the Mazovia Lowland).

Another historical dimension that has survived in the consciousness of Poles as a result of family tales and socially imposed patterns of behaviour and tradition is the 18th-century partition of the Polish lands into three zones of occupied by the neighbours: Russia, Austria (Austria-Hungary), and Prussia (Germany). This division survived, with slight modifications, until the end of the First World War when Poland regained independence (1918). Austria-Hungary occupied the south-eastern part of today's Polish territory called Galicia (which also covered part of contemporary Ukraine) and a small subregion of Cieszyn Silesia (from 1920 its western part belonged to Czechoslovakia). The western part of contemporary Poland belonged to Germany. After the First World War, substantial parts of Wielkopolska, Gdańsk Pomerania and Upper Silesia were incorporated into Poland as a result of uprisings of the Polish residents or people identifying with the newly formed Polish state. The remaining areas belonged to Germany until 1945 and passed to Poland on the strength of the decision of the "Big Three" in Potsdam. The Western Territories were colonised in the years 1945-1950 by the Polish population of the Eastern Territories and other parts Poland had lost to the Soviet Union; in most of those areas (with the exception of Opole Silesia) these re-settlers formed more than 90% of the population. Until the First World War, the eastern and central parts of contemporary Poland belonged to Russia; they came to be called Congress Poland informally (or in Russian, the Land of the Vistula). Some traditions of civil society that had formed in the latter half of the 19th century in Galicia and Cieszyn Silesia have survived until the present times in family tradition; two of their manifestations after the 1989 political transformation of Poland have been an above-average voter turnout at elections and substantial support for right-wing groups (cf. Matykowski, Tobolska 1994; Bartkowski 2003). During the post-1989 political-economic changes, intellectuals and the mass media tried to create sentimental Galicia regionalism in the form of a myth which Szul (1996) termed *Galicia felix*. According to this author, Galicia identity was supposed to be an alternative to Małopolska identity (based on a historical-geographical region of medieval Poland). However, Galicia regionalism relies on the symbols of the Austrian-Hungarian empire (most commonly the person of Franz Joseph I, the last emperor), which would have been considered anti-national provocation in newly independent Poland after 1918 (and during the Communist regime). A similar above-average level of electoral participation has been recorded in Gdańsk Pomerania and Wielkopolska. Some scholars claim (e.g. Kwaśniewski 1987) that the patterns of organisational behaviour and respect for public order in Wielkopolska (developed during the period of ethnic competition between Poles and Germans in the late 19th century) have survived until today in the form of Wielkopolska mentality. This mentality is a powerful factor of maintaining and raising regional awareness among Wielkopolska residents (cf. Matykowski, Prawelska-Skrzypek 1997).

The areas with a different historical heritage of the 19th century have been termed civilisational zones by Rykiel (1999), while Wódz and Wódz (1995) call the emotional ties of residents with those areas - provincialism.

After Poland had regained independence, administrative units were introduced that did not coincide with the boundaries of the Austrian, Prussian, and Russian sectors. For instance, Wielkopolska (or Poznań voivodeship) now included an area that had been under Russian administration in the years 1815-1914. However, fragments of the then-border have survived in social consciousness to this day, in the form of such symbols as the river Prosna and the railway station at Strzałkowo. Similarly symbolic barriers are the rivers Przemsza and Brynica in a coal-mining area of present-day Upper Silesia, once borders of the Russian, Prussian, and Austrian-Hungarian occupation sectors until the First World War. Residents of the Dąbrowa Górnicza Basin (formerly part of the Russian sector) still find it hard to integrate with Upper Silesia proper (the German sector). Rykiel (1989a) made an analysis of marriage links between the populations of the Basin, Upper Silesia, and the subregion of Chrzanów in the years 1962 and 1978. He found that while the strength of this paleo-boundary as a spatial barrier had weakened between these two dates, the closure of links within each of these territories exceeded 75%. In the 1990s there appeared differences in electoral behaviour - the Basin lends much support to left-wing parties. It should be emphasised, however, that these now nonexistent boundaries tend to blur, especially in the consciousness of the younger generation, for instance in the borderland between Wielkopolska and Lower Silesia (cf. Matykowski 1996).

Administrative Regionalism and Regionocentrism

The institutional territorial structure taking the form of a division into highest-order units (voivodeships) has also favoured the development of regionalism, especially in the conditions of civil society formation after 1989. The first decision of Poland into voivodeships after the Second World War was connected with the change of the state borders (a shift to the west). After 1945, three basic organisational-territorial structures could be distinguished at the voivodeship level:

a) in the years 1950-1975, Poland was divided into 17 voivodeships (at the close that period there were 22 voivodeships, but 5 of them were the country's biggest cities, which were also voivodeship capitals);
b) in the years 1975-1998, there were 49 voivodeships (in 1975 32 towns were made voivodeship centres; half of them had less than 50,000 inhabitants at that time); and
c) since 1999, Poland is divided into 16 voivodeships.

The institutionalisation of a region (in the form of a highest-order unit) should promote the development of regionalism. The 1975 change in the administrative division brought about a decomposition of the existing regional system (also in its geographical-historical version) and difficulties with the social perception of the country's new regional picture, especially with adjusting the new system to the old regional divisions vivid in social consciousness (cf. Budner, Matykowski 1993). Many new towns that had become the seats of new voivodeships used this promotion - in a centrally planned economy - to amass investment in their own areas, thus deepening the disparities between the centre and the hinterland. Naturally, this did not contribute to the growth of regional awareness, though it certainly enhanced the sense of self-importance in the residents of the new centres and strengthened their emotional ties with the new official name of their region. One of the few new administrative centres where the voivodeship authorities (and local leaders of the communist Party, the most influential body at that time) started to work on the consciousness of the inhabitants right after the new voivodeship had been established was Bielsko-Biała (in the south of Poland). Apart from the official name of Bielsko voivodeship, the term Podbeskidzie started to enjoy wide currency as one reflecting the region's natural conditions (the landscape of the Beskid Range). Although there had been a strong, historically-based subregionalism in the western part of the voivodeship (Cieszyn Silesia), distinct regional awareness had developed among the inhabitants of the entire area (Matykowski 1997). That is why, when the draft of changes in the administrative division was being discussed in 1998, this region saw social protests (and some of the MPs representing this constituency broke their party discipline when voting on the Changes in the Administrative Division Act). The 1999 administrative division largely coincides with that from the years 1950-1975, except that now most voivodeships bear the names of historical regions (e.g., Wielkopolska, Pomerania, West Pomerania, Mazovia, etc.), and two voivodeships have been given two capitals each, seated in competing towns (Bydgoszcz versus Toruń in Kujawy-Pomerania and Gorzów Wielkopolski versus Zielona Góra in Lubuska Land). The only seat of a 1950-1975 voivodeship that failed to acquire a voivodeship of its own again in 1999 is Koszalin (in West Pomerania). Social protests in a struggle for a voivodeship were initiated by workers of the service sector (who faced a loss of jobs in the voivodeship power apparatus), but at the close of 2003 there emerged a movement that had collected in excess of 135 thousand signatures under a petition to the Parliament to establish a voivodeship named Central Pomerania. The movement is the strongest in Koszalin (the potential seat of the authorities) and Kołobrzeg. A similar movement for the secession of Kalisz from Wielkopolska has been reported by many local activists (and left-wing parties) after 1999. Building emotional ties of a population (community) with its territory and launching movements that make use of syndromes of regionalism, but are oriented towards benefits (even if sometimes imaginary) for the residents of the main centre with a half or more of the region's population is called regionocentrism (Matykowski 2003a). With time, regionocentrism may change into authentic regionalism, but it can also be a source of destruction of a territorial community (e.g., the leaders of Słupsk, backed by a substantial proportion of its residents, campaigned in 1998 for the town to belong to Pomerania voivodeship rather than to never-established though contemplated Central Pomerania). Competition between towns has sometimes resulted in the destruction of the feeling of territorial solidarity and identity based on common historical-cultural roots and common interests (cf. Markowski 2000).

One of the biggest Polish cities that has been the seat of a voivodeship since 1919 is Łódź (pop. 789,000 in 2002). The city flourished in the mid-19th century as a result of industrialisation (the textile industry) and became a voivodeship capital as soon as Poland had regained independence. What is striking is the fact that this administrative region does not reflect any geographical-historical divisions (cf. Janiszewski 1959; Kiełczewska-Zaleska 1980; Otremba 1997), because Łódź lies in them in the peripheral zone of Mazovia. Hence, when a new division of the country was discussed in 1998 (and the proposal was put forward to give the new units the old-established names of historical regions), the name proposed for the Łódź-centred voivodeship was initially Łęczyca-Sieradz Land, a reference to the small but ancient towns of Łęczyca (pop. 16,000) and Sieradz (pop. 45,000). Thus, regionocentrism, manifesting itself in ostensibly similar phenomena as regionalism, may sometimes be unfavourable to, or hinder the development of, the latter. An example of such a discrepancy in social perception may be people's identifying with a big region, but regarding as regional symbols objects of a sub-regional or local rank (towns, historic personages, natural and economic objects).

ETHNIC MINORITIES AND ETHNOREGIONALISM

One of the sources of regionalism is the activation of ethnic groups resident in an area. The groups can sometimes be an important component of a regional community, and their position in the structure of this community can be one of the following:

(1) they can constitute the fundamental part of that population and be a significant source of the formation of regionalism;
(2) they can constitute one of the two principal elements (besides Poles) of a dichotomous regional community, and their competition can facilitate the development of regional movements (cf. Yiftachel 1997);
(3) they can constitute an important part of the regional community (especially when living in an area along a state border) whose goal is to establish and develop ties with representatives of the same ethnic group on the other side of the border; or
(4) they can only be a minor part of the regional community, but be a source of multiculturalism of the region and evidence of its separateness and specificity.

If there is a high concentration of such ethnic (or folk) groups, they can facilitate the development of subregionalism (whose range would correspond to that of a US county), that is, emphasising the separateness of a homeland region which in East-Central European conditions has been termed 'little fatherland' in Polish and 'Heimat' in German.

In the Polish literature on non-dominant ethnic groups at least three categories of such groups are distinguished:

a) ethnic groups defined on a national basis, also called national groups;
b) those distinguished on the cultural basis, but which are not part of another nation possessing its own nation-state; and
c) those considered to be a fragment of the Polish nation and hence whose separate identity is questioned, e.g. by Polish institutions and power apparatus; they are termed ethno-folk minorities in Polish.

As a result of agreements signed by the "Big Three" at the Yalta conference (February 1945) and that in Potsdam (July and August 1945), Poland faced a dramatic change of borders and ethnic structure. Poland lost its 'Eastern Territories' inhabited by Ukrainians, Belarusians, Poles, and Jews to the Soviet republics, while it gained new 'Western Territories' formerly belonging to Germany. These territorial changes and the Potsdam provisions concerning the transfer of Germans made the Polish authorities decide to change Poland into a mono-ethnic state. By a census based on the 1946 declarations of ethnicity, Poles constituted 85.7% of the total population, while at the start of the 1950s Poland was considered an extremely homogeneous country ethnically with 98% of Poles. In the years 1944-1950 about 3.2 million Germans left Poland, as well as 520,000 Ukrainians, Belarusians and Lithuanians (to the USSR on the basis of Polish-Soviet agreements), and 200,000 Jews.

Since the late 1940s no official records were kept of ethnic minorities (e.g. in censuses), but after the 1956 changes in the ruling Communist party some minorities were allowed to set up, under Party control, their cultural societies (cf. Table 1). In the Stalinist period of the

Communist rule in Poland, two organisations of ethnic minorities were allowed to be set up: the Socio-Cultural Society of Jews in Poland (in 1950) and the Belojanis Association of Political Refugees from Greece (in 1954). In the reckoning of the Communist authorities, these groups had a specific political role. The Jewish political (usually left-wing) parties operating in the years 1945-1950 had joined the Polish United Workers' Party (i.e. the ruling Communist party) or had been liquidated. Hence, activists of the Central Committee of Jews in Poland (established in 1945 and having also political activists as members, e.g. a fraction of a Communist party) and of the Jewish Culture Society set up an organisation relying on the values of the Yiddish culture. Members of the Association of Political Refugees from Greece were Communist guerillas and their families who came to Poland in the years 1948-1951 (about 13,200-14,500 persons). Among them Macedonians made up the biggest ethnic group (48.7%), and Greeks only slightly smaller (48.4%).

Further ethnic minority organisations obtained permission to act after the 1956 changes in the Communist Party (the so-called 'Polish October' events). In 1956 there appeared socio-cultural societies of Belarusians, Ukrainians, Czechs and Slovaks, and Russians; in 1957, of Lithuanians and Germans; and in 1963, the first organisation of Gypsies in Tarnów. It should be emphasised, however, that the German Socio-Cultural Society was set up in Lower Silesia (Wałbrzych), an area colonised after 1945 by Poles from the eastern borderland (the 'Eastern Territories') where there were very few Germans (only so-called specialists had been retained in industrial plants). One of the tasks of the organisation was to give legal advice to German nationals, including help in emigrating to one of the German states. In 1972 it expanded its activity to cover the whole of Poland.

Table 1. Estimated ethnic minority populations in Poland in the years 1961/1962 and 1980

Ethnic group	Population				Organisation(year of establishment)
	1961/1962		1980		
	thous.	%	thous.	%	
Ukrainians, Lemkos	180-200	0.59-0.66	345	0.97	Ukrainian Socio-Cultural Society (1956)
Belarusians	165	0.54			Belarusian Socio-Cultural Society (1956)
Russians	19	0.06	10	0.03	Russian Cultural-Educational Society (1950)
Slovaks	21	0.07	22	0.06	Socio-Cultural Society of Czechs and Slovaks (1957)
Czechs	2	0.01			
Lithuanians	10	0.03	12	0.03	Lithuanian Socio-Cultural Society (1957)
Germans	3	0.01	4	0.01	Socio-Cultural Society of Germans in Poland (1957)
Jews	31	0.10	25	0.07	Socio-Cultural Society of Jews in Poland (1950)
Gypsies	10	0.03	12	0.03	Socio-Cultural Association of Gypsies (1970)
Greeks, Macedonians	10	0.03	5.5	0.02	Beloyanis Association of Greek Political Exiles (1954)

Source: Kwilecki (1963), Sobczak (1982).

Another ethnic revival took place after August 1980 when, following the creation of independent trade unions, attempts were made to establish independent ethnic-based organisations (e.g., the Belarusian Student Association in 1981). In the 1980s German organisations started to operate illegally in Silesia (e.g. in Racibórz and Kamienna Góra).

The political changes of 1989 in Poland made it possible to create several new organisations. Right in 1989 there appeared the largest minority structure in Poland, viz. the Socio-Cultural Society of the German Minority in Opole Silesia, almost 200,000 strong (in 1999 it had 180,000 members). It was legally registered in 1990, and its headquarters was located at Gogolin. In turn, Opole (the capital of a voivodeship) became the seat of the Union of the German Socio-Cultural Societies in Poland (since 1991) and a few specialised and regional organisations (e.g. the German Educational Society). In 1995 in the Opole region a small organisation was set up which is in opposition to the principal German society, viz. the Union of German Upper Silesians at Głogówek. At the start of the 1990s, two German organisations were established in the Katowice region, namely the Socio-Cultural Society of Germans of Katowice Voivodeship (in 1990) and the German Community "Conciliation and Future" (in 1991), which put up competitive lists of parliamentary candidates in the elections of 1991, 1993 and 1997. However, in the 2001 election they decided to put up a common list.

German organisations mushroomed in the 1990s in the so-called Western Territories, especially in Warmia-Mazuria voivodeship. The first to register there (in 1991) was the "Heimat" Cultural Association of Germans at Szczytno. In the 1990s a further 25 local and sub-regional organisations have been set up with seats in 23 towns. The biggest include the Olsztyn Association of the German Minority (3,200 members) and the "Elk" German Association in Olsztyn (1,600 members).

In another census conducted in 2002, Polish residents were asked to define their ethnicity (nationality). 96.74% of respondents declared themselves as Polish, but as many as 2.03% failed to define their ethnicity at all. The reason may have been the decades-old fear of revealing their ethnic roots that many people still feel, but also assimilation processes. Only 1.23% reported their ethnicity as other than Polish, with the biggest minorities being Silesian (0.45%) and German (0.40%).

After the change of the Polish borders in 1945, representatives of the left-wing government and some élites proposed that the terms 'Pole' and 'Poland's citizen' become synonymous. As a result, a model of a mononational Poland was put forward which was justified by domestic policy (liberation from ethnic problems and conflicts) and by the postwar political order in Europe (Poland's place within Moscow's sphere of influence and relations with West Germany). A new view of the role and functions of ethnic minorities in Poland appeared only during the first Solidarity period in the years 1980-1981 (e.g., articles in the weekly "Tygodnik Solidarność"), and then after 1989 (the Round Table meeting). In the 1990s there was an upsurge, among the political and opinion-forming circles, of interest in and fascination with all kinds of cultural distinctness and multiculturalism (e.g., in the strategies of socio-economic development of voivodeships), especially in the context of the intended integration with the European Union (cf. Nijakowski 2002). Hence, after 1989 there appeared three ethnic groups that are also a significant source of regionalism: Germans in Upper Silesia (and Opole Silesia), Silesians in Upper Silesia, and Kashubians in Pomerania. Earlier, Silesians and Kashubians were only regarded as Poles differing in folklore.

As recently as the 1980s, the number of Germans in Poland was estimated at a mere 4-10 thousand when at the first democratic parliamentary election of 1991 the candidates of

German societies received an astonishing 138,200 votes. This electoral behaviour was especially conspicuous in the then Opole voivodeship (Opole Silesia), where Germans captured as much as 26.8% of the vote. However, at the successive elections German candidates in the region tended to receive a declining number of votes: 19.8% in 1993, 17.5% in 1997, and 13.6% in 2001. The drop in support resulted partly from the polarisation of political views among the German voters, partly from long-term migration of the voters to work in Western Europe (Matykowski 2003b), and partly from the fluid nature of their imagined ethnicity. The chief representative of Germans in the region is the Socio-Cultural Society of Germans in Opole Silesia (almost 200,000 strong in the 1990s). This estimate agrees with that obtained by Kurcz (1994) in the early 1990s for the then voivodeships of Opole and Częstochowa. It should also be kept in mind that Opole Silesia was colonised in the years 1945-1950 mostly by Poles from the Eastern Territories (now belonging to Belarus and Ukraine). From the start there had been stormy interactions between the immigrants and the indigenous population (with a hidden German or Silesian identity, but also including Poles). The community achieved some measure of regional integrity as a result of the introduction of local government (at the commune, poviat and voivodeship levels) in the 1990s, especially during the period of discussion about the administrative reform in 1998. It was the time when the Polish majority and the German minority joined forces in their struggle to retain Opole voivodeship against the alternative solution: including Opole Silesia in the 'greater' Upper Silesia. Still, at the local level conflicts between the two ethnic groups keep breaking out quite a lot.

Table 2. Ethnic minority populations in Poland on the basis of the 2002 census

Ethnicity	Number of declarations (in thous.)	Minority population (mid-1990s estimate)	Main centres
Silesian	173.2	not recognised as ethnic group	Silesia (Upper) and Opole
German	152.9	360-450	Opole, Silesia, Warmia-Mazuria
Belarusian	48.7	240	Podlasie
Ukrainian	31.0	220-250	Podkarpacie, Western Territories
Gypsy (Roma)	12.9	25-30	Scattered
Russian	6.1	17	towns of central and eastern Poland
Lemko	5.9	50-80	Podkarpacie, Małopolska, Western Territories
Lithuanian	5.8	15-20	Sejny poviat (Puńsk commune)
Kashubian	5.1	recognised not as separate ethnic group but as Poles	Pomerania
Slovak	2.0	18-20	Orava and Spisz
Jewish	1.1	10	big cities
Armenian	1.1	8	scattered (Armenian parish in Gliwice)

Source: Chałupczak, Browarek (1998), 2003 press information.

Table 3. Some forms of regionalism in Poland and its dimensions

Region	Type of regionalism	Alternative regional form, territorial disintegration	Regional institutions, regional actors	Centre	Components of regional identity	Frontier involved	Political dimension (political pressure)
Galicia	imaginary senti mental regionalism	alternative to Małopolska; integrating form of two new voivodeships (Małopolska and Podkarpacie)	informal creators: segments of intelligentsia (physicians, artists, journalists, etc.)	Cracow and biggest towns (Rzeszów, Tarnów, Nowy Sącz, Krosno); second symbolic centre: Lviv (Ukraine) in 19th c.	mythical identity (Galicia felix – sentimental memory of Austro-Hungarian Monarchy)	Slavonic-Hungarian-German frontier (19th/ 20th c.)	myth of Austro-Hungarian Monarchy
Małopolska	paleo-regionalism: cultural-scenic regionalism on historical basis	identified with voivodeship; identified with Galicia; expanding northwards (to former Russian partition in 19th c.)	Association of Małopolska Communes (especially before 1999)	Cracow – Poland's capital (11th c. – 1596)	culture and history (Wawel castle – seat of king in Cracow), nature: mountain and piedmont landscape	Polish-Ruthenian-Hungarian frontier (13th c.)	Poland's political centre (till 16th c,) and culture-forming centre; Małopolska as alternative to nationally indistinct Galicia
Podhale	folk-culture sub-regionalism	isolation or separation of Orava and Spisz	Association of Podhale Natives, Union of Podhale Communes	Zakopane and Nowy Targ – poviat seats	patois, folk costumes, religiousness, architecture, customs	fuzzy Polish-Slovak frontier (today) and Polish-Hungarian (previously)	right-wing voters; ecological protection of Tatra Mountains
Upper Silesia Great Upper Silesia'	regionalism in cross - road zone: multi-layer cultural and political regionalism	identified with voivodeship (or without Częstochowa area and Dąbrowa Górnicza Basin); joined to Opole Silesia; transborder form (joined with northern part of Czech Republic);	Upper Silesian Association, Movement for Silesian Autonomy (→ Association of Silesian Nationals, 1997, delegalized); voivodeship authorities	Katowice – capital of Silesian voivodeship (since 1922) Opole (?)	Silesian patois (with many Germanisms) – popular present-day option of links with German culture	Polish-German frontier and penetration zone (14th –20th c.)	anti-German uprisings (1919-1921), autonomy as voivodeship within Poland's borders (1922-1939); administrative integration and rivalry with Dąbrowa Coal Basin

Region	Type of regionalism	Alternative regional form, territorial disintegration	Regional institutions, regional actors	Centre	Components of regional identity	Frontier involved	Political dimension (political pressure)
Opole Silesia	two-layer ethnic re-gionalism (indigen-ous and incoming)	separatism from Great Upper Silesia (claims to Racibórz district); Olesno district joined to Opole Silesia (1999)	Association of Opole Silesia Communes (especially before 1999); Socio-Cultural Society of Germans in Opole Silesia; voivodeship authorities; informal creators (journalists, clerks)	Opole – capital of Piast principality (1283-1534); capital of German province 'Upper Silesia' (to 1945), capital of voivodeship (1950)	sense of cultural separateness of indigenous and incoming populations (conflict-based regionalism)	Polish-German frontier (14 th – 18th c.)	anti-German up-risings in eastern part (1919-1921), with participation on Polish side of ancestors of some of present residents considering themselves German; double citizenship and labour emigration to Germany
Dąbrowa Górnicza Coal Basin	counter-regionalism to Upper Silesia (its negative stereotypes)	in 1919-1939 as part of Kielce voivodeship (in 1945 joined to Upper Silesia)	Union of Coal Basin Natives; informal creators	Sosnowiec and Dąbrowa Górnicza – mining towns	negative stereotypes of Upper Silesians	frontier between Russian and German occupation zones (19th c.)	left-oriented voters (mining workers, etc.)→ 'Red Coal Basin Republic' (1905-1907)
Cieszyn Silesia	paleo-subregional-ism (cultural and economic)	identified with poviat; expanding northwards (to Jastrzębie-Zdrój) and eastwards	Communal Association of Cieszyn Silesia; poviat authorities	Cieszyn – capital of principality (1291-1653), seat of poviat	historical distinctness	Polish-Czech frontier (today) and Polish-German speakers frontier (previously)	territorial separateness in Austro-Hungarian Monarchy; Polish-Czechoslovak controversy over Cieszyn Silesia (1920), Polish minority on Czech side of border
Podbeskidzie	administrative regionalism	division between two voivodeships in 1999 (Upper Silesia and Małopolska)	local branch of 'Solidarność' trade union uses regional emblem „Podbeskidzie"; informal creators (journalists, teachers)	Bielsko-Biała – capital of voivodeship (1975-1998)	defence of administrative centre against degradation in 1990s (branch of voivodeship authorities since 1999); folk culture	frontier between Małopolska and Upper Silesia	acceptance of administrative reform in 1975, rejection reform in 1999

Table 3. (Continued)

Region	Type of regionalism	Alternative regional form, territorial disintegration	Regional institutions, regional actors	Centre	Components of regional identity	Frontier involved	Political dimension (political pressure)
Wielkopolska	paleo-regionalism and pragmatic (economic) regionalism	identified with voivodeship; separatism of Eastern Wielkopolska with centre at Kalisz (former Russian partition, 19th c.) joined to Konin district or Leszno district ('Southern Wielkopolska' version)	Union of Wielkopolska People; Association of Wielkopolska (especially before 1999); voivodeship authorities	Poznań – capital of principality (12th-13th c.), capital of Great Duchy of Poznań (as part of Germany, 19th c.), capital of voivodeship	organisational and economic behaviour	Polish-German penetration zone (especially 19th and 20th c.)	successful 'economic war' between Poles and German settlers (1880-1918), successful anti-German uprising (1918-1919)
(North) Podlasie („Great Podlasie")	two-layer ethnic/ religious regionalism (Catholic Poles and Orthodox Eastern Slavs); cultural-scenic imaginary regionalism	identified with voivodeship (weak connection with northern part – Suwałki district); expansive form: heart of Podlasie located in northern part of Lublin voivodeship and eastern part of Mazovia	voivodeship authorities; Association of Belarusians, St. Cyril and St. Methodius Orthodox Brotherhood; peasant and national-oriented parties	Białystok – capital of voivodeship	sense of cultural separateness (language and especially denomination; attachment to tradition, patriotism (Poles), stressing Orthodox-Church roots (Belarusians and Ukrainians)	frontier between Western and Eastern Slavs (today understood locally as boundary between Western and Eastern culture)	pro-Soviet behaviour of Belarusians in 1939 (invasion by USSR)
Mazovia	weak paleo-regionalism (cultural-scenic) mixed with regionocentrism of capital (Warsaw)	transitory status of frontiers (with Podlasie, Łódź region, etc.)	regional societies of scientists, local societies	Warsaw – capital of state (1596), capital of duchy of Mazovia (15th c.-1526); Płock –capital of Mazovia (12th c.) and principality (13th – 15th c.)	lowland landscape with Vistula river	'heart' of Poland; northern frontier between Poland and Prussia	typical conflict between core (capital) and rest of state

Region	Type of regionalism	Alternative regional form, territorial disintegration	Regional institutions, regional actors	Centre	Components of regional identity	Frontier involved	Political dimension (political pressure)
Kurpie	folk-culture subregionalism		Group of Kurpie Communes (episodic), local cultural societies	Myszyniec and Chorzele	Mazovia patois, folk religious customs and ethical principles	Polish (Mazovian)-Prussian frontier (17th c.)	Kurpie – defenders of Polish frontier against invasion (16th – 18th c.)
Gdańsk Pomerania	two-layer integrating regionalism on Kashubian ethnic basis	identified with voivodeship; expansion to east (Elbląg district) expansive conception of 'Vistula Pomerania' (including most of Kujawy and Pomerania voivodeship)	Pomeranian-Kashubian Association; voivodeship authorities; informal creators (regional party leaders)	Gdańsk - capital of German province of 'West Prussia' (1876-1919), political unit „Free City of Danzig" (1919-1939), capital of voivodeship (1945)	integration of Kashubian folk culture (dialect, costumes, customs) with culture of incoming population	Polish-German frontier (19th and 20th c.)	division of Kashubia between Poland and Germany (1920-1939)

Source: R. Matykowski and G. Prawelska-Skrzypek (1997), modified.

Even more unclear is the ethnic identification among the present-day residents of (Upper) Silesia. The Polish part of Silesia even had formal autonomy (a regional Diet) in the years 1922-1939, and after 1945 the indigenous population, while considered Polish, was recognised as distinct in cultural terms (the dialect, customs, family model). However, its distinctness had developed over the last few centuries in an area of overlap of two national cultures, German and Polish (hence frequent Germanisms in the Silesian dialect). In 1990 there appeared a Movement for the Autonomy of Silesia under the banner of restitution of the prewar Upper Silesia autonomy. In 1997 the group came up with the proposal to establish a Union of People of Silesian Ethnicity, claiming that about 20% of residents of the Katowice region felt they were Silesian. However, at the instance of the voivodeship authorities (the voivode, and practically the government), the court in Katowice refused to register the union. Following this event, a public-opinion poll was taken among a sample of about 1000 people concerning the separation of the Silesian ethnic minority. According to Gruszczyński (1999), 58% of respondents were against this initiative as against 28% who supported it (the rest had no opinion on the matter). At the 2002 census, the Silesian minority turned out to be the biggest ethnic group in Poland (cf. Table 2).

The Kashubians are a peculiar ethnic-cultural community that, despite adverse conditions through the ages, has preserved its own language (in Poland usually treated as a dialect of Polish, but listed as a separate Slavonic language in Jordan's (1996) American manual), its sense of separateness, its own system of values, and forms of material culture. From the mid-19th century, there developed a Kashubian-Pomeranian movement which displayed conflicting ideological and political orientations. By the mid-20th century, the various trends in this ethnic-regional movement included one seeking its roots and ties with the Slavonic family (Slavonic-Kashubian), ties with the Polish culture as a national culture (Polish-Kashubian), revival (Young Kashubian), autonomy (autonomous Kashubian), and strengthening its cultural separateness within the Gdańsk Pomerania territory (Pomeranian-Kashubian) (Bolduan 1996). In 1956 the movement assumed an institutional shape in the form of the Kashubian-Pomeranian Association. Latoszek (1996) estimated the number of Kashubians in the late 1980s at 330,000, but at the 2002 census only about 5,000 people confirmed their Kashubian ethnicity.

Conclusion

Poland's history in the 19th and 20th centuries did not favour the development of the sense of regional belonging and distinctness. The Polish national identity had, and still has, many centralist and anti-regional features (cf. Wódz 2000). This has been confirmed by a survey research conducted among urban youth for whom the most important plane (level) of territorial identification is that of the nation-state, followed by those of their home town, Europe, and only finally region (Jałowiecki 1996b). That is why Jałowiecki (1996a: 45) claims that "regionalism seems to be in fact a marginal phenomenon, and one, too, that is evaluated rather negatively". Still, in the consciousness of the young people polled by Jałowiecki one can often find such social constructs of a region in Poland as Wielkopolska (81% of indications), Małopolska (74%), Pomerania (69%), Mazovia (59%), Silesia (59%), and Mazuria (44%). Moreover, some respondents divided Silesia into two regions: Upper

(15%) and Lower Silesia (13%). In turn, when analysing regional movements by the then system of 49 voivodeships, Rykiel (1993) found that regionalism did not occur in 26 administrative units and assumed the form of quasi-regional political movements in 17 of them. A synthetic analysis of regionalism in Poland was carried out by Matykowski and Prawelska-Skrzypek (1997) on the basis of their own research and results published by other scholars. They distinguished regionalisms (a) smaller in range than the then voivodeships, i.e. the subregionalisms of Cieszyn Silesia, Podhale and Kurpie, (b) coinciding in range with those voivodeships (Podbeskidzie, North Podlasie/Białystok region, Opole Silesia), and (c) larger than the then voivodeships and close to or larger than the present units (Wielkopolska, Upper Silesia, Pomerania/Kashubia, and Galicia/Małopolska). A short characterisation of the components of those regionalisms is presented in Table 3.

REFERENCES

Bahrenberg G., 1993. Dimensions of regionalism. W: E. Dirven, J. Groenewegen, S. van Hoof (red.). Stuck in the region? Changing scales for regional identity. "*Nederlandse Geografische Studies*", 155.

Bartkowski J., 2003. *Tradycja i polityka. Wpływ tradycji kulturowych polskich regionów na współczesne zachowania społeczne i polityczne*. Warszawa, Wydawnictwo Akademickie Żak.

Belcher D., 1973. *Giving psychology away*. San Francisco, Canfield.

Bolduan T., 1996. *Nie dali się złamać. Spojrzenie na ruch kaszubski 1939-1995*. Gdańsk, Oficyna Czec.

Budner W., Matykowski R., 1993. Regionalizm i świadomość regionalna w Wielkopolsce. In M. Latoszek, ed. *Regionalizm jako folkloryzm, ruch społeczny i formuła ideologiczno-polityczna*. Gdańsk, 133-154

Chałupczak, Browarek 1998. *Mniejszości narodowe w Polsce, 1918-1995*. Lublin, Wydawnictwo UMCS.

Chojnicki Z., 1996. Region w ujęciu geograficzno-systemowym. In T. Czyż, ed. *Podstawy regionalizacji geograficznej*. Poznań, Bogucki Wydawnictwo Naukowe.

Chojnicki Z., Czyż T., 1992. Region – regionalizacja – regionalizm. "*Ruch Prawniczy, Ekonomiczny i Socjologiczny", 2, 1-17.

Cooke Ph., 2002. *Knowledge economies. Clusters, learning and cooperative advantage*. London, Routledge.

Deas I., Ward K.G., 2000. From the "new localism" to the "new regionalism"? The implications of regional development agencies for city-regional relations. "*Political Geography*", 19, 273-292.

Dobrowolski P., 2000. Regionalizm i współpraca międzyregionalna na tle europejskich procesów integracyjnych. In P. Dobrowolski and M. Stolarczyk, eds. *Polityka, przedmiot badań i formy jej przejawiania się*. Katowice.

Domański R., 1990. *Zasady geografii społeczno-ekonomicznej*. Warszawa, PWN.

Dziewoński K., 1967. Teoria regionu ekonomicznego. "*Przegląd Geograficzny*", 39, 33-50.

Fishman J. , 1956. An examination of the process and function of social stereotyping. "*Journal of Social Psychology*", 43, 27-64.

Gibb R.A., Michalak W.Z., 1994. The European Community and East-Central Europe. "*Tijdschrift voor Economische en Sociale Geografie*", vol. 85, 5, 401-416.

Giddens A., 1984. *The constitution of society. Outline of the theory of structuration.* Cambridge, Polity Press.

Giordano B., 2000. Italian regionalism or "Padanian" nationalism – the political project of the Lega Nord in Italian politics. "*Political Geography*", 19, 445-471.

Gruszczyński L. A.,1999. Problem "narodowości śląskiej" w opinii mieszkańców województwa katowickiego. In J. Sztumski and M. Gramlewicz, eds. *Badania nad sytuacją mniejszości niemieckiej na Śląsku po 1989 roku.* Katowice, Wydawnictwo Uniwersytetu Śląskiego.

Häkli J., 1994. Territoriality and the rise of modern state. "*Fennia*", 172, 1, 1-82.

Hartshorne R., 1959. *Perspective on the nature of geography.* Chicago, Rand McNally.

Hartshorne R., 1961. Istota geografii. Podsumowanie wniosków. "*Przegląd Geograficzny*", 33, 585-591.

Haliżak E., 2000.Regionalizm w stosunkach międzynarodowych. In E. Haliżak and R. Kuźniar, eds. *Stosunki międzynarodowe. Geneza, struktura, dynamika.* Warszawa, Wydawnictwo Uniwersytetu Warszawskiego.

Hard G., 1987. Das Regionalbewußtsein im Spiegel der regionalistischen Utopie. "*Informationen zur Raumentwicklung*", H. 7/8, 419-440.

Hine R.C., 1992. Regionalism and the integration of the world economy. "*Journal of the Common Market Studies*", 30, 115-123.

Jałowiecki B., 1996a. Przestrzeń historyczna, regionalizm, regionalizacja. In B. Jałowiecki, ed. Oblicza polskich regionów. "*Studia Regionalne i Lokalne*",17 (50), 19-88.

Jałowiecki B., 1996b. Świadomość regionalna młodzieży licealnej. In B. Jałowiecki, ed. Oblicza polskich regionów. "*Studia Regionalne i Lokalne*", 17 (50), 174-199.

Janiszewski M., 1959. *Regiony geograficzne Polski.* Warszawa, PZWS.

Jordan T., 1996. *European culture area.* New York, HarperCollins.

Kerscher U., 1992. Raumabstraktionen und regionale Identität. Eine Analyse des regionalen Identitätsmanagements im Gebiet zwischen Augsburg und München. "*Münchener Geographische Hefte*", 68.

Kiełczewska-Zaleska M., 1979. Rozwój geografii a koncepcja podziału Polski na regiony geograficzne. *Geografia w Szkole*, 3, 99-105.

Kiełczewska-Zaleska M., 1980. O znaczeniu regionów geograficzno-historycznych w geografii Polski. *Przegląd Geograficzn*, 53, 705-715.

Knight D.B., 1984. Regionalism, nationalism, and the Canadian state. "*Journal of Geography*", 5, 212-220.

Kurcz 1994. Mniejszość niemiecka w Polsce. *Kultura i Społeczeństwo*, 4, 145-164.

Kwaśniewski K., 1986. Mentalność wielkopolska. In R. Domański and S. Kozarski, eds. *Województwo poznańskie. Zagadnienia geograficzne i społeczno-gospodarcze.* Warszawa, PWN.

Kwaśniewski K., 1993. Regionalizacja i regionalizm a podział administracyjny. W: M. Latoszek (red.). *Regionalizm jako folkloryzm, ruch społeczny i formuła ideologiczno-polityczna.* Gdańsk.

Kwiatkowski P., 1984. Ideologia regionalizmu w Polsce międzywojennej. *Kultura i Społeczeństwo*, nr 4.

Kwilecki A., 1963. Mniejszości narodowe w Polsce Ludowej. *Kultura i Społeczeństwo*, 4, 85-103.

Latoszek M., 1996. *Pomorze. Zagadnienia etniczno-regionalne. gdańsk,* Gdańskie Towarzystwo Naukowe.

Lefebvre H., 1974. *La production de l'Espace*. Paris, Anthropos.

Lovering J., 1999. Theory led by policy? The inadequacies of the new regionalism in economic geography illustrated from the case of Wales. *International Journal of Urban and Regional Research*, 23, s. 379-395.

Matykowski R., 1996. Rola świadomości regionalnej w kształtowaniu granic regionu poznańskiego. In T. Czyż, ed. *Podstawy regionalizacji geograficznej*. Poznań, Bogucki Wydawnictwo Naukowe, 127-140.

Matykowski R., 1997. Śląsk Cieszyński a Podbeskidzie. Świadomość regionalna mieszkańców województwa bielskiego (spojrzenie geograficzne). In I. Bukowska-Floreńska, ed. Śląsk Cieszyński i inne pogranicza w badaniach nad tożsamością etniczną, narodową i regionalną. *Studia Etnologiczne i Antropologiczne*, 1, 99-114.

Matykowski, 2003a. Teoretyczne podstawy geograficzne badań nad regionalizmem. In E. Orłowska and J. Klementowski, eds. *Kulturowy aspekt badań geograficznych. Studia teoretyczne i regionalne*. Wrocław, PTG – IGiRR UW, 35-49.

Matykowski R., 2003b. Mniejszość niemiecka a wyniki wyborów prezydenckich w województwie opolskim: analiza przestrzenna. In M. Śmigielska, J. Słodczyk, eds. *Śląsk Opolski w warunkach integracji europejskiej*. Opole, PTG w Opolu.

Matykowski R., Prawelska-Skrzypek G., 1997. *Dimensions socio-culturelles de la conscience régionale en Pologne. Colloque sur les approches culturelles en Géographie*. Paris, 8-11 Décembre 1997 (mimeo).

Matykowski R., Tobolska A., 1994. *The 1991-1993 parliamentary elections in Poland: From the birth of democracy to success of the paleosystem. IGU Commission Geography and Public Administration, Hruba Skala,* 18-21 August 1994 (mimeo).

Murphy A. B., 1991. Regions as social constructs: the gap between theory and practice. *Progress in Human Geograph*, 15, 1, 22-35.

Ossowski S., 1967. Zagadnienie więzi regionalnej na Śląsku Opolskim. In Z zagadnień *psychologii społecznej,* vol. 3. Warszawa.

Otremba T., 1997. *Wyżyna Polska.* Gdańsk, Wydawnictwo Regnum.

Paasi A., 1986. The institutionalization of regions: a theoretical framework for understanding the emergence of regions and the constitution of regional identity. *Fennia*, 164, 1, 105-146.

Piskozub A, 1987. *Dziedzictwo polskiej przestrzeni. Geograficzno-historyczne podstawy struktur przestrzennych ziem polskich.* Wrocław, Ossolineum.

Rykiel Z., 1989a. Powiązania małżeńskie a problemy integracji społecznej. In Z. Rykiel, ed. Struktury i procesy społeczno-demograficzne w regionie katowickim. *Prace Geograficzne IGiPZ PAN*, 151, 67-92.

Rykiel Z., 1989b. Wyobrażenia i stereotypy Śląska. In Z. Rykiel, ed. Struktury i procesy społeczno-demograficzne w regionie katowickim. *Prace Geograficzne IGiPZ PAN*, 151, 107-120.

Rykiel Z., 1993. Typologia ruchów regionalnych w Polsce. W: K. Handtke (red.). *Region, regionalizm – pojęcia i rzeczywistość.* Warszawa.

Rykiel Z., 1999. Regionalizm ekonomiczny a regionalizacja szans rozwojowych w Polsce. In J. Łoboda i S. Grykień (red.). *Przekształcenia regionalnych struktur funkcjonalno-przestrzennych.* Wrocław, t. IV, s. 227-245.

Rykiel Z., 2001. *Krytyka teorii regionu społeczno-ekonomicznego.* Białystok, Wydawnictwo Wyższej Szkoły Finansów i Zarządzania w Białymstoku.

Shamai S., Kellerman A., 1985. Conceptual and experiment aspects of regional awareness: An Israeli case study. *Tijdschrift voor Economische en Sociale Geografie,* 76,88-99.

Skorowski H., 1993. etyczne aspekty regionalizmu. In M. Latoszek ed. *Regionalizm jako folkloryzm, ruch społeczny i formuła ideologiczno-polityczna.* Gdańsk, Wydawnictwo Gdańskie, 65-77.

Sobczak L.,1982. Mniejszości narodowe w Polsce. *Czasopismo Geograficzne*, 2, 205-208.

Sowa K. Z., 2000. *Socjologia, społeczeństwo, polityka.* Rzeszów, Wydawnictwo Wyższej Szkoły Pedagogicznej.

Szczepański M.S., 1995. Regionalizm górnośląski w społecznej świadomości. Socjologiczne studium przypadku. In M.W. Wanatowicz. *Regionalizm a separatyzm – historia i współczesność. Śląsk na tle innych obszarów*. Katowice, Wyd. UŚ.

Szczepański M.S., 1999. Tożsamość regionalna – w kręgu pojęć podstawowych i metodologii badań. In G. Gorzelak, M.S. Szczepański, and T. Zarycki, eds. *Rozwój, region, społeczeństwo.* Warszawa, s. 75-88.

Szczepkowski J., 1977. Struktura przestrzenna regionu bydgosko-toruńskiego. Ewolucja i dynamika. *Prace Geograficzne IGiPZ PAN*, 118.

Szul R., 1996. Galicja – teatr czy rzeczywistość. In B. Jałowiecki, ed. Oblicza polskich regionów. *Studia Regionalne i Lokalne*, 17 (50), 224-237.

Tuan Yi-Fu, 1977. *Space and place*. London, Arnold.

Whittlesey D., 1954. The regional concept and regional method. In *American geography: inventory and prospect*. Syracuse, University of Syracuse Press, 26-37.

Wódz J., Wódz K., 1995. Regionalizm, dzielnicowość, tożsamość narodowa. Próba socjologicznej analizy dynamiki zjawisk. In M. Wanatowicz, ed. *Regionalizm a separatyzm – historia i współczesność. Śląsk na tle innych obszarów*. Katowice, Wydawnictwo Uniwersytetu Śląskiego.

Yiftachel O., 1997. The political geography of ethnic protest: nationalism, deprivation and regionalism among Arabs in Israel. *Transactions, Institute of British Geographers*, 22, 91-110.

In: Economic and Political Developments in Poland
Editor: Maureen P. Larsen
ISBN 978-1-61209-951-4

Chapter 5

THE SERVICE SECTOR IN THE NEW SOCIO-ECONOMIC REALITY

Waldemar Wilk*

Geography and Regional Studies, Warsaw University, Poland

ABSTRACT

The current stage of development of the service sector in Poland is the consequence of many factors. Some of the factors are those that influenced the organization of services during the time when the centrally planned economy was in place, while the other factors are those that brought about the changes in the service sector during the socio-political transformation beginning in the late 1980's. In the first group of factors, it is impossible to overstate the effects of: services being counted in the national income, forced industrial investments being prioritized over other sectors of the economy, many services being intentionally internalized within government-run businesses, as well as the low level of the society's assets. In the second group of factors, one should look at the current picture of the service sector in Poland and take into account the effects of new processes: the development of private enterprise, privatization, the deregulation of many service markets; the nature and scale of foreign direct investment, as well as the increase in the gross national product and changes in household consumption behavior.

During the last decades, development of the service sector has been accompanied by the creation or the widening of local inequalities in the development of service infrastructure (supply-side), as well as by changes in reported demand for business services and for consumer services (demand-side). It should be noted that attempts at portraying the changing role of the Polish economy's service sector, as well as changes within the sector, have not had much success due to a lack of satisfactory and official statistical data. Statistics concerning the service sector are still disproportionately meager in comparison to the sector's significance in the Polish economy. In addition, in many instances it is impossible to trace changes over a certain period of time, due to changes in data-collection methodology and changes in the industrial classification system. In those cases in which it was possible, an attempt was made nonetheless to show variation in the

* wwwilk@uw.edu.pl.

indicators for the longest-possible time period. Sometimes this was possible only in the qualitative sense.

The Decline of the Service Sector in the Centrally Planned Economy

Regardless of how highly one rates the development of the service sector during the period between the two World Wars, following 1945, and especially from the 1950's onwards, it is possible to observe significant changes in the politics of service sector development. As the basis for these changes one should point to the ideologically dependent status of the service sector within the total national income. The emphasis on the dominance of the material sector over the immaterial sector differed. Service-related industries included within the material sphere (and, in consequence, included in computations of the national income) were: transport, communications, trade, urban development and the skilled trades. Most other services, in important fields such as research and education, healthcare, public administration, banking, insurance and the judicial system, found themselves outside of the material sphere. This favoritism towards the material sphere was echoed in investment politics, in accordance with which a sizeable part of the expenditures were made towards forced industrialization and development of activities related to the production of investment goods, as opposed to consumer goods.

In effect, the economic system which came to be in the years immediately following WWII did not, in the following years, undergo changes to the same extent as could be observed in the economies of the highly developed counties of Western Europe as well as even in other Comecon (Council for Mutual Economic Assistance) countries. One of the indicators of stagnation (and eventually of slow economic growth) for the service sector is its share in the job market. Over a period of nearly 40 years, up to the year 1988, the share of service sector employees in the overall number of people employed grew from 20 to 35%, all while the preeminence of the industrial sector was increasing (Figure 1). One can determine how stagnant the tempo of these changes actually was only by comparing the situation in Poland to that in other countries (namely Czech Republic, Hungary and the former Yugoslavia), in which the service sector's share in the job market rose from 40 to 50% during that same time period. In comparison to western countries (USA, Great Britain, Sweden and France), where towards the end of the 1980's, at least ⅔ of all those working were employed in the service sector, this difference is even more marked.

A similar pattern can be observed in the case of investments made. Until the end of the 1970's, the biggest expenditures were made in the area of manufacturing (up to 45% of all investment spending in 1975). Between 1950 and 1988, the agriculture sector's share in the investment fund fluctuated between 12 and 16%. The general service sector's investment share began to experience significant growth from 1980 until the collapse of the centrally planned economy, when it amounted to over 50%. Housing and urban development had the greatest share of all the investments (about ⅓). Expenditures in areas such as transport and communications, education, culture and health care, were much lower (Jakubowicz 1993:27).

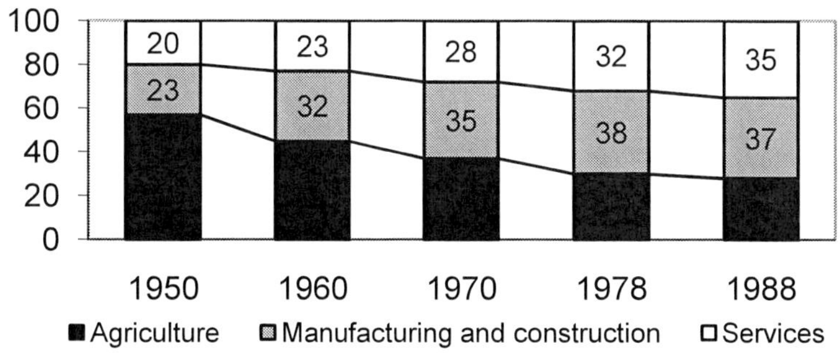

Source: authors calculations based on *Statistical Yearbook of Poland* (various years).

Figure 1. Economically active population in Poland by sectors of the economy (in percent).

The development of services (consumer services in particular) in the centrally planned economy, in which public enterprise (usually government-run) played a significant part, could be described as an attempt to satisfy the basic needs of citizens (households). Under such circumstances, it is no surprise that the focus was on the development of those services which would allow the fulfillment of people's basic needs, located at the very bottom of the A.H. Maslow's hierarchy of needs. And yet, even in these aspects (grocery items, housing, house furnishings and health care) one can speak of inadequate quantities and especially poor quality. This concerned, among other things, the small assortment of consumer goods one could choose from (grocery items and house furnishings), and the low standard of the apartments being built (with regard to size and furnishings).

The domination of the supply side of consumer services by the public sector was in effect supposed to improve access to these services for all of the country's citizens, including those living in rural areas. Such attempts were sometimes made while financial records were not fully kept, and costs and effects not analyzed, because the only norms, which were strictly observed were those regarding the spatial distribution of services. Yet, even in this one aspect (of equal access), there were serious obstacles. Among them should be mentioned the characteristic settlement pattern, made up of a large number of small and dispersed rural centers. In effect, especially since the 1980's, there had been an emphasis on the need to even out the supply and demand for services on a regional scale. This is how regional differences in the infrastructure of services and their consumption became sanctioned, and the effect was especially visible in large cities.

For many decades, the service sector in Poland was faced with low demand, as is illustrated by the share of services in overall consumption, which up to 1960 did not exceed 10% (Niewadzi 1975). The 1970's and early 1980's did not see a significant increase in this figure, which did not exceed 20% for the latter period. On the contrary, in 1985 a decrease was noted when the share of services in overall consumption fell to 17%. In reference to service consumption, at times it was actually suggested that a return to the cottage industry had taken place (Olearnik, Styś 1989:81). This was manifested by an increase in the role of self-service in the functioning of the household, which in turn was the result of many factors, among which are highlighted the high cost of services (in relation to earnings), the low quality of the services provided as well as the unsuitable location of service establishments.

As many household services were beginning to be offered again (repair, renovation, beauty), the number of unregistered businesses on the market also began to rise. This grey area mainly encompassed tailoring, renovation and construction, as well as automotive and other services (ibid.: 81-82).

Up till the mid-1970's, most immaterial services (e.g. education, health care) were offered free of charge and only about ¼ of their consumption was financed directly by the personal assets of the citizenry, while the rest was financed by the state budget.

In comparison to the market for consumer services geared towards private persons and households, it is much more difficult, if not outright impossible, to fittingly analyze the market for services geared towards businesses. What makes the task difficult is the lack of credible data (including statistics) concerning the size and nature of businesses offering such services. During the entire period preceding the political changes of the late 1980's, a considerable share of services came from within the companies themselves, what statistical data do not show. The high level of internalization was the result of several factors, the most important being that the preferred way of structuring companies involved highly hierarchical administrative structures. In effect, within the Polish economy we were dealing with a highly advanced, vertical integration of enterprise. This system had many advantages in view of the economic conditions at the time, one of which was the possibility of greatly reducing risks associated with supply chain management.

Permanent shortages in many areas forced companies to develop their own departments which were devoted exclusively to solving the problem of the short supply of (mainly material) goods, so that production could proceed without interruption. Since decision-making was focused on the area of supply, and the need to control the flow of goods often led to significant development of the companies' own storage space, this was not conducive to the development of companies specializing in wholesale trade.

The self-sufficiency of companies in the realm of what are considered typical business services also stemmed from the relaxed controls on companies with regard to bookkeeping. The limited scope of bookkeeping activities was not conducive to the development of companies specialized in providing this type of service to other firms. The situation was similar with services such as marketing, advertising and public relations. Because scarcity was the norm, the suppliers/producers were able to dominate and even dictate the terms in many areas of the economy. There was no incentive for companies to develop their own sale-boosting services or to purchase them. Neither did the ease with which all the products were liquidated, nor the lack of competition, impel companies to analyze the market situation or to collect data regarding potential clients and their preferences, so there was a lack of the typical services devoted to market research.

The weak connection to foreign markets and the relatively rare occurrences of export and import operations were no stimuli for the development of shipping services. The lack of an exchangeable currency, the lack of regard for the businesses' own ways of managing their finances, as well as the controlled manner in which state budget funds were being invested, had to contribute to the low level of development in the banking and insurance industries.

Towards the end of the 1980's, at the eve the great socio-economic transformation, the combined results of all of the above-mentioned factors led to a situation, which could be dubbed as the developmental gap in services (Rogoziński 2000:135). The preference for the material sector as the one driving development contributed to marked stagnation in the service sector. The condition of the service sector in Poland in many respects deviated from the European average, not only with regard to quantitative aspects (the service sector's role in the job market, national income and export, as well as the condition of the infrastructure of a given service, such as communications), but also with respect to the qualitative aspects (e.g. technological advancement, quality of services provided, outdated management techniques). This is the situation, which the service sector found itself on the eve of the great political transformation.

THE SERVICE SECTOR IN AN ECONOMY UNDER RECONSTRUCTION

Since 1989, the increased importance of the service sector is one of the most significant and remarkable changes accompanying the ongoing transformation of the Polish economy and society. The role of the sector, measured as a portion of the employed population, is not yet as significant as in other countries, since it is barely approaching 50%, compared with 70% in highly developed countries. However, since the beginning of the 1990's, a clear and steady increase in the services can be observed (Figure 2). Much more significant is their role in generating the gross national product - currently ⅔ of the entire Polish GDP.

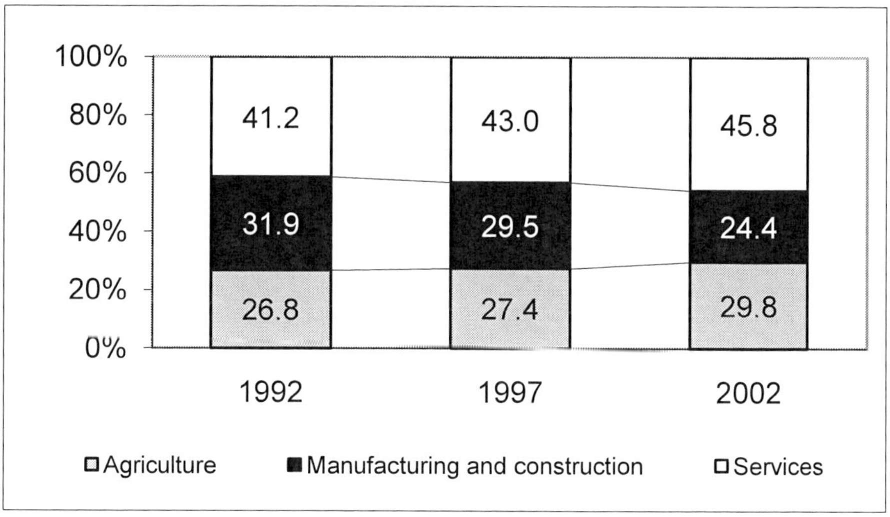

Source: See Figure 1.

Figure 2. Changes in employment by sectors (1992-2002).

Particularly in urban areas, the creation of many new service-related jobs has helped lower the unemployment rate, which, along with the discontinuation of the so-called canon of full-time employment, was one of the effects of the transformation. The restructuring of many facets of the economy constricted the job market, in manufacturing in particular (Figure 2). The removal of various restrictions placed upon the economy by the state in the previous period also contributed to an increase of the market for services. New laws regulating private enterprise, deregulation in many areas, and the privatization of large, state-run companies, are the main factors for the quick growth of the service sector.

As the result of the changing economic situation during the last decade, the process of the fast growth of service sector jobs observed in Poland since 1989, changed between the years 1992 and 2002. While in the manufacturing sector there has been a steady decrease in the number of employees, in the service sector this trend has appeared only after 1999. Relative to the situation in 1992 (when the new industry classification system came into effect), by 2002, the employment growth indicator for the service sector was 106, up from 100, what it had been ten years earlier. In the case of the manufacturing sector, including construction, this same indicator shrunk to 73.

The service sector's share in the job market also tends to vary with location. In 2001, this indicator ranged from under 10% to almost 80% among the different districts (Figure 3). Apart from the largest urban agglomerations, the highest relative percentages of people employed in the service sector were noted in the western and northern districts of Poland. This indicator was also high in the regions of Śląsk (Silesia) and Warmia. The service sector was most weakly represented in districts in central Poland (Mazowsze/Mazovia, apart from Warsaw), as well as those in the east and southeast.

Apart from the changing face of services as an industry, also visible were the changing trends within the internal structure of the third sector. To a lesser extent, this also concerned the market shares of two groups of services: market and non-market (mainly public) (Table 1). Their shares have not changed significantly over the last decade and have remained at a ratio of 2:1, for market services and non-market services, respectively.

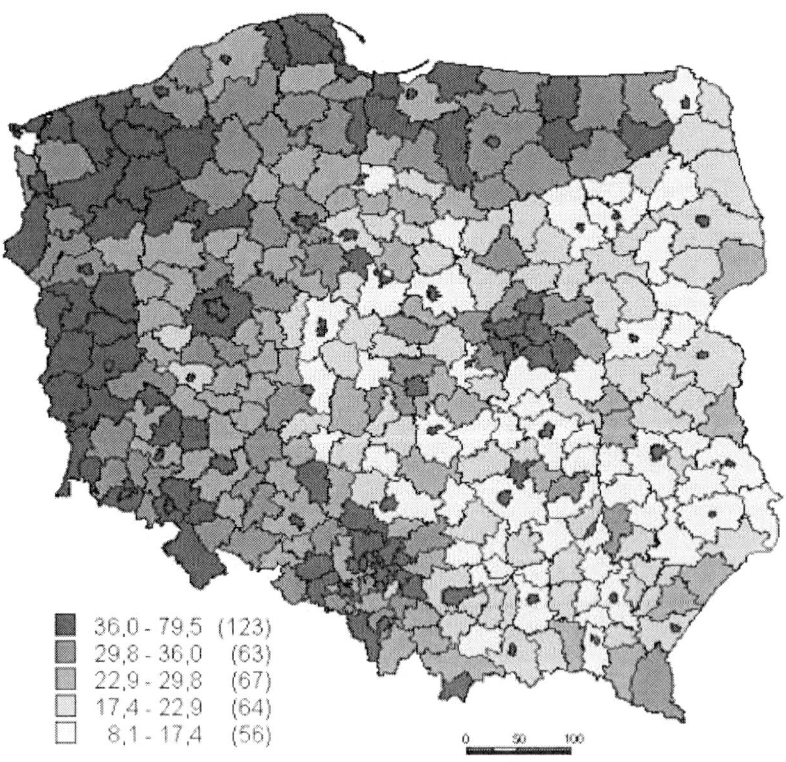

Source: own analysis based on *Powiaty w Polsce 2001*, 2002, Central Statistical Office, Warsaw.

Figure 3. The percentage of the total working population employed in the service sector, 2002.

Table 1. Changes in the numeration and organization of the service sector during 1992-2002

No.	Section of Polish Industrial Classification System	1992		1997		2002	
		'000	%	'000	%	'000	%
1	Trade and repair	1871,3	30,2	2060,6	30,0	1931,5	29,3
2	Hotels and restaurants	164,4	2,7	201,8	2,9	210,3	3,2
3	Transport, storage and communications	912,9	14,7	864,7	12,6	689,8	10,5
4	Financial intermediation	188,3	3,0	305,2	4,4	279,3	4,2
5	Real-estate and business services	542,8	8,8	699,1	10,2	867,7	13,2
6	Public administration and defense	292,4	4,7	431,8	6,3	522,2	7,9
7	Education	811,9	13,1	902,1	13,1	891,3	13,5
8	Healthcare and social work	1009,3	16,3	1029,2	15,0	845,8	12,8
9	Other services	397,4	6,4	370,6	5,4	344,7	5,2
	Market services (1-5, 9)	4077,1	65,9	4502,0	65,6	4323,3	65,7
	Non-market services (6-8)	2113,6	34,1	2363,1	34,4	2259,3	34,3
	Total services (1-9)	6190,7	100,0	6865,1	100,0	6582,6	100,0

Source: see Figure 1.

Wholesale and retail trade still constitutes the dominant category within the service sector in Poland, representing nearly ⅓ of all employment within it. The remaining categories' shares are much lower, ranging from around 13% (education, real-estate and business support) down to 10%. The hotel and restaurant industry is definitely the one most weakly represented.

If we consider the service sector in view of changes in the number of jobs, we will see that up until 2002, public administration and defense was the category which was experiencing the most growth (growth indicator of 179, compared to 100 in 1992). Growth was slightly lower for real-estate and business support (160) and financial intermediation (148). Three other types of services had a growth indicator above 100: hotels and restaurants (128), education (110) and trade (103). Transport and communications (76), healthcare (84), and other personal, social and community services (87) found themselves at the other end of the spectrum.

The relative importance of individual categories (measured as their share in the total of service sector jobs) experienced significant changes during the 10 year period analyzed. Due to changes in the number of jobs, four categories lost and five categories gained importance during the period from 1992 to 2002 (Figure 4).

The services which experienced the biggest increase were business services (+4,4%) and public administration (+3,2%), which experienced additional growth in 1999, when changes in the industrial classification system were instituted and financial services related to compulsory on-the-job insurance were moved from financial intermediation to the category encompassing public administration and defense as well as compulsory social security. A relative decrease of importance was most visible in the case of jobs in the transport and communications (-4,2%) as well as health care (-3,5%) divisions.

In the case of the service sector, a change in the number of jobs indirectly indicates a change in the number of businesses, since businesses in this sector are usually small, family-owned, and have few employees. In 2002, 76% of all registered businesses happened to be in the service sector. The size of the firm also depends on the type of services it offers (the level of specialization) and varies depending on the type of industry.

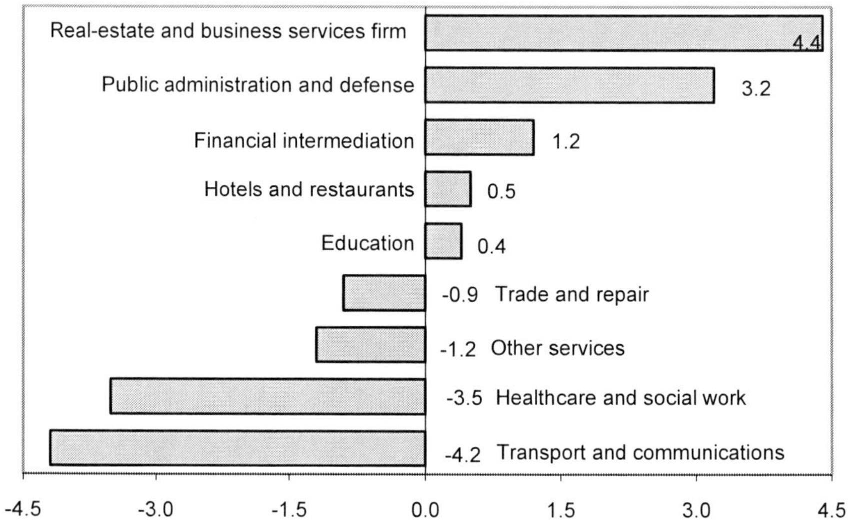

Source: see Figure 1.

Figure 4. Changes by division in the percentage of the total employed in the service sector (1992-2002).

The 1990's were a time of significant transformation in the organization of ownership within the service sector. The increasing role of the private sector is the combination of the effects of several processes, of which the ones most often mentioned are: the privatization of state-run companies, the increase in foreign direct investment, as well as the development of private domestic enterprise. These processes are closely tied to each other and so it is difficult to analyze any one of them separately. In Poland, the state's relinquishment of its economic assets happened at different rates in different categories of the service sector, and often the strategic investors taking over all or a part of the assets (the control package) were companies based in countries of the European Union and/or in the USA.

According to the data of the Polish Information and Foreign Investment Agency (*FDI in Poland*, 2003), from mid-2003 on, foreign companies have collectively invested 64,5 billion USD. These investments (worth over 1 million USD each) are nearly equally divided between the service sector and the manufacturing sector. The presence of foreign capital is most visible in several areas, especially in financial intermediation, trade and communications. Direct investments in financial intermediation amount to 14,3 billion USD, or over ⅕ of the entire FDI. The biggest investors that have taken control of Polish banks include HypoVereins Bank, Citigroup, EBRD, Allied Irish Bank and Credit Agricole. The investments of major retailers are just as visible, especially in urban areas. Major European and global retail companies have been expanding their retail chains in Poland for several years. The individual investments of these French (Carrefour, Casino), German (Metro Group AG) and British (Tesco) retail firms have each surpassed the 800 million USD mark. France Telecom, controlling the Polish landline telephone service provider Telekomunikacja Polska S.A. (TP S.A.), is still the biggest overall investor (with 3,2 billion USD). Foreign investment in other service areas is less spectacular, but the influence of foreign capital is still visible in the hotel and restaurant industry, as well as in real-estate and business services, and in other service categories.

The public sector still has a large share in areas, which traditionally constituted the state-controlled domain, meaning public administration and defense, education, health care and other (community) services. The state continues to play an important role in providing rail transport service and mail service.

The combined effects of privatization, foreign investing and the development of domestic enterprise have led to a quantitatively and qualitatively transformed organization of the service sector. The increase in foreign connections and the increasing presence of multinational corporations on the Polish market, the establishment of a market economy and the emergence of competition, the widespread increase in private business ownership by Polish citizens, as well as changes in their affluence level and ways of consumption, have all helped create the new types and develop the already existing types of services on the Polish market.

Briefly surveying the changes in each of the industry categories, we can point out new types of services or quickly developing services. In the case of *trade*, a new type of phenomenon is the growing presence of firms possessing foreign capital, directing the continuously expanding distribution chains of both wholesale and retail trade. The creation of nationwide or regional chains has introduced forms of retail trade which are new to the Polish market, and range from large establishments with lots of retail space (hypermarkets and supermarkets, shopping centers, shopping and service centers) to small establishments offering products in limited quantity, but at competitive prices (discount sales). A relatively new phenomenon is the direct sale of (mainly cosmetic) goods. The increase in catalogue (mail-order) sales is also notable. Internet sales are also on the rise, albeit not without encountering some difficulties. An increasingly common way of organizing service activities, and not only in the realm of trade, is by franchising. During the last couple of years, a tendency towards the integration and consolidation of companies has also been visible.

Within the *hotel and restaurant* industry as well, both hotel chains, and bar and restaurant chains, have been developing. The hotel infrastructure still remains insufficient. During the 1990's, most money was invested in projects involving the building of high-standard hotels in most large cities. As a result, even in the largest cities there is a shortage of budget-class accommodations, though this varies in degree, depending on the region. In rural regions, a new type of phenomenon is agro-tourism, in the case of which the base of available accommodations is constantly growing and developing. In the restaurant industry, the popularity of bars and fast food restaurants is increasing. This is also true of restaurants offering different types of ethnic food. The market for catering and phone-order home-delivery services has also emerged, mainly in large cities.

Changes in many areas of the economy could not have been as quick, if at all possible, without significant changes in the *transport* industry, especially in the realm of communications. In the area of passenger transport, there has been a noticeable, gradual departure from relying upon the rail system, in favor of flexible automotive transport, in which there is a large number of active private companies providing services. Often, the services they provide also include shipping and logistics. Firms providing courier services are also growing in number and developing in scope.

Very significant changes have taken place in the area of communications, the insufficiency of which for a long period of time had been a major obstacle for the inflow of foreign capital. The privatization and the loosening up of restrictions placed upon the market allowed quick changes to take place in telecommunications. The existing infrastructure of the fixed-line telephone network was modernized by the introduction of digital switchboards and fiber-optic technology. Following the introduction of one analogue mobile telephone network, development of a digital mobile phone network began in the mid-1990's. The rate of mobile telephony development was so high that by 2002, the number of subscribers in the three digital networks (nearly 14 million), significantly exceeded the number of fixed-line telephone service subscribers. The development of telecommunications has made possible the introduction of new services that utilize voice and data transmission channels. The list of internet providers is long and new local and regional cable television networks are being created. Numerous private local radio stations, as well as national and local television stations, have come into existence. The increased availability of telephone services has also been conducive to the reorganization of customer service departments at many companies (to the creation of call centers).

Financial intermediation services have also undergone a significant transformation. In the course of only a decade, the banking sector has been reorganized, beginning with the separation of the functions of the central bank from those of the commercial banks. Gradually, banks with foreign capital started gaining the biggest share of the market, so that they currently own most of the assets and bank offices. Although banks which are universal and operate on a national scale dominate the market, increasingly more banks are specializing. The stock market has begun to operate and retirement funds have become established. With regards to property insurance and life insurance, development of the insurance market is proceeding at varying rates. Changes stimulated by technological development include inter-bank activity (the sum of electronic settlement transactions), new services (networks of automatic teller machines, electronic and internet banking), and the increasing frequency of electronic transactions (the usage of Visa and Eurocard/Mastercard pay-cards).

Given the conditions in Poland, a new type of phenomenon is the development of many *business services*, and especially a wide spectrum of consulting services, from strategic management consulting, through legal, technical (information technology - IT) and financial consulting, to personal consulting. Serious changes have also taken place in bookkeeping and audit services. There has been significant development of marketing services, from advertising agencies, through market research firms, to logistics and shipping services. More and more frequently, many of the work functions of the company are outsourced to outside firms. The increase in outsourcing concerns: IT, financial (bookkeeping), legal, transport, personnel management and building maintenance (cleaning and security) services.

In the area of *public administration*, it should be pointed out that a new system was introduced on all three levels, from the lowest (*gmina* or commune), through the middle (*powiat* or district), to the highest (*województwo* or voivodship) autonomous administrative unit. Each new change in administrative division also leads to the reorganization of functions at each of the three administrative levels. For the ordinary citizen (the user of the services) or business owner in particular, the territorial division reform that took place in 1999 meant that it was necessary to make adjustments. The introduction of the intermediate district level meant that many of the functions of the lowest communal level were transferred to the district level (e.g. control over building codes and over secondary education). A serious problem for the Polish state administration and the local self-governing bodies is that not many of their services can be accessed through the Internet. An overwhelming majority of administrative services still require the physical presence of the interested party at the appropriate office. The high cost of creating virtual offices, training the staff and informing the public about the possibility of using the internet for this purpose is a serious obstacle in the development of this form of services.

The 1990's witnessed the rapid development of existing *educational institutions* and the creation of numerous new ones. This relates to virtually all levels of the educational system, from the elementary to the university level. The most significant changes were related to the transfer of the authority over most elementary and secondary schools from the state to the local (communal and district) level. Not any less significant were changes related to the creation of many new schools by community groups and institutions, as well as by private companies. This is testimony to the growing initiative of local communities, even if the direct cause behind the creation of some of the new schools was dissatisfaction with the level of teaching at the public schools.

A new phenomenon, notable in scale, is the development of higher education institutions, and private schools in particular. Within a short time period, one hundred and several dozen new institutions were created, and not exclusively in large cities. They are often located in centers which have previously never had any academic traditions. In the period from 1990 to 2002, the number of students grew several-fold, from around 400 thousand to around 1 800 thousand. The education offered at most of the schools is either professional or finance-oriented.

Within *health care*, the third category of services usually associated with the public sector, one can notice changes in the services offered due to the increasing range of new technological solutions, which can be applied in many areas of health care. Surely, one change of an organizational nature is the increasing involvement of the private sector within the medical service sector. This includes privately managed medical and dental offices. Private and often highly specialized medical clinics and hospitals represent a phenomenon, which is becoming increasingly more common in large cities.

An analysis of the changes which have taken place in the service sector in Poland over the last decade, including organizational changes and the appearance of new services and the disappearance of more traditional services, would not be complete without looking for the reasons on the consumers' end. The consumers have been becoming more individualistic in their choices. The range of life styles and attitudes has expanded and become more diverse. This has been concurrent with the rise of the Poles' affluence level and the progressive spreading out of their income levels. Current studies point out that consumption in Poland is increasingly service-oriented (Bywalec 2002). Among the reasons for the increasing consumption of services, and their increasing role in the consumption patterns of households, is the improved supply of consumer goods on the market. The increase in the supply of goods and services and the transformation from a seller-oriented market to a buyer-oriented market has made possible the formation of individual consumption patterns. During the years 1991-2002, there was a marked decrease in the individual (household) consumption of food and beverages (including alcohol and tobacco products) from over ⅓ to ¼ of all expenses. Simultaneously, the share of services increased from 39 to 43% (Bywalec 2002: 21). The breakdown of household expenses still depends however on household size and type (working, farming, retired, etc.). The increasing disparity between income levels will undoubtedly contribute to further diversification of consumption.

The City and the Countryside: Two Extremes in Relation to Services

The dynamic of the service sector's increasing role in the economy had been varied not only with regard to each category within the sector, but also within each region of Poland, in association with the region's level of socio-economic development and the effects of processes (such as privatization) which had taken place up to that point. The clearly visible concentration of certain services in cities and especially in large urban centers is also caused by purely economic factors. In many types of specialized (business) services, demand reaches the required threshold only in urban centers. To a certain degree, the fact that firms offering services are overrepresented in large urban centers (relative to demographic and economic potential), is related to the low level of power decentralization. Firms often wish to be located near official information sources and decision-making centers. In the case of many consumer services, one can still notice that not enough capital is being invested in rural areas. The level of service infrastructure development in these areas is often lower than in the cities and the quality of services is also not as high.

Regional differences in the availability of services will now be illustrated by the example of three service categories, in which the role of foreign direct investment (FDI) has been especially significant: financial intermediation, trade and communications. All together, by mid-2003, 27,5 billion USD of FDI, what constitutes 85% of all investments made in the service sector, had been allocated in these three categories. And it is in these categories that changes in spatial distribution are most visible.

Financial Intermediation

It is difficult to say whether forecasts made in the early 1990's regarding the direction and rate of changes in the Polish financial sector are currently being confirmed. To some analysts (e.g. Caselli, Pastrello 1992:229) the prospect of establishing a system of financial firms and institutions in Poland, similar to those in the West, seemed unlikely. The characteristics of the local economy always necessitate the creation of local solutions, and yet in its basic form, the Polish banking system currently resembles other European Union countries solutions.

With regard to size and spatial layout of bank office networks, the increasing contributions of foreign capital resulted in significant changes in this category of services. In the year 2000, for the first time the number of offices belonging to banks run mostly on foreign capital exceeded the number of Polish bank offices. A similar change took place regarding the composition of the workforce. Progressive consolidation of the banking sector, and successive mergers and acquisitions, lead to an increased concentration of these services; what from a geographical point of view leads to changes in the strategy for the development of service networks.

In mid-2003, 45 commercial banks (about ¾ of the total) had their head office in Warsaw, while in other cities there were only 16 head offices. When one takes into account the strength which banks posses (in the form of own capital or assets), in the capital city, there is an even greater concentration of these banks with the most capital and assets. In addition, this fact is supported by the list of foreign banks represented in Poland, 17 of which are located exclusively in Warsaw (*Lista central...*, 2003).

The presently being built and the already created banking offices are located mainly in cities and towns. In 2000, commercial banks jointly owned around 5 000 offices, most of which were located in cities and towns. Only 4% of the offices were located in rural regions. One may be puzzled that at the same time, nearly ¼ of Polish cities and towns were lacking a commercial bank office. Included in these 200 cities and towns were almost all small towns with a population no greater than 2 000 (39 of 42 of these towns did not have a bank office), and over half of the towns with a population between 2 000 and 5 000 (140 towns out of 239). Even some larger towns did not have a bank office. This was even true for every one out of nine towns with a population between 5 000 to 10 000.

This rather pessimistic image of the availability of bank services for town residents should be verified however by including credit unions in the analysis, in addition to commercial banks. The presence of a credit union office is seen as competition and partly justifies the unwillingness of commercial banks to expand their networks into small towns. Cost benefit analysis usually points to insufficient demand for banking services due to the low income level of the residents (as well as their inability to save money) and a weakly developed service sector. The specificity of credit union activity and distribution has involved serving the populations of rural areas and small towns, which still function as farming communities. Including credit unions in the analysis markedly improves the rate of availability of banking services in smaller urban centers. Among nearly 200 towns without a commercial bank office, only 15 also did not have a credit union branch. One should mention that most credit unions situated their branch offices (as well as headquarters) in rural regions, what improves the availability of banking services for the still numerous rural population.

Table 2. Bank offices in 2000 by city population size and by number of offices in the city

Population (in thousands)	**No. of cities in the given category**	**No. of bank offices**	**No. of bank offices in the city**				**No. of residents per 1 bank office**
			Min	Max	Mode	Mean	
0-2	42	42	0	3	1	1,0	1635
2-5	239	332	0	4	1	1,4	2403
5-10	181	432	0	7	2	2,4	2964
10-20	182	688	1	8	4	3,8	3841
20-50	139	931	2	20	5	6,7	4576
50-100	50	763	6	33	16*	15,3	4407
100-200	22	651	11	47	41	29,6	4386
> 200	19	1511	25	177	149*	79,5	4657
Warsaw	1	447	447	447	447	447	3393
Total	*875*	*5797*	*0*	*447*	*1*	*6,6*	*4106*

* Multimodal distribution.

Source: Own calculations based on the branch address databases of respective banks.

Considering commercial bank and credit union offices jointly, it can be pointed out that their distribution is not even throughout the cities of Poland. Towards the end of 2002, there were 5 800 bank offices, in 875 cities and towns (Table 2). Among all the cities, Warsaw could boast the highest number of offices – nearly 450. In the remaining cities one could observe a tendency according to which the increase in population was accompanied by an increase in the number of bank offices. In the smallest towns (of up to 5 000 inhabitants) there often was only one office. On the other hand, cities which are the capitals of districts (most having 10 000 to 50 000 inhabitants) could boast 4 to 5 bank offices. The average number of bank offices in voivodship capitals (usually with over 200 000 inhabitants) was several dozen.

Variation from city to city, also within the respective city population size categories, compels one to reflect upon the availability of banking services. If one measures availability as the number of residents per one branch office, then in the year 2000, that number was 4 100 residents for cities (Figure 2). For small towns (of up to 10 000 residents) this figure was more favorable (from 1 600 to 3 000 residents). In the subsequent population size categories, the availability rate was a little lower, while the categories with the relatively lowest level of banking infrastructure development were cities with 20 000 to 50 000 residents and cities with at least 200 000 residents (with the exception of Warsaw).

Regional variation in the banking services availability rate among Polish cities and towns is presented in Figure 5, which shows deviations from the mean number of residents per one local bank office. The situation is relatively favorable in highly urbanized areas such as Upper and Lower Silesia, the agglomeration around Warsaw and the environs of other large cities. Lack of banking services is noticeable in small towns in southeastern and eastern Poland, in towns along the German border, as well as in Wielkopolska.

The various strategies for building bank office networks (building from the ground up; acquiring already existing offices as a way of gaining control or creating a merger) and the relative novelty of the Polish banking system have without a doubt influenced the current spatial development of the bank office network. Usually, this development is studied in relation to specific factors which banks take into account when choosing the location of new offices. The factors most often analyzed in bank localization politics (Grzegorczyk 1996:109) are: population potential, economic potential, infrastructure and employment.

Studies done up to this point have made it possible to ascertain that the number of bank offices in a given city is strongly dependent upon the social and economic characteristics of the city (the number of residents, the number of those employed, as well as the number of business entities). The condition of the banking infrastructure has shown to have the least effect (Wilk 2003:165). By using multiple correlation and regression analyses, it has been determined that over 98% of the variation in the number of bank offices in Polish cities can be explained by analyzing variations in the number of the three abovementioned elements (population, employed, business entities). In view of this fact, it is not surprising, that banks, which are profit-driven, develop their office networks in the largest urban and economic centers, not in rural regions, where – especially in the absence of farming – the development of private enterprise is low.

Retail Trade

Trade, and retail trade in particular, is always mentioned among the services the face of which has been significantly altered in Poland in recent years. This is caused by significant changes in the way that retail trade functions, with regard to ownership, size, the way the facilities are equipped, the involvement of foreign business entities and many other factors that are significant in this segment of the market.

In the 1990's, the role of the private sector grew significantly in the area of trade. Currently, trade is one of the most privatized areas of Poland's national economy. In 1990, the public sector's share in all of retail trade was nearly 64%, only to decrease to 2% by 2002. At the same time, the number of stores in the public sector fell from 14 000 to less than 1 800 (out of a total of 450 000 stores). The role of stores, which are controlled by foreign capital is steadily increasing. At the end of 2002, there was 3 300 such establishments, which equals to less than 1% of all retail stores, but because they are mostly large facilities, their share in the total retail space is 8.5%.

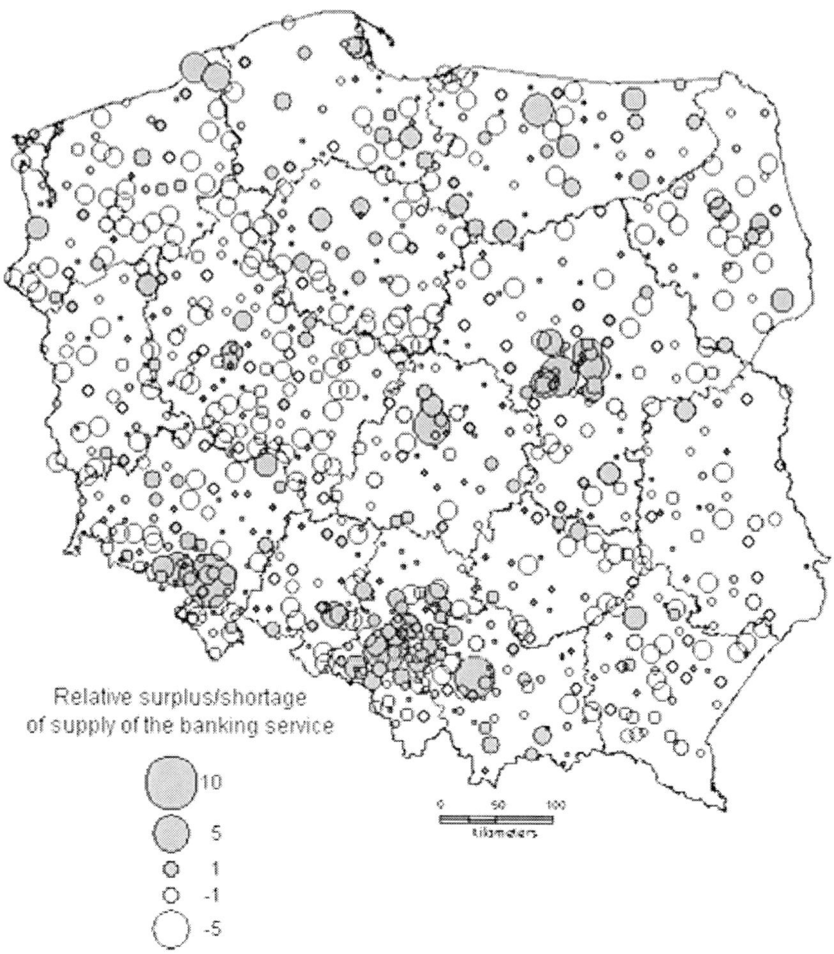

Source: See table 2.

Figure 5. The relative surplus or shortage of supply of banking services in cities and towns (the number of standard deviations from the mean number of people per one local bank office).

The influence of foreign companies upon the face of the market in the area of trade is most apparent in the development of supermarket, hypermarket and discount store chains – chains of stores which all have a lot of retail space. In 2002, the number of supermarkets was approaching 2 000, and the number of hypermarkets was over 200. The bigger the retail space of the store, the greater the likelihood of it being owned by a foreign company. While half of the supermarkets (stores with up to 2 500 sq. m of retail space) are owned by Polish firms, ¾ of the hypermarkets are owned by foreign firms. Many of these establishments are a significant component of the over 100 newly-built shopping centers.

Although foreign retail investments are being made in all regions of the country, some regions are more popular among foreign investors. In 2002, ⅓ of the 216 hypermarkets operating in Poland were located in two voivodships: Śląskie and Mazowieckie. It is understandable that the largest cities, where the greatest number of hypermarkets has been built, were the main locations that were targeted by the investors. These cities – Warsaw, Łódź, Kraków, Wrocław, Poznań and Gdańsk – are the capitals of voivodships, while also being the biggest cities in Poland. The distribution of supermarkets is also similar to that of hypermarkets, with the exception that there are markedly more supermarkets in the Silesia than in Mazovia. Overall, ¼ of all supermarkets are located in either one of these regions. The Wielkopolskie Voivodship also boasts a relatively large share of supermarkets.

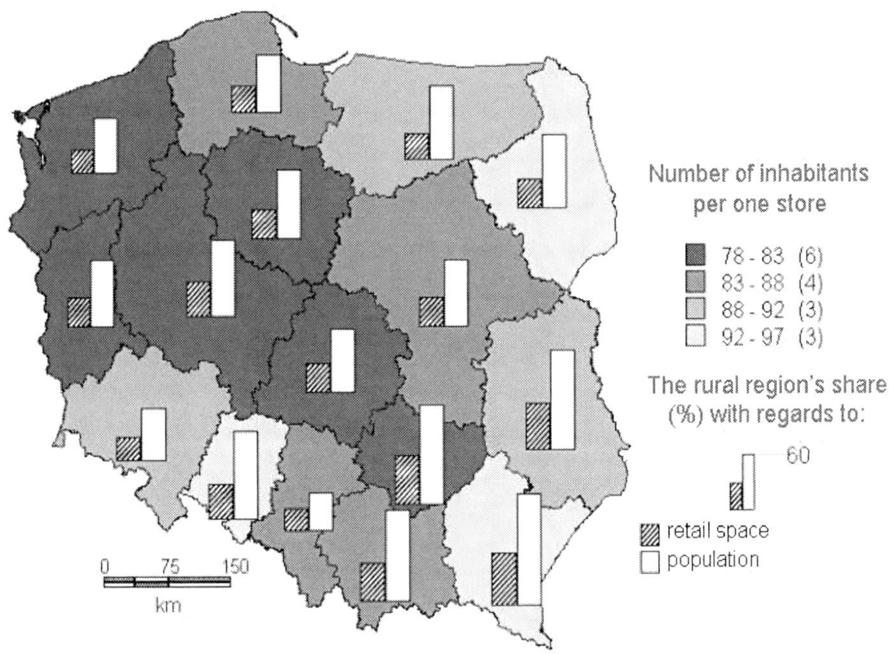

Source: own calculations based on *Rynek wewnętrzny w 2002 r.* (*Internal Market in 2002*), Central Statistical Office, 2003, Warsaw.

Figure 6. The distribution density of stores and a characterization of rural regions in 2002.

For the most part however, retail trade in Poland is conducted by small and often family-owned firms which are housed in small shops that can be found in all the cities and towns as well as in most villages. In 2002, around 105 000 stores (23%) were located in rural regions. The rural stores usually have less retail space than those operating in the cities. The rural stores' share of all retail space is a mere 17,5%. At the same time, rural regions are inhabited by 38% of Poland's population. The percentage of the overall retail space situated in rural areas varies depending on the region (Figure 6). It is decidedly the highest in southeastern

Poland (Podkarpackie, Świętokrzyskie, Lubelskie Voivodships) and the lowest in Silesia (with the exception of the Opolskie Voivodship).

Even though statistically every village had two stores at the time, they were usually small. The distribution of stores in rural regions is still half as dense as in urban regions. In 2002, there were 139 people per one rural store, while that number was only 68 in urban regions. The overall number of people in Poland per one store is 85. This index varies depending on the region (Figure 6). The distribution density of retail locations is the greatest in northwestern and central Poland (not including the Mazovia). The lowest indicators in regards to access to retail networks can be observed in the eastern part of the country (the Podlaskie and Podkarpackie Voivodships).

Telephony

Although it would be difficult to say that the state of the Polish fixed-line telephone network is satisfactory, one should note that during the years 1989 to 2002 there was a significant increase in the rate at which the infrastructure for the fixed-line telephone network was being built. In 1989 there were merely 3,1 million fixed-line telephone service subscribers. By 2002, their number had grown more than threefold. (There were nearly 11 million in 2002.) (Figure 7.) The telephone network density indicator rose during that time from 82 to 286 subscribers for every 1 000 residents. In spite of significant changes, it is difficult to term the current situation as satisfactory, especially in relation to service in other European Union countries.

The development level of the infrastructure of services can be measured by its technological advancement. The 1990's witnessed the gradual modernization of the technology used in landline telephone services in Poland. This especially pertains to telephone switchboards and cables. During the 1990's, intercity telephony had become completely automated. Additionally, most of these connections are now made by digital switchboards.

The development and modernization of the telephone network's infrastructure requires a great deal of financial investment. A phenomenon specific to the development of local telephone networks in Poland during the last decade was the significant financial contribution made by local communities, even while the project was still in its initial stages. This pertains to rural regions in particular, where the telephone network is the least advanced. Very often the contribution of the local community committees represented 50% of the total cost. It was not until 1989-1996 that cooperation between TP S.A. and the local communities made it possible to bring telephone service to nearly 300 000 new subscribers (which is over ¼ of all new rural subscribers whose service was connected at the time).

The density of both the fixed-line and mobile telephone networks varies greatly by region, but there is also a very noticeable difference in density between urban and rural regions. The situation of the Polish telephone service market leads one to believe that this market is structured in a way that is similar to that of markets in developing countries (Salomon, Razin 1988:125). The large discrepancy in network density between urban and rural regions is the typical phenomenon. The network density mark is quite high in Mazovia and Upper Silesia (Figure 8). The landline telephone network is the least developed in the less urbanized regions of southestern Poland, where the economy is driven by agriculture.

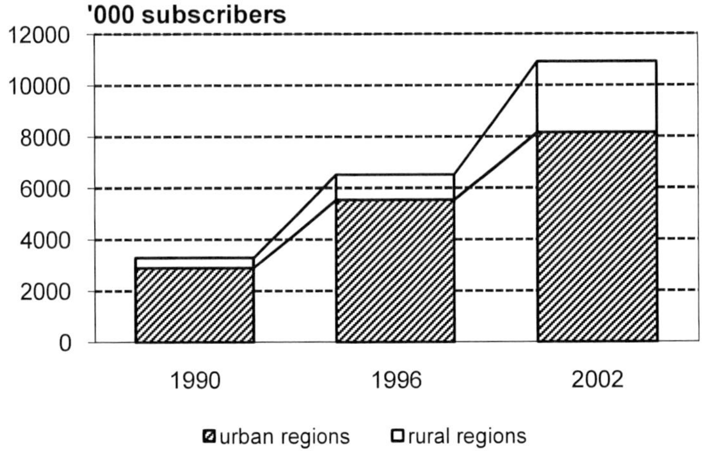

Source: see Figure 1.

Figure 7. Increase in the number of landline telephone service subscribers from 1990 to 2002.

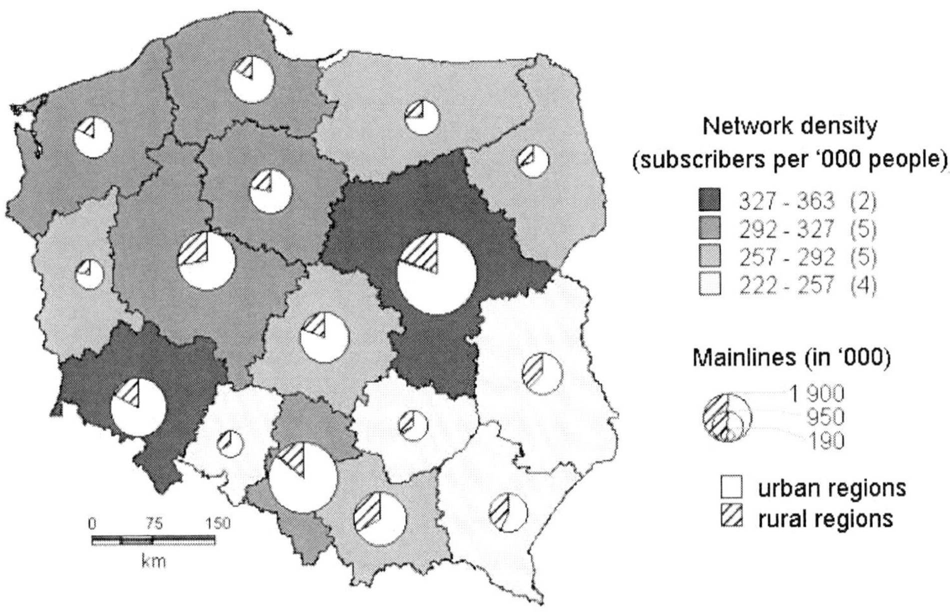

Source: own analysis based on the *Rocznik Statystyczny Województw 2002* (*The Statistical Yearbook of Voivodship 2002*), 2003, Central Statistical Office, Warsaw.

Figure 8. Number of subscribers and the density of the fixed-line telephone service network in 2001.

Telephone service network density (number of subscribers per 1 000 inhabitants), landline telephony (main lines, in thousands): urban regions, rural regions.

The discrepancy in telephone network development is especially visible between the cities and rural regions. This is also the result of preexisting conditions of an economic nature. Investment projects in telecom are made in areas where a quick return of expenditures is guaranteed. The rural fixed-line telephone service is not as lucrative as its urban counterpart, which takes in many subscribers. Given the situation existing in Poland, it is estimated that in the country, the average cost of installing one telephone line is 1,5 to 2 times greater than it is in the city. This is mainly due to the fact that residences are scattered over a large area, what makes accessing individual homesteads difficult.

From 1990 to 2002, funds invested into the development of rural landline telephone networks made it possible to reduce the discrepancy in telephone network density between urban and rural regions. In 1990, this inequality was 4,9:1; by 1996 it had been reduced to 3,5:1; and by the end of 2002 to 1,8:1. The degree of network density in rural areas is growing constantly, from 27 subscribers per 1 000 residents in 1990, to 67 subscribers in 1990, and to 188 subscribers towards the end of 2002.

The contrast between urban and rural regions is also visible in the case of mobile telephone networks. Every one of the three mobile service providers began by making service available in large cities and along the major thoroughfares connecting them. Only later the area of coverage was expanded to include more sparsely populated regions (e.g. main tourist destinations). The area of coverage for these networks corresponds therefore with the main routes and junctions, along which the exchange of goods and services is the most frequent, and the population is the most highly concentrated. This is also where the potential demand for mobile telephony is the greatest, making possible the quick return of expenditures. Since they are peripheral to the Polish economy, a portion of rural areas is located outside of the area covered by the mobile telephony networks.

The underdeveloped infrastructure of the telephone network may seriously limit the chances of including the rural population in the process of building an information-age society. Without the infrastructure, it is difficult to assure Internet access and the transmission of data. For similar reasons, it is difficult to build profitable cable television networks in areas of sparse rural settlement.

Besides the three industry categories mentioned above, within the socio-economic dimension in Poland, there is great regional variation in the overall distribution of firms of the service sector. Looking at urban and rural regions, one can observe relatively little variability in the availability of services that are offered by organizations which are part of the public sector (education, healthcare, administration), and do not function according to market principles. Significant disparities become visible however once one considers the spatial distribution of firms providing business support. At times, high competition and the search for attractive markets cause the business support firms to concentrate in densely built over and highly exploited urban regions. Still not enough capital is being invested in rural regions where agriculture is crumbling while other forms of economic activity are underdeveloped; and where the loose network of settlements is often made up of villages that are slowly becoming deserted.

It appears that the process of evening out the disparities in the development of service infrastructure, and in the accessibility of services – present both between different geographic regions in Poland and between the urban and rural regions in general – will be long and difficult. The reasons for this are: the still relatively low degree of urbanization and the still significantly high number of rural settlements (high rural population). The prospect of securing European Union Structural Funds looks hopeful, but even under those circumstances, contributions from local funds are necessary, and it is therefore essential to engage the local communities in the process.

References

Bywalec Cz., 2002, Serwicyzacja konsumpcji w Polsce [Consumption in Poland Becoming Service-Oriented] (in:) Czubała A., Wiktor J.W. (eds.) *Kierunki rozwoju marketingu usług. Teoria i praktyka.* [*The Course of Development of Service Marketing. Theory and practice.*] Chrzanów: Wyższa Szkoła Przedsiębiorczości i Marketingu, pp.15-25.

Caselli G.P., Pastrello G., 1992, The Service Sector in Planned Economies of Eastern Europe: Past Experiences and Future Perspectives, *Service Industries Journal*, *12*(2):220-237.

FDI in Poland, 2003, Polska Agencja Informacji i Inwestycji Zagranicznych (PAIiIZ) [The Polish Information and Foreign Investment Agency], www.paiz.gov.pl [accessed 20.10.2003].

Grzegorczyk W., 1996, *Strategie marketingowe banków* [*The Marketing Strategies of Banks*], Warszawa: Wydawnictwo Naukowe PWN.

Jakubowicz E., 1993, *Podstawy metodologiczne geografii usług* [*Methodological Foundations of the Geography of Services*], Wrocław: Wydawnictwo Uniwersytetu Wrocławskiego.

Lista central banków krajowych (bez banków spółdzielczych) i oddziałów banków zagranicznych działających w Polsce [*A list of the headquarters of domestic banks (excluding credit unions) and of foreign bank branches operating in Poland*], 2003, Narodowy Bank Polski, www.nbp.pl/banki [accessed 20.10.2003].

Niewadzi Cz., 1975, *Usługi w gospodarce narodowej* [*The Service Sector Within the National Economy*], Warszawa: PWE.

Olearnik J., Styś A., 1989, *Usługi w rozwoju społeczno-gospodarczym* [*The Role of the Service Sector in Socio-economic Development*]. Warszawa: PWE.

Rogoziński K., 2000, *Usługi rynkowe* [*Market Services*], Poznań: Akademia Ekonomiczna w Poznaniu.

Wewnętrzny Rynek w *2002 r.* [*Internal Market in 2002*], 2003, Warszawa: Główny Urząd Statystyczny.

Salomon I., Razin E., 1988, The Geography of Telecommunications Systems: The Case of Israel's Telephone System, *Tijdschrift voor Econ. en Soc. Geografie*, *79*(2):122-134.

Wilk W., 2003, Accessibility of service in Poland on the example of the retail banks, (in:) A. Kowalczyk (ed.) *Geographical Space at the Turn of the Century.* Warsaw: Warsaw University, Faculty of Geography and Regional Studies, pp.159-166.

In: Economic and Political Developments in Poland
Editor: Maureen P. Larsen

ISBN 978-1-61209-951-4

Chapter 6

FOREIGN INVESTMENT CAPITAL IN POLAND AND ITS SPATIAL DISTRIBUTION SINCE 1990

Magdalena Wdowicka
Institute of Socio-Economic Geography and Spatial Management,
Adam Mickiewicz University, Poznań, Poland

INTRODUCTION

In 1989 Poland was the first among the post-communist states of Central and Eastern Europe to start a deep, fundamental systemic transformation that has changed the country's political, social and economic conditions irrevocably. The Polish economy had to grapple with a host of problems, largely posed by its communist heritage, especially in the initial period of the transformation. They included an obsolete economic structure, a worn-out stock of machines, high unemployment, soaring inflation, low accumulation, a budgetary deficit, foreign debt, and other. Poland still needs capital badly to continue the opening of the economy and its restructuring, but suffers a deficiency of domestic sources of financing. This is a major obstacle reducing the pace and range of the systemic changes, given the fact that the country is still striving to make up for its civilisational backwardness, modernise and supplement the existing manufacturing potential, and create an efficient, growth-enhancing infrastructural system. But first of all, it has to build an efficient economic system meeting the standards of advanced countries.

Poland's present capital resources are inadequate to deal with its economic situation, hence the country has to look for and employ external sources from which to finance developmental processes. One of them is the inflow of foreign capital, especially foreign direct investment (FDI), which is treated as the most advantageous form of capital flow. The change of regime in 1989 has made it possible for Poland to join in globalisation processes, including its opening to foreign investment, which has become a new development moulding the country's economic processes. This is due to the fact that the inflow of foreign capital is accompanied by additional elements highly significant for economic growth: the transfer of new technology and know-how, and modern, more efficient methods of labour organisation, management, and marketing. Foreign direct investment is also connected with access to foreign markets and the creation of new jobs. Among the many benefits associated with the inflow of foreign investment capital, especially worth mentioning are the acceleration of the systemic transformation and enhancement of the competitiveness of the Polish economy. Foreign investment promotes the stability of the country's economy, the building of market institutions, privatisation, the restructuring of its industry and foreign trade, and its integration with the world economy. That is why foreign direct investment can be a major factor of socio-economic development in Poland and the other post-socialist states.

The aim of this study is to present the inflow of foreign investment capital to Poland since the beginning of the transformation period, spatial differences in investment processes, barriers to investment, and the role of foreign investment in the transformation of the Polish economy.

Table 1. Foreign direct investment in the European Union and in the United States, 1995-1998

Country	Cumulative stock of FDI in country, 1998		Country's cumulative stock of FDI abroad, 1998	
	$ million	% global investment	$ million	% global investment
Belgium & Luxembourg	164,093	4.01	128,799	3.13
Denmark	31,762	0.78	35,821	0.87
Finland	15,523	0.38	32,810	0.80
France	179,186	4.38	242,347	5.89
Germany	228,794	5.60	390,090	9.47
Greece	22,048	0.54	851	0.02
Ireland	23,871	0.58	6,477	0.16
Italy	105,397	2.58	170,746	4.15
Netherlands	169,522	4.15	262,996	6.39
Portugal	21,130	0.51	7,534	0.18
Spain	118,926	2.91	68,392	1.66
Sweden	53,790	1.31	93,487	2.27
Great Britain	326,809	7.99	498,624	12.11
Austria	25,386	0.62	16,808	0.41
European Union total	1,486,237	36.35	1,955,782	47.50
USA	875,026	21.40	993,552	24.13

Source: own calculations on the basis of the 2000 International Statistics Yearbook, GUS.

THE VALUE AND STRUCTURE OF FOREIGN CAPITAL

Poland's share in global foreign investment is still minor (0.6%), despite a marked increase over the recent years. By the end of 1998, the total stock of FDI in the world exceeded $4 trillion. Each year the biggest proportion of capital goes invariably to the most advanced countries. The leader is the USA, and in Europe, Great Britain, The Netherlands, Germany, France, Belgium, and Luxembourg. These are also countries that invest the most abroad. Among non-European countries, the major world investors include Japan, Canada, and China.

The region attracting the bulk of FDI at the world scale is the European Union. By the end of 1998, a total of $1.5 trillion were invested in its member states, which amounted to 36% of the global stock of FDI, as against 21% in the United States and a mere $82.7 billion, or 2%, in the countries of Central and Eastern Europe (cf. Table 1, Table 2).

Among the countries of Central and Eastern Europe, Poland ranks first, both in terms of the yearly foreign capital inflow and the cumulative stock of foreign investment since 1990. It is followed by Hungary, Russia, and the Czech Republic.

Table 2. Foreign direct investment in the countries of Central and Eastern Europe

Country	Cumulative stock of FDI in country, 1998	
	$ million	% global investment
Poland	21,722	0.53
Czech Republic	13,457	0.33
Slovakia	2,062	0.05
Hungary	18,255	0.45
Bulgaria	1,352	0.03
Romania	4,250	0.10
Ukraine	2,801	0.07
Belarus	466	0.01
Russia	13,389	0.33
Lithuania	1,625	0.04
Latvia	1,488	0.04
Estonia	1,822	0.04
Total	82,689	2.02

Source: own calculations on the basis of the 2000 International Statistics Yearbook, GUS.

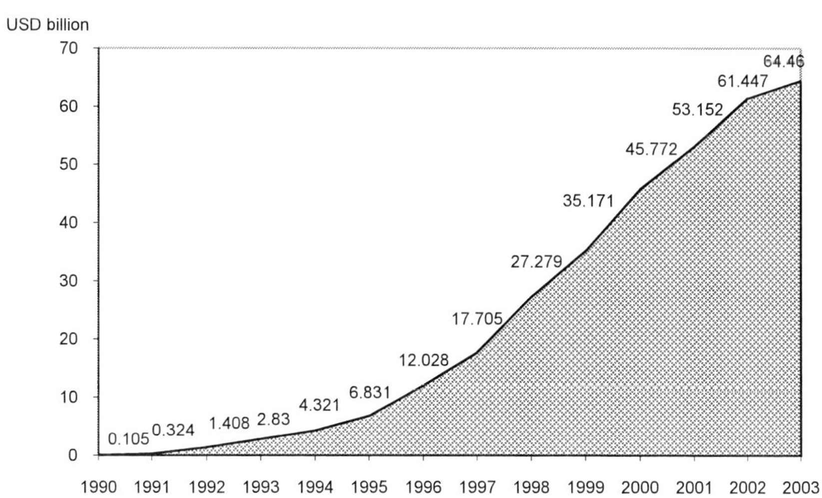

Source: own compilation on the basis of data of the Polish Information and Foreign Investment Agency.

Figure 1. Foreign direct investment in Poland, 1990-2003 (in USD billion).

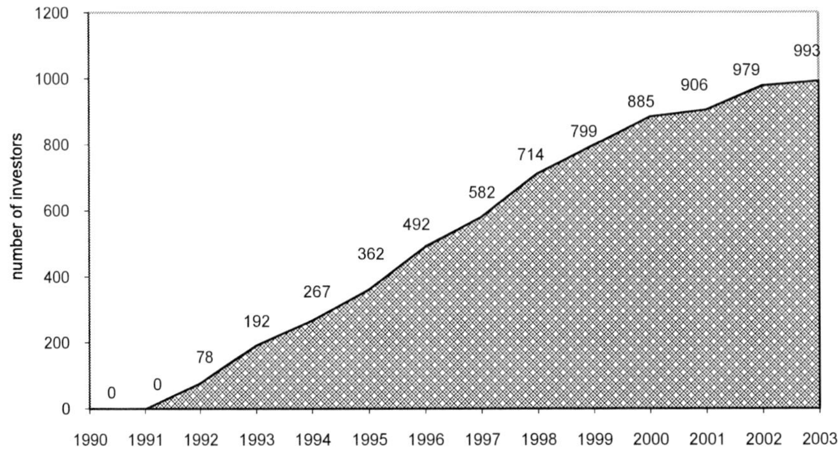

Source: own compilation on the basis of data of the Polish Information and Foreign Investment Agency.

Figure 2. Foreign investors over $1 million each in Poland, 1990-2003.

By the end of June 2003, Poland's cumulative foreign direct investment since 1990 totalled $68.3 billion (of which firms that had invested in excess of $1 million each accounted for $64.5 billion). The growing presence of foreign capital in Poland can be assessed in terms of an increase in the number of foreign investors and an increment in the value of capital they bring into the Polish economy (cf. Figure 1, Figure 2). When analysing annual capital inflows since the start of 1990, one can note that the record year has been 2000 with $10.6 billion in FDI; only 1998 comes close with $9.6 billion. The other years show much lower amounts of inflowing foreign capital. The FDI invested over the study period displays a clear linear development trend. The observed capital increment has been less than proportionate (cf. Figure 3).

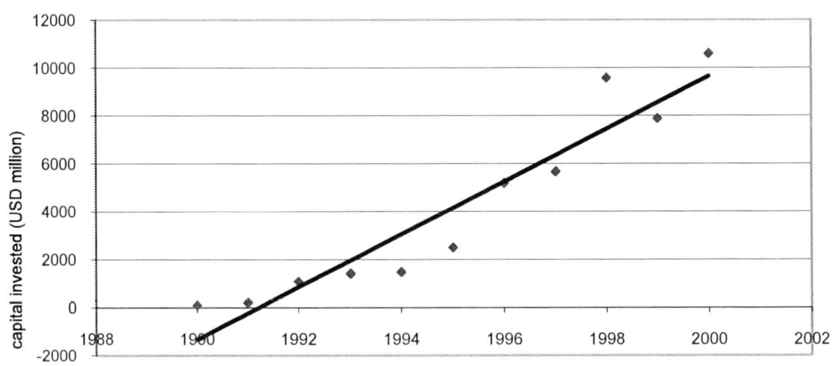

Source: own compilation.

Figure 3. Development trend of foreign direct investment in Poland, 1990-2000.

The Polish economy is ever better prepared for the reception of foreign capital. The upsurge in FDI flows to Poland in the mid-1990s was largely due to amendments to the law controlling foreign investment activity in Poland. What enhanced investment activity at that time was, beyond doubt, the signing by Poland of the Interim Association Agreement with the European Community in 1992 (which regularised foreign capital flows among the associate members), Poland's accession to the OECD in 1996, and to NATO in 1999. Other factors that helped to quicken foreign investors' interest in launching an activity in Poland was the country's rapid rate of economic growth and the stability of its political situation.

Since 2001, however, FDI has been on a decline. This reflects the downward tendency of the Polish economy, which has been caused mainly by the running down of the process of privatisation of large state enterprises with the participation of foreign strategic investors, deterioration in macroeconomic indicators, and changes in internal rules in Poland, among others those concerning special economic zones. The downturn in the world economy has also had a detrimental effect. Also worth remembering is the fact that the prospect of Poland's imminent membership of the European Union has reduced the profitability of firms (owing to an increase in operational costs, including wages).

An encouraging development has been an increase in the number of countries investing in Poland. In 1993, there were firms from 24 countries, as against 36 in 2003. The biggest group, at 227, or 23%, included German investors, followed by those from the USA (124), The Netherlands (106), and France (92). Much fewer investors came from Ireland, Greece, Russia, Liechtenstein, South Korea, Croatia, the Czech Republic, Slovenia, Hungary, China, Turkey, Portugal, Australia, Cyprus, and Israel, with single businessmen from South Africa, Taiwan, and the Philippines (cf. Figure 4). Also worth noting is the steadily growing number of transnational corporations bringing international capital into companies, which is undoubtedly an effect of globalisation.

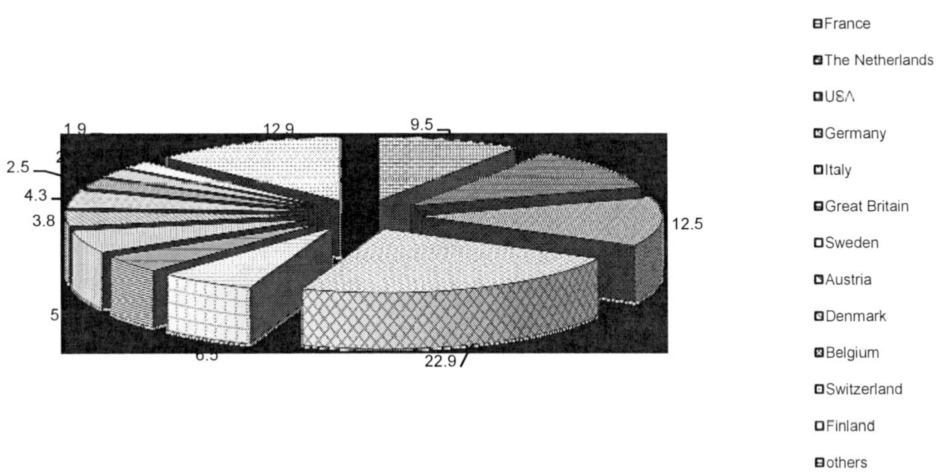

Source: own compilation on the basis of data of the Polish Information and Foreign Investment Agency.

Figure 4. Foreign investors of over $1 million each, by source country (in %).

In terms of the value of capital invested in Poland by the individual countries, the situation is somewhat different (cf. Figure 5). In the years 1993-1997, the leading foreign investor was the United States; in 1998-1999, Germany; and in 2000 France overtook both these countries in terms of the cumulative value of its investment since the start of the transformation. In 2003, The Netherlands took second place with $8.9 billion, right after France with $12.5 billion. The countries investing most in Poland are those belonging to the European Union. By mid-2003, they have invested a total of $47.4 billion, or 74% of all foreign capital. Investors from North America have invested $8.5 billion (13.2%) so far, while the proportion of capital from Asia is a mere 3.2% ($2.0 billion).

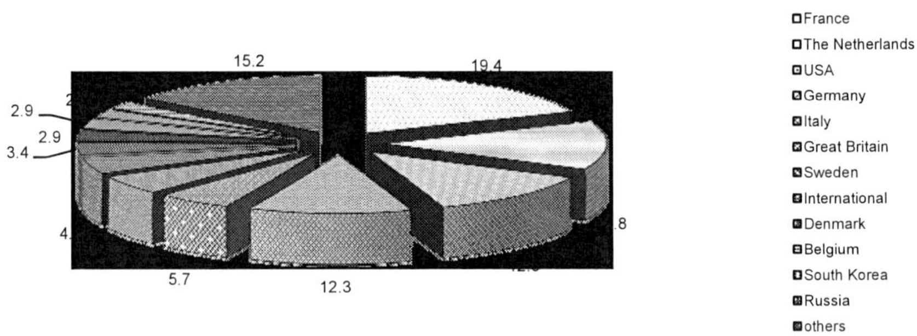

Source: own compilation on the basis of data of the Polish Information and Foreign Investment Agency.

Figure 5. Foreign investment in Poland by source country (in %).

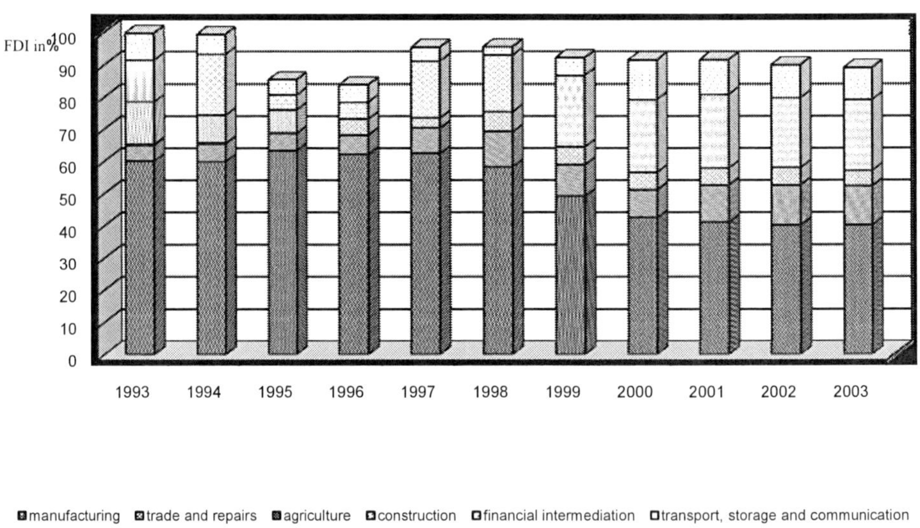

Source: Own compilation.

Figure 6. Changes in the structure of foreign investment in Poland by line of business, 1990-2003.

The structure of FDI by line of business may be of interest. From the very beginning of the transformation, most capital has gone invariably into manufacturing, in particular to the production of foodstuffs, beverages, and tobacco goods. In the late 1990s, however, there was a marked decline in industrial investment and a shift to other sectors of the economy, especially financial intermediation, transport and communications, which may be evidence of Poland's gradual inclusion in the globalisation process. The share of the financial sector in the total stock of FDI grew from 13% in 1993 to 22.1% in 2003, while investment in transport and communications increased from 8.2% to 10% over that period. In turn, there was a slump in construction (from 13.3% in 1993 to 4.6% in 2003). Agricultural investment has been very low throughout the study period (cf. Figure 6).

Since the beginning of 1990, most capital has been invested in manufacturing ($25.9 billion, or 40.2% of total investment). Next come financial intermediation ($14.3 billion), trade and repairs ($7.8 billion), transport and communications ($6.4 billion), and construction ($3.0 billion) (cf.Figure 7). The least foreign capital has been invested in agriculture as well as mining and quarrying, which is due to the still unresolved restructuring problems of these sectors of the economy.

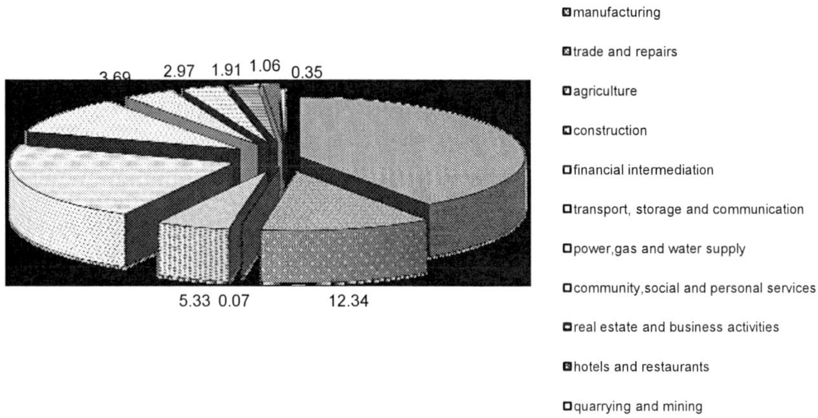

Source: Own compilation on the basis of data of the Polish Information and Foreign Investment Agency.

Figure 7. Structure of foreign investment by line of business (in %).

The biggest among foreign firms in Poland is France Telecom, which has invested $3.2 billion to date. The remaining leaders include Fiat ($1.7 billion), Daewoo ($1.4 billion), HVB ($1.3 billion), Citibank ($1.3 billion), RAO Gazprom ($1.3 billion), Vivendi ($1.2 billion), United Pan-Europe Communications ($1.2 billion), UniCredito Italiano ($1.2 billion), EBRD ($1.2 billion), KBC Bank ($1.1 billion), and Metro Group AG ($1.1 billion).

REGIONS ATTRACTIVE AND NOT ATTRACTIVE TO FOREIGN INVESTMENT

The economic climate for foreign direct investment in Poland has for years been perceived as one of the best among the transforming economies. This assessment has been reflected in foreign capital inflows. The most significant development in terms of investment processes in Poland has been creating the foundations of a market economy and its immediate opening to the world, which has radically changed the prevailing climate for FDI and made it possible for foreign investors to enter the Polish market. The opening of the economy consisted primarily in its joining the tendencies of development in the world economy, and its aims were a stronger economic performance, technological progress, an internal and an external economic balance, and ultimately, economic growth.

Among the most important changes that enabled the Polish economy to open to foreign investors were the liberalisation of the foreign direct investment law, the liberalisation of foreign trade turnover and rules of currency exchange, allowing foreign capital to participate in the privatisation of state enterprises, and progress in the building of a system and institutions proper to a market economy. These measures turned out to be highly significant, because until 1989 foreign capital could only be invested in so-called Polonia enterprises (i.e., those set up by members of the Polish community abroad) and companies of the joint-venture type, owing to the complicated procedures and bureaucratic intricacies in force then. Restrictions of various kinds, e.g. on the transfer of profits, and lack of any guarantee did not encourage businessmen, even those potentially interested in the Polish market, to invest here.

Poland's investment attractiveness was especially high in the other half of the 1990s. This was largely due to the economy breaking through the recession barriers fairly efficiently and entering a stage of accelerated economic growth with sinking inflation and with the upward tendency in unemployment being less steep. The ever wider opening of Poland to the world economy, adjustment of the Polish legal system and institutional economic structures to the European Union standards, the gathering of strength by the financial sector, more intense foreign trade, rising standards of living, advances in privatisation, and an improvement in Poland's financial and credit standing with international institutions were the main factors of the country's attractiveness in the assessment of foreign investors and their basic incentives to start economic ventures here. These factors were a reliable guarantee that an advanced marked economy meeting the Western standards was going to be built in Poland in a short time. They also lessened investment risk by laying more stable foundations of the investors' trust in the host country. For investors from the EU, Poland has become a more friendly country, and one closer to the solutions they are familiar with at home; for those from outside the Union, Poland is an attractive area from which access to the uniform EU market is easier.

Poland's attractiveness to investment capital is determined by a variety of features, the most important of which include:

(1) the market size - it is the biggest market in Central Europe with almost 40 million consumers, nearly four times as many as in Hungary or the Czech Republic, and medium income by world standards;
(2) an advantageous location - an attractive, strategic geographical situation in the centre of Europe ensuring easy access both to the western and eastern markets; it also opens up the prospect of access to the European Union market;
(3) low labour costs and a possibility of their reduction (cheap labour - monthly wages are several times lower than in Western Europe);
(4) labour supply (the labour market with ca. 18 million workers is highly diversified; there is a high proportion of skilled labour);
(5) high-quality factors of production;
(6) natural resources;

(7) well-developed industrial base (the industrial potential created in the times of a planned economy is being restructured and privatised, and new management methods are being introduced);
(8) an improvement in the country's financial and credit standing (smaller investment risk after Poland signed agreements with the Paris and London Clubs in 1994 concerning the conversion of Polish debt); and
(9) the newly created legal system (cf. Jodkowski 1995, Liberska 1996).

Naturally, Poland's attractiveness investment-wise is not the same throughout its territory. There are areas that are a great magnet for investors and those that have to struggle hard to obtain any significant investment. There are several factors determining spatial differences in the investment attractiveness of the various parts of Poland, the most important among them being the socio-economic transformation, which has differed in intensity and rate from region to region since its very beginning. According to some authors (Czyż 1998; Szlachta 1996; Kożuch 1998), transformation processes have even contributed to a deepening of the existing regional disparities inherited from the past and fixed during the years of the planned economy. One of the major causes of this state of affairs has been the shortage and comparatively low mobility of capital, which is a resultant of the given region's capital supply and readiness to invest. Investment capital tends to flow to the wealthiest regions, which additionally aggravates spatial disparities in development.

In the present article an attempt is made to assess the many-dimensional differences in the investment attractiveness of Poland's individual regions (voivodeships). The study accommodates a larger number of variables, which made it necessary to employ multivariate statistical analysis. To this end, use was made of principal components analysis which allowed an identification of the chief dimensions of differences in Poland's investment attractiveness (Maćkiewicz, Ratajczak 1993). Then cluster analysis was employed to classify and determine similarity relations holding in the set of Polish regions.

The following variables were studied: population density (x1), employment per 1,000 population (x2), per cent employment in market services (x3), number of economic entities registered under the REGON system (X4), number of companies with foreign capital (x5), total investment in millions of zlotys (x6), budgetary revenues of communes per inhabitant in zlotys (x7), budgetary expenditure of communes per inhabitant in zlotys (x8), graduates of higher schools (x9), number of units in the research and development (R&D) sector (x10), paved public roads per 100 km^2 (x11), and sewerage piping in km (x12).

This set of variables was transformed into principal components (using a correlation matrix) in such a way that the first component (V1) accounted for 63% of the total variability of the twelve variables in the set of Poland's sixteen voivodeships, the second (V2) for 19%, and the third (V3) for 13.2% (a total of 95.2% of the set's variability).

An analysis of the coefficients of determination of the components and the input variables allows the nature of the components to be interpreted (cf. Table 3). The first principal component is highly ($\alpha < 0.001$) correlated with the variables: number of economic entities, number of companies with foreign capital, investment outlays, budgetary revenues of communes, budgetary expenditure of communes, graduates of higher schools, and number of units in the R&D sector. Hence, it can be termed a component of economic activity, budgetary revenues of communes, and knowledge resources. The second principal component is significantly ($\alpha < 0.001$) correlated with population density and road density, hence it can be called a component of market absorptiveness and spatial accessibility. The third component is significantly correlated with employment per 1,000 population, hence it can be termed a component of occupational activity.

Thus, in the light of the analysis, there seem to be three clearly distinct dimensions of spatial differences in Poland's level of investment attractiveness:

(1) economic activity, the associated level of communal income, and knowledge resources,
(2) market absorptiveness and spatial accessibility, and
(3) the population's occupational activity.

Table 3. Principal components analysis for the voivodeships of Poland

Principal components	Variables mos strongly correlated with components
V1	X_4-number of economic entities registered under the REGON system (R=0,96) X_5-number of companies with foreign capital (R=0,96) X_6-total investment in millions of zlotys (R=0,98) X_7-budgetary revenues of communes per inhabitant in zlotys (R=0,89) X_8-budgetary expenditure of communes per inhabitant in zlotys (R=0,88) X_9-graduates of higher schools (R=0,98) X_{10}-number of units in the research and development (R&D) sector (R=0,97)
V2	X_1-population density (R=0,81) X_{11} -paved public roads per 100 km^2 (R=0,88)
V3	X_2 -employment per 1,000 population (R=0,91)

Source: Own compilation.

An analysis of the values of the particular components provided a basis for a classification of the voivodeships. In terms of economic activity, level of budgetary revenues and knowledge resources, the top-ranking voivodeships are Mazovia, Silesia and Wielkopolska, and the worst, Opole, Lubuska Land and Świętokrzyska Land. Mazovia, Silesia and Wielkopolska are also the best in terms of market absorptiveness, spatial accessibility, and the population's occupational activity. Opole is invariably the worst again.

As the last stage of the research, a synthetic classification of the voivodeships was made taking into consideration the values of the first two principal components. The results are presented in Figure 8. An analysis of the dendrite allowed four classes of regions to be distinguished:

class 1 - voivodeships enjoying a very high level of investment attractiveness: Mazovia;
class 2 - voivodeships showing a high level of investment attractiveness: Silesia;

class 3 - voivodeships showing an above-average level of investment attractiveness: Wielkopolska, Lower Silesia, and Małopolska; and

class 4 - voivodeships showing a low level of investment attractiveness: Opole, Lubuska Land, Świętokrzyska Land, Podlasie, Podkarpacie, Warmia-Mazuria, Lublin, Kujawy-Pomerania, West Pomerania, Pomerania, and Łódź (cf. Figure 9).

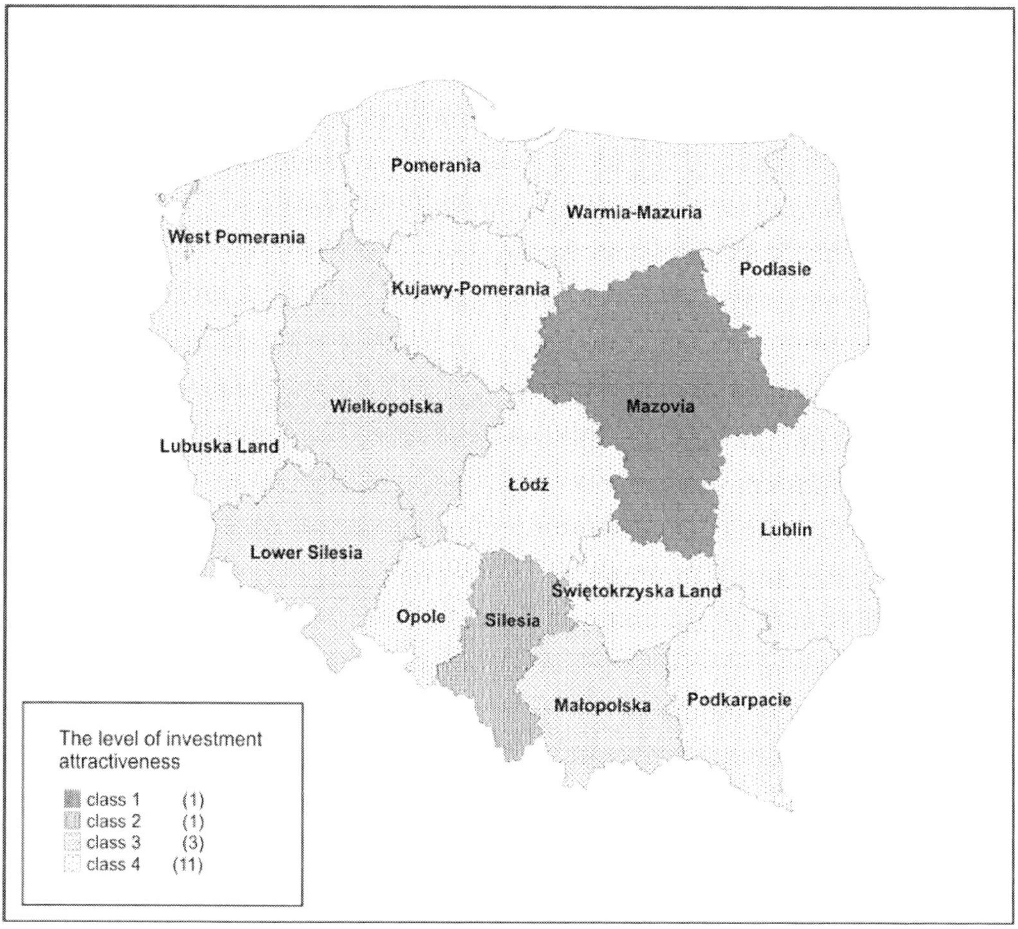

Source: own compilation.

Figure 9. Investment attractiveness of the voivodeships of Poland.

The results of the classification presented on the map show that the regions investors find the most attractive are strong, well-developed voivodeships of western, southern and central Poland. Most regions of low attractiveness are situated in eastern and northern Poland. They are typically agricultural voivodeships with poor industry and infrastructure, delayed systemic changes, and low market absorptiveness. The low investment attractiveness of these parts of the country is the result, on the one hand, of the heritage of the past (underinvestment, agricultural orientation, and distance from the principal administrative and communication centres), and on the other, of their seeming inability to overcome this unfavourable image.

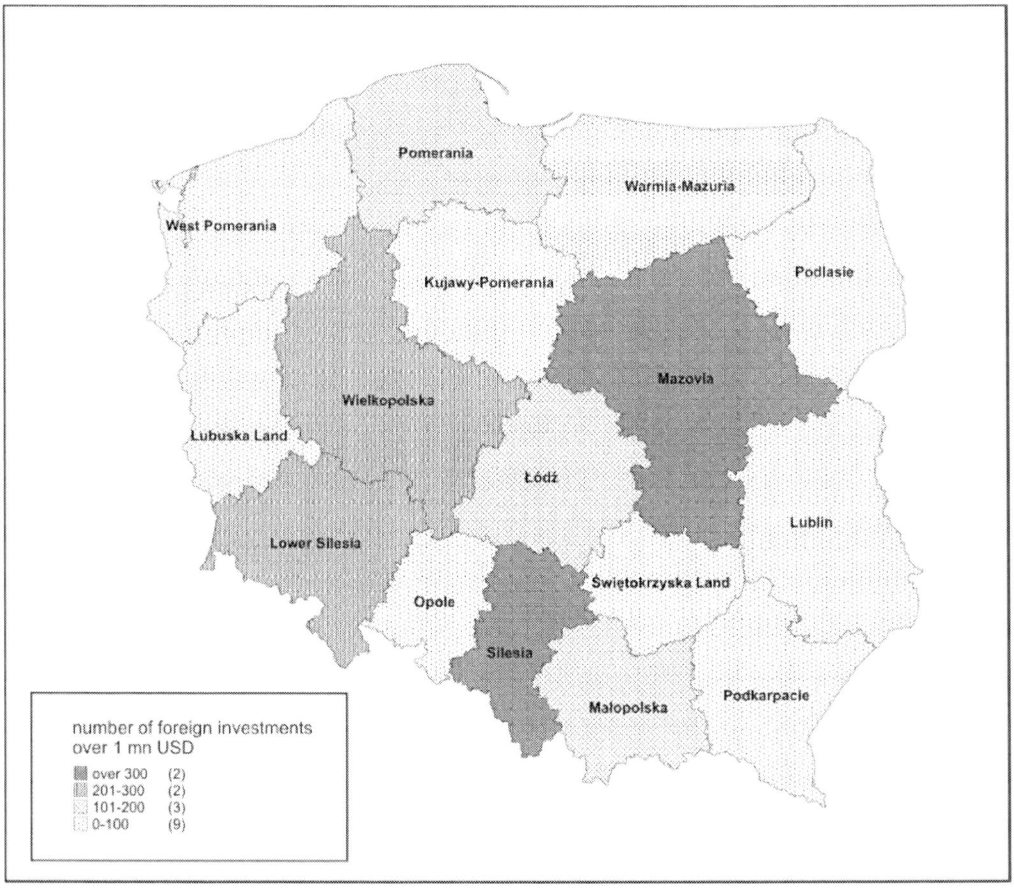

Source: own compilation on the basis of data of the Polish Information and Foreign Investment Agency.

Figure 10. Distribution of foreign capital in Poland in 2002.

The differences in Poland's investment attractiveness largely coincide with the inflow of foreign capital to the particular regions (cf. Figure 10). The spatial distribution of FDI in Poland since 1990 has been extremely uneven. Foreign capital tends to concentrate in the best-developed voivodeships: Mazovia, Silesia, Wielkopolska, and Lower Silesia. They attract the biggest number of companies with foreign shareholders and the highest values of capital (cf. Figure 11). Since the very start of the transformation, Mazovia has drawn the highest proportion (29.6%) of entrepreneurs who have invested in excess of $1 million each. The region accounts for 34.5% of all companies with foreign capital. The next-ranking voivodeships with the biggest proportion of serious investors (in excess of $1 million each) have been Silesia (13.1%) and Wielkopolska (9.7%). The smallest number of foreign investments have been made in voivodeships of north- and south-eastern Poland (Podlasie, Świętokrzyska Land, Lublin, Podkarpacie, Warmia-Mazuria). This is due to the fact that investors tend to locate capital in the largest cities (the metropolitan areas of Warsaw, Poznań, Katowice, Wrocław, Cracow, Szczecin, Gdańsk, and Łódź) because of their better-developed technical infrastructure, easier access to highly skilled labour, and availability of office space. Thus, the directions of capital inflow show investors to give marked preference to the main, fully developed urban-industrial centres of Poland, especially given the present system of communications. Foreign capital seeks locations with a diversified social and economic structure, a strong R&D and training backup, an extensive network of business-environment institutions, and ready accessibility, i.e., wealthy places functioning as growth centres.

Table 4. Effect of selected factors on the choice of location of foreign investment (in%)

Motive of choice of investment location	Big effect on location decision	Average effect on location decision	Slight effect on location decision	Motive was disre-garded
nearness of major domestic and international roads	78.5	7.5	3.0	11.0
nearness of railways	21.0	5.8	13.9	59.3
nearness of airport	16.9	10.5	17.4	55.2
nearness of Poznań city	70.3	9.3	4.1	16.3
location with respect to future A2 motorway	33.7	13.4	8.7	44.2
nearness of state border	27.9	9.9	8.1	54.1
cheap labour	18.6	12.8	18.6	50.0
skilled labour	49.4	10.5	10.5	29.6
presence of institutions favourable to business, e.g. banks, consulting firms	30.3	14.5	5.8	49.4
low land prices	22.1	15.1	10.5	52.3
marketing activity of local authorities	14.6	9.3	12.2	63.9
favourable attitude of local authorities	33.1	11.6	7.6	47.7
high quality of service in offices	17.5	12.8	11.0	58.7
professional, comprehensive information about commune	15.8	11.6	8.7	63.9
tax relief granted by commune	13.4	5.8	11.0	69.8
technical infrastructure on investment site	54.1	16.3	5.2	24.4
unambiguous land ownership	46.5	12.2	1.7	39.6
market absorptiveness	57.0	4.6	2.4	36.0
location with respect to parent company	21.5	6.4	4.1	68.0
favourable experiences of other firms investing in commune earlier	25.6	9.9	7.0	57.5
prior knowledge of region	40.7	14.5	6.4	38.4
place of origin of partner	15.7	4.6	4.1	75.6
level of commune's economic development	29.7	18.6	11.6	40.1
advancement and directions of socio-economic transformation of commune	19.8	16.9	12.2	51.1
nearness of sources supplying raw materials, other materials, or parts	11.7	11.0	6.4	70.9
availability of services meeting needs of company's employees	8.1	14.0	16.9	61.0
availability of services meeting needs of company's employees	8.7	7.6	8.1	75.6
tourist attractiveness of commune	8.1	4.1	5.8	82.0

Source: results of a survey research among foreign investors in the Poznań metropolitan area.

The above conclusions were corroborated by a survey study of motives that had inclined foreign investors to launch an activity in the Poznań metropolitan area. The respondents set the greatest store by the area's ready accessibility. Almost 80% of firms conceded that a great influence on the location decision was the nearness of major domestic and international roads. Highly significant was also the neighbourhood of a large urban centre; this motive was acknowledged by 70% of respondents. For 57% of firms with foreign capital, equally important was the area's market absorptiveness. High on the list of location incentives was also the proper development of land for investment. For 54% of investors, an important consideration was the presence of technical infrastructure on the chosen site, and for 46.5%, unambiguous land ownership (cf. Table 4). Also worth noting is the fact that nearly 70% of investors considered high qualifications of the local labour, and only 18.6% thought low labour costs were important. A comparatively high proportion of respondents set great store by the presence of institutions favourable to business (30.3%) and a high level of economic development (29.7%).

These preferences of investors widen the existing disparities in Poland's economic development and increase the concentration of economic activity in the most advanced centres.

Barriers to Investment

The leading position Poland occupies among the countries of Central and Eastern Europe in terms of FDI worth and the comparatively high marks for investment attractiveness it is given by various international institutions and opinion-forming circles should not dim the awareness of the threats and barriers that still keep hindering investment in Poland. Further economic and institutional changes are vitally necessary to facilitate the operation of foreign firms, because Poland is only one of the many countries soliciting foreign investment and the competition in the world capital market is very stiff.

The quarterly studies which the Foreign Trade Research Institute has been conducting for several years among enterprises with the participation of foreign capital in Poland show that foreign investors see four basic groups of barriers to their activity:

(1) demand barriers - an insufficient demand in the domestic or international market, competitive imports;
(2) supply barriers - lack of skilled workers, a shortage of raw materials and semi-finished products for reasons other than financial, an antiquated stock of machines;
(3) financial barriers - unfavourable terms of credit, difficulties in obtaining credit, heavy budgetary burdens; and
(4) systemic barriers - erratic paths of privatisation, unclear and inconsistent legal rules (cf. Marczewski 2002).

The first two groups can be seen as barriers connected with the operation of the markets of goods and factors of production (market barriers), while the other two, as barriers connected with the regulatory and institutional spheres of the economy (regulatory and institutional barriers).

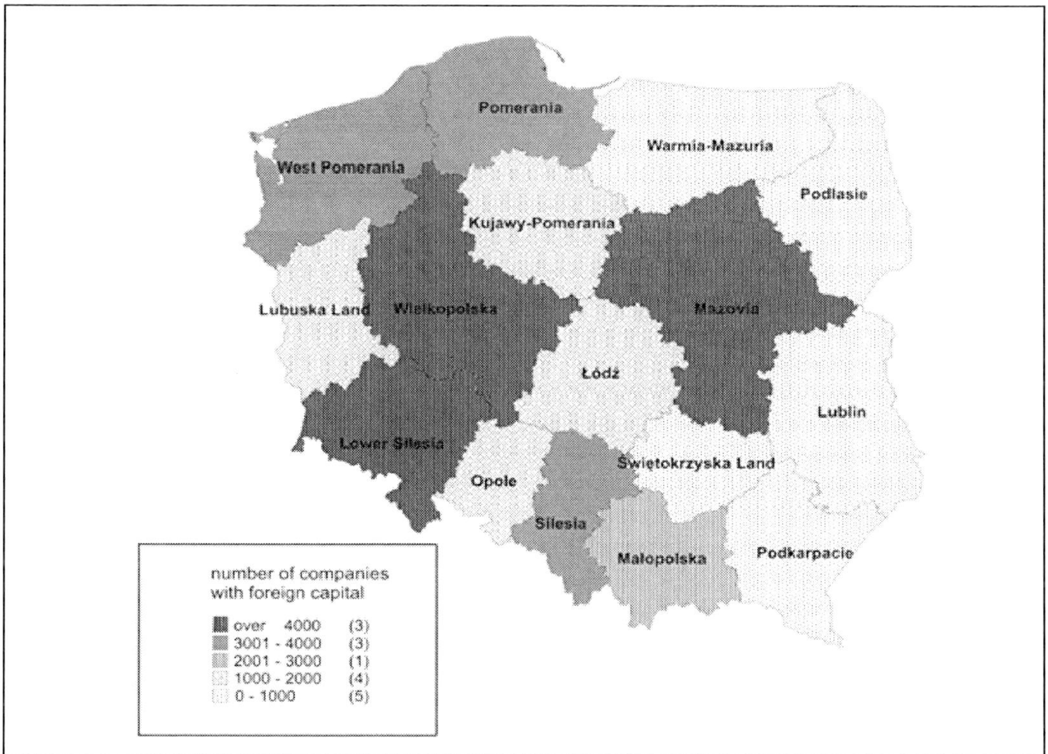

Source: own compilation on the basis of data from the 2002 Statistical Yearbook, GUS.

Figure 11. Distribution of companies with foreign capital in Poland.

Market barriers turn out to be the most daunting for foreign investors, especially the insufficient demand at home (76.3%) and abroad (60.1%). This situation results from both, a slackening rate of economic growth and dwindling export opportunities owing to an economic downturn in the economies of Western Europe (especially Germany) and the United States. The barrier that the foreign investors feel much less acutely is competitive imports (32%). An even smaller role is played by the supply barriers. It is only rarely that foreign firms find it difficult to acquire highly skilled workers (3.4%) or suitable materials (3.1%).

An unfavourable development has been an increase in regulatory and institutional barriers, particularly those created by fiscal and monetary policies. Almost a half of respondents (46.7%) complain of budgetary burdens, despite the gradual reduction in the rates of the corporate income tax. Foreign investors criticise both the instability of the tax system and tax assessment. This is due to the financial burden of excessively high social insurance contributions (for old age and disability pensions) and the contraction of the economy.

About 24% of firms see a barrier in the unfavourable terms of credit in Poland. Apart from the low profitability of obtaining a credit, the respondents emphasise the nuisance of the inefficient banking system and long, complicated credit-granting procedures that are well below the Western standards.

Worth noting among the systemic barriers is the increase in the significance of the barrier of vague legal rules (37.8%). This is due to the inconsistency of the law, constant modifications of rules, loopholes in the law which allow clerks to interpret it in arbitrary ways, and inadequate legal guarantees for foreign investors. This barrier reflects the bureaucratic ineptitude of Poland's economic life.

Among the remaining barriers to foreign investment activity in Poland, the respondents include:

(1) instability of tariff policy and high tariffs,
(2) an insufficiently developed service system,
(3) obstacles in the purchase of land and buildings by foreigners,
(4) unsorted ownership of many plots of land on which investors would like to carry out an activity,
(5) poorly developed communications infrastructure, and
(6) insufficient help and initiative that foreign investors get from local communities (cf. Liberska 1996; Cichowski 1998; Kożuch 1998).

An adverse effect on foreign investment has been the slackening rate of economic growth. It should be kept in mind that in the modern world economy it is foreign direct investment that follows economic growth, not the other way round. Unfortunately, Poland has lost its position as one of the fastest developing countries in Central and Eastern Europe. Economic stagnation, a high budgetary deficit, or a bad situation on the labour market, if persistent, can bring about a definite decrease in foreign investment because the climate they create is not favourable to investors.

A certain expansion of Poland's economy could be observed in 2003. Inflation now stands at a low level, and the current-account deficit has improved dramatically. A result of lower inflation should be an improvement in consumer feeling and a greater tendency towards buying. In turn, lower interest rates and the weakening of the zloty should benefit exporters and help to reverse the downward tendency in investment outlays. On the other hand, however, Poland's economic growth is being hampered by excessive public spending and tax rates. Also unfavourable is too low a rate of the zloty against the euro.

There may be a rise in foreign capital inflow after Poland has joined the European Union. The basic incentives will be the convenience of a homogeneous market and Poland's location offering a springboard to other big foreign markets.

The Role of Foreign Capital in the Economic Transformation

Foreign investment has played a special role in the transformation of the Polish economy. It is treated as one of the most crucial exogenous factors capable of making economic growth more dynamic both at a macro- and a micro-scale, i.e., at the levels of the entire national economy as well as regional and local economies (cf. Małuszyńska 1996; Dziemianowicz 1998; Chrupek 1999). At the national scale, foreign capital engagement mainly brings financial, technological, employment, and broadly understood structural effects. At the local and regional scales, foreign investment especially affects the labour market and local business circles (Domański 2001).

Foreign direct investment has a wide and diversified impact on the various spheres of the economy. It can be felt directly or directly, and produce more or less readily measurable benefits. By participating in the construction of a market-economy system, affecting major macroeconomic variables and the sectoral structure of the economy, and finally facilitating the transfer of new technologies and management methods, FDI helps to accelerate the systemic transformation processes. Foreign capital also stimulates the competitiveness of the Polish economy on international markets. As a result, it contributes to economic growth and hence, to a higher level of general well-being in the country.

The Creation and Development of the Market Economy

Foreign direct investment particularly affects the building of a market-economy system. Its inflow contributes to the expansion of the goods, service, capital and labour markets, and the creation of a new ownership structure based on private property (Wojnicka 1997).

By bringing new products, FDI plays a big role in the diversification of goods supply on the market, which in turn affects domestic consumption patterns. Foreign capital also has an indisputable share in the formation of a market of business services indispensable for an efficient market economy, viz. consulting, marketing, or new financial services. It can also contribute substantially to the development of the capital market, e.g. by purchasing shares of companies listed on stock exchanges, or by issuing securities.

An integral element of the building of a market economy is privatisation. Advances in this field largely depend on the inflow of foreign capital, given the shortage of domestic capital in Poland. Over the last years of the systemic transformation, FDI has played a major role here, especially in the privatisation of big and medium-sized enterprises naturally requiring larger capital inputs. Foreign capital has had a small part in the privatisation of small businesses.

In firms privatised with the help of a foreign strategic investor, several favourable adaptive changes can be observed. The most important include modernisation of the firm, a much higher increase in production than in domestic businesses, desirable changes in the product range, a faster rate of replacement of old technologies with new ones, higher management efficiency, and finally gaining access to new markets, which is also connected with an increase in the proportion of exports in total sales. These changes often follow from the foreign investor's commitment to earmark financial means, in a specified future, for the development and improvement of performance of the enterprise he has bought.

The growth of the private sector, especially that of small and medium-sized businesses, is also facilitated by smaller-capital FDI which involves establishing new plants on greenfield sites or entering into joint ventures with domestic firms. Economic growth will depend on whether foreign investments, rather than supplanting their domestic equivalents, are going to lead to improvement in the latter's performance by stimulating competition in the given sector (Wojnicka 1997).

The Balance of Payments and other Financial Effects

Mentioned among the most important benefits of foreign capital inflow is its effect on the chief macroeconomic variables of the recipient country, and in particular, its balance of payments. The impact of FDI on the balance of payments is always advantageous in the initial stage, since the incoming foreign capital is part of the balance credited to the capital account. In a later period this impact may change depending on the export-import activity of the investors and the extent of profit retransfer (cf. Hunya 1996). A crucial issue is what proportion of profits earned by the foreign investors in Poland is transferred abroad and what is reinvested at home. The OECD agreements on the avoidance of double taxation offer foreign investors the possibility of transfer pricing, a way for a multinational company to shift profits to countries with lower tax rates. As a result, owing to transfer pricing practices, FDI can in fact reduce the budgetary receipts of the country where the profit was actually generated, but where fiscalism is comparatively high.

FDI has a particularly strong impact on the trade balance component of the balance of payments (Czerwieniec 1990). The situation most advantageous for the Polish economy is when a foreign investor, having established a manufacturing plant, helps to boost the country's exports and restrict imports. An algebraic formula for these benefits looks as follows (Root 1984):

Payment benefits = K + X + S,

where:

K - the initial inflow of investment capital,
X - exports of a Polish-based subsidiary company of a foreign firm,
S - imports substitution (replacement of imports by the output of the subsidiary company).

At present, however, the foreign firms operating in Poland are generating an excess of imports over exports (Durka, Chojna 1999; Domański 2001). This situation probably results from the fact that they bring means of production, i.e. machines and equipment, from abroad. This can turn out to be beneficial for Poland in the long run, because it contributes to modernisation and expansion of the country's production potential, and hence to its greater export capacity in the future.

On the other hand, foreign firms display a much greater inclination to export than companies with exclusively domestic capital, and their exports are much more diversified (Wojnicka 1997). This is connected, first, with better technology employed by foreign investors, thus improving efficiency and quality of production and as a result increasing the output, and secondly, with obtaining access to new markets. Foreign firms can distribute their export production using the marketing and distribution networks they maintain. In turn, the high quality of goods for export is crucial because of the much stiffer competition they encounter than goods produced exclusively for the domestic market.

The most important direct advantage of the inflow of foreign investment capital is increased tax receipts it generates (Czerwieniec 1990). On the other hand, however, tax rates can be reduced by exemptions and tax relief granted to the investors[1].

The general balance of capital flows in Poland, accommodating reinvestment and transfer of profits, various payments to parent companies, taxes and all forms of their reduction, and costs of attracting investors, has been definitely in surplus (Domański 2001). The foreign capital inflow covers a substantial part of the country's current-account deficit, and making good the deficit helps to accelerate the rate of economic growth. And the growth rate is the higher, the more capital is invested in manufacturing rather than expanding the country's currency reserves.

As to other macroeconomic variables, FDI can contribute to a dropping inflation rate. The more investments are implemented, the greater is the supply of goods and services, which results in falling prices. A decline in inflation is favourable to the country's development, because it reinforces economic certainty through greater predictability of future prices and costs, and implies a lowering of the nominal interest rate (credit price), thus stimulating the economic activity of firms.

Employment

FDI is ascribed a significant role in employment. Its impact on the labour market is both quantitative and qualitative, and depends on the nature of the particular investment and needs of the investors. The beneficial effect of foreign capital in quantitative terms is connected with the creation of new jobs, particularly in the case of labour-intensive types of investment. The situation is especially advantageous for the labour market when an investment is located on a greenfield site. Employment then rises even during the construction stage, and so it does again when the establishment goes into operation. Greenfield investments tend to employ the local population. In most cases the investors also make use of the local managerial staff, which corroborates the importance of qualified labour as a significant factor of investment location.

An increase in employment can also result from the expansion of an existing enterprise. However, more typically, in firms privatised with the help of foreign capital the output grows while the number of employees declines. This results from the introduction of more modern technology which improves labour efficiency.

Foreign investment also has an indirect impact on employment manifesting itself in the activation of local suppliers, setting up of new distribution channels, and networks of services offered to foreign subsidiaries. There is also a possibility of a rise in employment in the other sectors of the economy produced by a multiplier effect.

In terms of the qualitative effects of FDI, especially worth mentioning is the upgrading of employees' skills as a result of training and contact with modern models of management, organisation of production, and high technology. Most foreign employers earmark substantial outlays for intensive upgrading courses for their personnel, as a result of which there is a general improvement in their qualifications, responsibility, and labour efficiency (Jodkowski

[1] The Companies with Foreign Capital Participation Act of June 1991 guaranteed foreign investors individual corporation tax exemptions granted by the Ministry of Finance.

1995; Gieorgica 1998; Starzyk 1998; Olesiński 1999). A part of the personnel are trained abroad (Jodkowski 1995; Domański 2001).

Modern Technologies and Management

One of the most highly regarded benefits of FDI in Poland has been the transfer of high technology, know-how, modern management models, and methods of organisation of production and marketing.

Larger foreign ventures in the form of FDI worth several million US dollars and more are usually connected with the implementation of new technologies, novel product designs, and modern management techniques which improve labour efficiency. This, in turn, brings about an increase in output and a lowering of production costs, as well as a rise in profits and the venture's profitability. Naturally, improvement in the efficiency of use of the factors of production largely depends on the advancement of the technology transferred and the ability of domestic producers to absorb it. Moreover, the employment of a more modern technology and better organisation of production allows improvement in the quality of goods manufactured, which greatly enhances the competitiveness of the firm. As a result, Polish-based enterprises can compete with firms from abroad more successfully and expand their exports to more advanced countries. The more novel ways of organising production, well-tried abroad, allow the introduction of solutions which result in a single plant being able to manufacture a diversified range of products of better quality while making better use of materials, suppliers, floorspace, and workers.

It is believed that the spread and efficient use of high technology is an important source of economic growth. The inflow of foreign capital and high technology also contributes significantly to changes in the structure of the economy.

Changes in the Sectoral Structure of the Economy

By locating capital and high technology in the particular sectors of Poland's economy, foreign investors can accelerate the growth of some and the decline of others. In this way they produce a change in the country's industrial specialisation and structure. The most favourable is investment made in industries displaying the greatest growth potential and innovativeness and making use of technologies generated by Polish scientific thought whose development is impeded, however, by the shortage of domestic capital (Wojnicka 1997).

Foreign capital has also a crucial share in attracting to Poland the so-called global sectors, including the financial and information ones. This is manifested in the location of branches of foreign banks offering new and higher-quality financial services. The development of the information sector, in turn, ensures faster access to the global resources of information, thus allowing Poland to reduce the civilisation gap dividing it from the advanced countries.

Local Business Circles

At the local level, foreign investment affects primarily local business circles. In building enterprises along the lines developed by the mature market economies of their home countries, foreign investors set a model for Polish entrepreneurs to pursue. Thus, the impact of FDI goes far beyond foreign-owned companies. The imitation effect, that is, the employment by domestic firms of solutions implemented in those with foreign capital participation, manifests itself in a variety of forms. First, the implementation of high technology in foreign firms forces domestic producers to modernise manufacturing, primarily in order to be able to face the stiffening competition. The introduction of high technology, in turn, raises the requirements of technical know-how, level of education, and quality of work on the part of personnel, hence it has an educational effect. On the one hand, it manifests itself in higher qualifications and efficiency of workers, and on the other, it necessitates changes in the management of the Polish firms and the introduction of efficient marketing involving a fundamental change in the market policies of enterprises in general (cf. Bąk, Kulawczuk 1996). In this way, the models of the organisation of production and management spread to competitors, suppliers, and other co-operating firms. It brings about an improvement in the quality and technological level of production and an expansion of the domain of higher efficiency and competitiveness. The situation is similar in the case of wages. By offering above-average pay, foreign investors indirectly cause an increase in wages in domestic firms.

Moreover, foreign investment stimulates the economic activity of local communities and popularises the spirit of entrepreneurship. It releases initiative among local workers, managers, politicians, and a large segment of public opinion. Not infrequently, one can meet a situation when a big foreign investment attracts competitors besides smaller co-operating firms.

Negative Aspects of the Implementation of Foreign Investment

Apart from the indisputable benefits for the economy and its growth, foreign direct investment can also bring it some threats. They usually appear when the goals of the foreign investor and the host country are divergent. The adverse effects include a general reduction in employment in plants privatised with the participation of foreign capital, largely as a result of growing labour efficiency; a limitation of the role of the domestic R&D backup; substantial imports and poor use of Polish suppliers by some plants; destruction of domestic entrepreneurship by stiffening competition and preferences for foreign capital; and intentional activity aimed at ruining plants in order to eliminate competition.

In spite of these negative developments that can accompany the inflow of foreign capital, most FDI researchers agree that Poland needs foreign investment badly if the Polish economy is to attain again the fast growth rate it experienced in the mid-1990s. This is the basic priority of economic policy closely connected with Poland's aspiration to join the European Union on terms of partnership, which requires intensive measures to reduce the difference in the levels of economic development between the country and the advanced European states (Sadowski 1999).

Conclusion

Since the very start of the systemic transformation in Poland, foreign investment has been playing an important role in many sectors of the Polish economy. However, the role of foreign capital has been different in the particular regions of the country. Over the study period, FDI tended to reinforce primarily the best-developed voivodeships, which could fast adapt to the changing economic conditions and growing international competition, and benefit from the situation in a variety of ways. Thus, foreign investment capital did not affect the development of the whole country equally, but only some of its regions. As a result of new capital being attracted by existing investment, the polarisation among voivodeships with a low and a high level of foreign investment widened.

In the face of ever sharper competition among the countries of Central and Eastern Europe, it is hard for Poland to keep its investment attractiveness. Since 2001 one can observe a slackening dynamics of FDI inflow, mainly due to a lower attractiveness and a narrower scope of privatisation and a contraction of the Polish economy.

In the nearest future one should not expect a sudden increase in foreign investment in Poland because of the government's failure to implement an active policy of attracting foreign capital. With a more restricted privatisation offer, there are no big projects of a greenfield type of investment. Still, a factor that can keep Poland attractive to foreign investors is the Financial Support for Investment Act (in force since April 2002) which defines the rules and forms of financial support for enterprises making investment or creating new jobs.

Other important factors affecting the magnitude of the FDI flow to Poland will be an improvement in the economic situation, acceleration of economic growth, and joining the European Union. As a result of these developments, the inflow of foreign direct investment may increase in the years to come.

References

Bąk M., Kulawczuk P. (red.), 1996, *Wpływ inwestycji zagranicznych na gospodarkę Polski (Effect of foreign investment on the Polish economy),* PAIZ/ Instytut Badań nad Demokracją i Przedsiębiorstwem Prywatnym, Warszawa.

Chrupek Z., 1999, *Stan zagranicznych inwestycji bezpośrednich w Polsce* (The state of foreign direct investment in Poland) [w:] Sadowski Z. (red.) *Kapitał zagraniczny w Polsce- warunki działania*, PTE, Warszawa, 89-118.

Cichowski L., 1998, *Przepływ kapitału i technologii* (Capital and technology flows), Wydawnictwo Politechniki Poznańskiej, Poznań.

Czerwieniec E., 1990, *Zagraniczne inwestycje bezpośrednie w gospodarce krajów rozwiniętych* (Foreign direct investment in advanced economies), Poznań.

Czyż T., 1998, *Polaryzacja rozwoju regionalnego w okresie transformacji społeczno-gospodarczej w Polsce* (Polarisation of regional development during the period of socio-economic transformation in Poland), [w:] Parysek J., Rogacki H. (red.) *Przemiany społeczno-gospodarcze Polski lat dziewięćdziesiątych*, Bogucki Wydawnictwo Naukowe, 47-63.

Domański B., 2001, *Kapitał zagraniczny w przemyśle Polski. Prawidłowości rozmieszczenia, uwarunkowania i skutki* (Foreign capital in Polish industry. Distribution regularities, determinants, and effects), IG i GP, Uniwersytet Jagielloński, Kraków.

Durka B., Chojna J., 1999, *Share of companies with foreign participation in Polish foreign trade* [w:] Durka B., 1999, *Foreign investments in Poland*, Instytut Koniunktur i Cen Handlu Zagranicznego, Warszawa, 43-63.

Dziemianowicz W., 1998, *Rola władz samorządowych w stymulowaniu napływu bezpośrednich inwestycji zagranicznych* (The role of local government in stimulating the inflow of foreign direct investment), [w:] Olesiński Z. (red.) *Bezpośrednie inwestycje zagraniczne w Polsce*, PWE, Warszawa, 214-232.

Gieorgica J., 1998, *Wpływ inwestycji zagranicznych na wprowadzenie nowych technologii społecznych* (Effect of foreign direct investment on the introduction of new social technologies), [w:] Olesiński Z. (red.) *Bezpośrednie inwestycje zagraniczne w Polsce*, PWE, Warszawa, 87-110.

Hunya G., 1996, *Contribution of Foreign Direct Investment to Economic Recovery and Restructuring*.

Jodkowski A., 1995, *Zagraniczne inwestycje bezpośrednie w Polsce jako element kształtowania konkurencyjności* (Foreign direct investment in Poland as an element shaping competitiveness), Raporty – Studia nad konkurencyjnością, Instytut Rozwoju i Studiów Strategicznych, Warszawa.

Kożuch B., 1998, *Inwestycje zagraniczne a wzrost konkurencyjności regionu* (Foreign direct investment and an increase in a region's competitiveness), [w:] Olesiński Z. (red.) *Bezpośrednie inwestycje zagraniczne w Polsce*, PWE, Warszawa, 191-213.

Liberska B., 1996, *Zagraniczne inwestycje bezpośrednie w Polsce* (Foreign direct investment in Poland), [w:] Mujżel J., Wojtyna A., Mączyńska E. (red.) *Bezpośrednie inwestycje i kredyty zagraniczne*, Raport nr 18, Rada Strategii Społeczno-Gospodarczej przy Radzie Ministrów, Warszawa, 58-78.

Maćkiewicz A., Ratajczak W., 1993, *Principal components analysis*, Computers & Geosciences, 19/3, 303-342.

Małuszyńska E., 1996, *Lokalizacja inwestycji zagranicznych w zachodnich województwach Polski* (Location of foreign investment in Poland's western voivodeships), Biuletyn PAN KPZK, Zeszyt 174, 89-104.

Marczewski K., 2002, *Koniunktura i bariery działalności gospodarczej w ocenach inwestorów zagranicznych* (The trade cycle and barriers to economic activity in the opinion of foreign investors), [w:] Durka B. (red.) *Inwestycje zagraniczne w Polsce*, IKiCHZ, Warszawa, s. 113-126.

Olesiński Z., 1999, *Foreign investors in the local environment* [w:] Durka B. (red) *Foreign investments in Poland*, Instytut Koniunktur i Cen Handlu Zagranicznego, Warszawa, 102-118.

Root F.R., 1984, *International trade and investment*, Cincinnati, Ohio.

Sadowski Z. (red.), 1999, *Kapitał zagraniczny w Polsce - warunki działania* (Foreign capital in Poland: conditions of operation), PTE, Warszawa.

Starzyk K., 1998, *Bezpośrednie inwestycje zagraniczne a transfer technologii w procesie transformacji gospodarczej* (Foreign direct investment and technology transfer in the process of economic transformation), [w:] Olesiński Z. (red.) Bezpośrednie inwestycje zagraniczne w Polsce, PWE, Warszawa, 263-282.

Szlachta J., 1996, *Główne problemy polityki rozwoju regionalnego Polski na przełomie XX i XXI wieku* (Main problems of Poland's regional development policy at the turn of the 21st century), [w:] *Strategiczne wyzwania dla polityki rozwoju regionalnego Polski*, Friedrich Ebert Stiftung, Warszawa, 16-27.

Wojnicka E., 1997, *Bezpośrednie inwestycje zagraniczne w Polsce 1976-1996* (Foreign direct investment in Poland, 1976-1996), Zeszyty IBnGR, nr 4.

In: Economic and Political Developments in Poland
Editor: Maureen P. Larsen
ISBN 978-1-61209-951-4

Chapter 7

APPROACHING THE ENDGAME: POLISH PUBLIC OPINION AND THE CHANGING EURO-DEBATE IN THE RUN UP TO THE 2003 EU ACCESSION REFERENDUM

Aleks Szczerbiak
Sussex European Institute, University of Sussex
Brighton, United Kingdom

ABSTRACT

Recent years have seen a significant fall in support for Polish EU membership and the emergence of a sizeable bloc of anti-EU public opinion. While, the new ex-communist led government elected in September 2001 adopted a more flexible approach to the accession negotiations this produced a mixed public reaction and the fact that they have been forced into a coalition with an agrarian party will constrain their room for manoeuvre during the negotiating endgame. Nonetheless, overall levels of support for Polish EU membership appear to have consolidated at a relatively high level and it is extremely likely that most Poles will vote Yes in the 2003 accession referendum. The only real threat to a Yes vote appears to be if the referendum is turned into a plebiscite on the socio-economic transition as a whole. However, the greater concern for the pro-EU camp is that the referendum fails to achieve the turnout required by the Polish Constitution for it to be valid.

The September 2001 Polish parliamentary election received considerable comment both domestically and internationally because of its perceived impact on the EU accession negotiations. On the one hand, the election led to the formation of a new government committed to adopting a more flexible negotiating strategy in order to accelerate the EU accession process. On the other hand, it also saw parties and groupings that had expressed hostility or even outright opposition to Polish EU membership win a significant share of the vote.

Table 1. Polish support for EU membership, 1994-2002

	June 94	May 95	May 96	March 97	April 97	Aug 97	May 98	Aug 98	Dec 98	May 99	Nov 99	Feb 00	May 00	Sept00	Mar 01	May 01	June 01	July 01	Oct 01	Dec 01	Jan 02	Feb 02	Mar 02
Yes	77	72	80	72	72	72	66	63	64	55	59	55	59	55	59	55	54	53	56	60	57	54	55
No	6	9	7	12	11	12	19	19	19	26	26	26	25	26	25	28	29	25	24	22	22	25	29
Don't know	17	19	13	16	18	15	15	18	17	19	15	19	16	19	16	17	17	22	20	18	21	21	16

Source: CBOS. Poparcie dla wejścia Polski do Unii Europejskiej i opinie o konwencji Europejskim. Warsaw: CBOS. March 2002.

Table 2. Benefits of European Integration, 1993-2000

Who benefits most from Polish-EU relations?	July 93	March 94	May 95	May 96	Aug 97	Aug 98	May 99	Nov 99	May 00	Sept 00	Mar 01	Dec 01	Feb 02
EU countries	41	38	31	19	28	39	39	47	44	50	54	51	59
Poland	5	8	11	11	11	7	8	8	8	6	6	6	5
Both equally	27	26	33	46	35	30	30	27	29	26	25	25	19
Don't know	27	27	26	24	27	24	23	18	19	18	15	18	17

Source: CBOS. Stosunek do integracji Polski z Unią Europejską po ogłoszeniu nowego stanowiska negocjacyjnego. Warsaw: CBOS. January 2002; and CBOS. Opinie o integracji Polski z Unią Europejską. Warsaw: CBOS. March 2002.

At the time of writing (July 2002) Poland's EU accession negotiations are entering their final, decisive stage. In autumn 2002 they are scheduled to enter their 'endgame' when the most difficult and controversial issues (regional aid, agriculture and the budget) are due to be discussed. These negotiations must be completed successfully before the end of the year in order for Poland to be admitted in the next enlargement wave scheduled for 2004. In autumn 2003, therefore, Poles will have to vote in an EU accession referendum.

This paper examines the state of Polish public opinion and the changing euro-debate at this critical conjuncture for Polish-EU relations. It begins by examining and accounting for changing patterns of support for Polish EU membership over the last few years. Section two moves on to examine the impact on the Polish euro-debate of both the new government's negotiating strategy and the presence, for the first time, of a sizeable anti-EU bloc of parliamentary deputies. Finally, section three considers how public attitudes towards EU membership are likely to evolve over the coming period in the run up to the referendum.

The paper argues that the new ex-communist led government's more flexible negotiating strategy produced both a hostile political and mixed public reaction. The fact that the September 2001 election saw parties and groupings critical of and even hostile to EU membership obtaining a substantial share of the vote and significant parliamentary representation has also, to some extent, polarised the terms of the Polish euro-debate. Moreover, the fact that the former communists and their allies fell short of winning an overall parliamentary majority and have been forced to form a government with an agrarian party critical of the EU has constrained their room for manoeuvre somewhat. It will continue do so during the negotiating endgame on issues such as agricultural subsidies where the EU is proposing to phase in payments to Polish farmers over a ten year period.

Nevertheless, the pro-EU camp has fairly solid grounds for remaining cautiously optimistic that it will win the accession referendum. The Polish public appears to have been unmoved by recent controversies and overall levels of support for Polish EU membership remain relatively high. Poles also have a fairly realistic attitude towards the costs and benefits that are likely to flow from EU membership and pro-EU voters are more likely to turn out than anti-EU ones. If the current government, pro-EU opposition and Catholic Church hierarchy form a relatively united front on this issue and present the accession referendum primarily in historical terms as representing a major civilisation and geo-political choice, then it is highly likely that they will win the accession vote. The anti-EU camp's best hope is to frame the referendum debate in terms of a plebiscite on the socio-economic transition and portray EU membership as something that will only benefit the minority of transition winners. Nevertheless, even if the pro-EU camp secures a convincing Yes vote, there remains the (probably even greater) danger that the referendum will fail to achieve the 50% turnout required for it to be valid under the Polish Constitution.

Decline and Stabilisation: Changing Patterns of Support for Polish EU Membership

Until a couple of years ago Polish EU membership was the subject of an overwhelming political elite consensus and enjoyed extremely high levels of public support. However, in the late 1990s, Poland saw a significant fall in support.[1] As Table 1 shows, the number of Poles supporting EU membership declined steadily from 77% in June 1994 (the year that Poland formally submitted its application) and a peak of 80% in May 1995 to only 55% in March 2002.[2] At the same time, a significant segment of anti-EU opinion began to emerge with the number of opponents increasing from only 6% in 1994 to 29% in 2002. However, it is striking that from mid-1999 onwards public support began to stabilise at around 55-60% in favour while the number of opponents has fluctuated between 22-30%. Precise figures vary between different polling organisations but the overall trend in terms of support for EU membership has clearly been one of steady decline and then subsequent stablisisation.

Perhaps even more significantly, beneath the surface of what remained relatively high levels of public support there were a number of potentially significant indicators suggesting that the prospect of EU membership provoked considerable anxieties even among the pro-EU majority. In particular, the decline in overall support was also reflected in increasing uncertainty about whether or not (and by how much) Poles would actually benefit from EU membership compared with current member states. As Table 2 shows, having fallen from 41% in July 1993 to only 19% in June 1996, the number of Poles who believed that existing EU member states would derive the greatest benefit from Polish accession increased steadily to 59% in February 2002. At the same time 19% of Poles believed that accession would be equally beneficial to both Poland and the EU while only 7% cited their country as the main beneficiary.

Similarly, while most Poles continued to think that EU accession would bring their country more benefits than losses they were more uncertain when it came to whether they would benefit as individuals. For example, a March 2001 CBOS survey found that 56% of respondents said that EU membership would benefit Poland and only 16% said it would be disadvantageous (10% said it would make no difference and 18% did not know). On the other hand, only 32% felt that EU membership would benefit them *personally* while 50% said it would make no difference and 11% did not know (8% said that it would be disadvantageous).[3] Similarly, a June 2001 OBOP/Polityka survey found that 31% of respondents felt that EU membership would bring Poland more gains than losses while 27% thought the losses would outweigh the gains (25% said that they would be equal and 17% did not know). However, only 21% felt that it would bring them more gains personally while 24% said that it

[1] For a full analysis of this see: A. Szczerbiak. 'Spadek i stabilzacja. Zmieniające się wzorce poparcia dla członkostwa Polski w Unii Europejskiej,' in E. Popławska, ed. *Konstytucja dla rozeszerzającej się Europy.* Warsaw: Instytut Spraw Publicznych. 2000; and A. Szczerbiak. 'Polish Public Opinion: Explaining Declining Support for EU membership.' *Journal of Common Market Studies.* Vol 39 No 1. March 2001. pp107-124. For other interesting accounts of how EU membership has impacted upon Polish domestic politics see: G. Blazyca and M. Kolkiewicz, 'Poland and the EU: Internal Disputes, Domestic Politics and Accession,' *Journal of Communist Studies and Transition Politics.* Vol 15 No 4. December 1999. pp131-143; L. Kolarska-Bobińska, ed. *Polska Eurodebata.* Warsaw: ISP. 1999; and F. Millard. 'Polish domestic politics and accession to the European Union,' in K. Henderson, ed. *Back to Europe: Central and Eastern Europe and the European Union.* London: UCL Press. 1999. pp203-219.

[2] The analysis in this paper rests heavily on data published by the two leading Polish polling organisations, the Centre for Research on Public Opinion (Centrum Badania Opinii Społecznej: CBOS) and the Institute for Research on Public Opinion (Ośrodek Badania Opinii Publicznej: OBOP), and the Institute of Public Affairs (Instytut Spraw Publicznych: ISP) research institute. All the usual limitations of relying on such data are, of course, applicable. These include the margin of error arising from (in some cases) relatively small samples and the inability to subject the data to more rigorous statistical analysis, together with the fact that information is not always available in the precise form required.

[3] See: CBOS. Przewydiwane skutki integracji Polski z Unią Europejską. Warsaw: CBOS. March 2001.

would bring them greater losses and 23% said it would have no impact (18% said the effect would be neutral and 14% did not know).[4]

Similarly, while most Poles continued to think that EU accession would bring their country more benefits than losses they were more uncertain when it came to whether they would benefit as individuals. For example, a March 2001 CBOS survey found that 56% of respondents said that EU membership would benefit Poland and only 16% said it would be disadvantageous (10% said it would make no difference and 18% did not know). On the other hand, only 32% felt that EU membership would benefit them *personally* while 50% said it would make no difference and 11% did not know (8% said that it would be disadvantageous).[5] Similarly, a June 2001 OBOP/Polityka survey found that 31% of respondents felt that EU membership would bring Poland more gains than losses while 27% thought the losses would outweigh the gains (25% said that they would be equal and 17% did not know). However, only 21% felt that it would bring them more gains personally while 24% said that it would bring them greater losses and 23% said it would have no impact (18% said the effect would be neutral and 14% did not know).[6]

Increasing anxiety about the possible impact of EU accession was confirmed by data on the effects that Poles thought that it would have on specific sectors of the economy and living standards more generally. In February 2002, for example, 53% of Poles said it would have a negative effect on individual farms while only 26% said that it would be positive (the analogous figures for June 1994 were 24% and 40% respectively). Similarly, 35% of Poles said that EU membership would have a negative effect on the functioning of public sector enterprises compared with only 33% who felt it would be positive (37% and 32% in 1994). Even the number who believed that EU membership would have a positive effect on the private business sector fell from 67% in 1994 to 42% in 2002 while those who said it would have a negative effect increased from 6% to 29% over the same period. In terms of the impact on the economy more generally, the number who said that it would have a positive effect on their living standards fell from 57% in 1994 to 42% in 2002. The number who said that it would have a negative impact increased from 10% to 23%.[7] Indeed, in an earlier analysis of changing Polish attitudes towards EU membership, I argued that the best way to characterise the state of public opinion was that Poles *consented* to the idea of EU accession but were not particularly *enthusiastic* about it.[8]

There are number of factors that account for these shifts in public support during the course of the accession negotiations that began in March 1998. Firstly, given the existence of an overwhelming pro-EU consensus among political elites, Polish opponents of EU membership may have been reluctant to identify themselves previously and earlier polling data may have artificially overstated the true levels of public support. Secondly, given there was also very little serious debate about the potential costs and benefits of EU accession, the previous very high levels of support may not have represented a conscious and considered declaration. Thirdly, given the difficult issues that needed to be tackled, the accession

[4] See: 'Bez entuzjazmu.' *Polityka*. 7 July 2001.

[5] See: CBOS. Przewydiwane skutki integracji Polski z Unią Europejską. Warsaw: CBOS. March 2001.

[6] See: 'Bez entuzjazmu.' *Polityka*. 7 July 2001.

[7] See: CBOS. Opnie o integracji Polski z Unią Europejską. Warsaw: CBOS. March 2002.

[8] One Polish commentator has characterised this as a "shallow consensus" in favour of EU membership. See: E. Skotnicka-Illasiewicz, 'Poland on its Way Towards Membership of the EU and NATO: Hopes and Anxieties in a View of Public Opinion Polls.' *Yearbook of Polish European Studies*. Warsaw: Warsaw University Centre for European Studies. 1998. pp243-263.

negotiations themselves inevitably focused to a large extent on the concessions that had to be made by the Polish side. This, in turn, raised the profile of the European issue in Polish politics in a very negative way, with Brussels viewed increasingly as a focus for conflict and hostility. In this sense, the more recent polling data are, it could be argued, simply a more accurate reflection of the true levels of support for Polish EU membership and, therefore, simply represented a kind of 'reality check.'

Fourthly, and perhaps most significantly, the period since the beginning of the accession negotiations saw a striking politicisation of the debate on Polish EU membership. Partly this was because a crack appeared in the previously overwhelming pro-EU elite consensus with the emergence of the first organised and potentially significant political forces to adopt an overtly anti-EU stance. However, a more significant development was probably the way that the debate on EU membership began to be conducted among those political forces that were ostensibly pro-EU. This was not so much about whether or not the country should join *per se* but about the terms on which (and the kind of EU that) it should join. As one commentator has noted, this led to a tendency to turn political debates about EU membership into 'ideological' confrontations between the right-wing Solidarity Electoral Action (Akcja Wyborcza Solidarność: AWS) led government and the ex-communist Democratic Left Alliance (Sojusz Lewicy Demokratycznej: SLD) opposition.[9] One of the most important aspects of this politicisation of the Polish Euro-debate was the division of the pro-EU camp into those who (allegedly) favoured a 'soft' negotiating stance and those who (allegedly) favoured a 'tough' one. The former, it was argued, were prepared to 'give in' to Brussels while the latter placed numerous conditions upon and posited reservations concerning support for EU membership.[10] As one Polish commentator put it, the overall effect of this kind of rhetoric was to create the impression that Poland was negotiating with an enemy and that EU membership was a regrettable necessity rather than something to be sought positively.[11]

THE POST-ELECTION SCENARIO AND THE CHANGING POLISH EURO-DEBATE

In spite of this increasing public anxiety, it was widely assumed that the decisive September 2001 election victory of the unambiguously pro-EU SLD, which contested the election in coalition with the small Labour Union (Unia Pracy: UP) party, would speed up the progress of the EU accession negotiations.[12] Being weak, unstable and containing a substantial Eurosceptic current, the previous AWS-led government found it difficult to make any significant concessions to the EU in a number of key negotiating areas. It rigidly demanded an eighteen-year transition period on the sale of Polish land to foreigners refusing

[9] See: J. Kucharczyk. 'Porwanie Europy,' *Rzeczpospolita*, 4 March 1999.

[10] For a good example of this see the kind of rhetoric employed by AWS candidate Marian Krzaklewski in the October 2000 presidential election campaign. See: A. Szczerbiak. *Europe as a Re-aligning Issue in Polish Politics? Evidence from the October 2000 Polish Presidential Election*. Sussex European Institute Working Paper No 48/Opposing Europe Research Network Working Paper No 3. Brighton: Sussex European Institute. June 2001. pp10-13.

[11] See: J. Kucharczyk, *European Integration in Polish Political Debates 1997-1998*. Warsaw: ISP, February 1999; and 'Porwanie Europy.'

[12] See: 'Po pierwsze Unia Europejsa.' *Rzeczpospolita*. 5 June 2001; and P. Apanowicz. 'Elastyczność, ale bez przesday.' *Rzeczpospolita*. 6 September 2001.

the EU's offer of seven years. It also rejected the EU's proposal of allowing member states to introduce transition periods of up to seven years before citizens from the candidate countries would be given unrestricted access to Western labour markets.[13] The SLD-UP coalition's election rhetoric certainly gave the pro-EU camp reason to hope that the government would adopt a more flexible approach to these issues and perhaps even subsequently on the most difficult negotiating areas: regional aid, agricultural subsidies and budget contributions. During the campaign, SLD leader and subsequent premier Leszek Miller argued that Polish membership of the EU "would be the final confirmation that we are the joint hosts of the continent,"[14] while the alternative was being "on the margins and thereby wiping out any chance to modernise our country."[15] Consequently, Miller argued that it was essential that the next government made a "rational compromise" on the sale of Polish land to foreigners and access to the Western labour markets.[16] Another SLD leader Józef Oleksy (who went on to become chairman of the parliamentary European affairs committee) argued that "we are aware that the Union is the stronger partner in these discussions, that is why a certain elasticity is essential, although certainly not at the cost of (sacrificing) Poland's most important interests."[17]

Consequently, it came as little surprise when, in November 2001, the new SLD-UP led government announced a new negotiating strategy that involved making a number of concessions in order to speed up the accession negotiations. Initially, the government announced that it would broadly accept the proposed transition periods on access to Western labour markets as non-negotiable (although it would seek to persuade individual member states not to take full advantage of them). More controversially, it also announced that it would reduce the proposed transition period on the sale of Polish land to foreigners from eighteen to twelve years with no restrictions on the purchase of land for investment purposes.[18] Even more controversially, a couple of days later the new SLD Foreign Minister Włodzimerz Cimoszewicz announced a series of further concessions when presenting the new Polish negotiating position in Brussels. These included: reducing the transition period on the sale of recreational land to seven years, a three year transition period on the sale of farm land to foreign leaseholders and no transition period for the sale of domestic dwellings.[19]

However, the government's new negotiating strategy produced a somewhat mixed reaction from the Polish public. A December 2001 CBOS survey found that 82% of Poles continued to supported transition periods on the sale of Polish land to foreigners (a considerable hardening of attitudes on this issue compared with the previous year) with only 7% against (11% did not know). More positively for the government, 43% of respondents supported its proposal for a twelve year transition period for the sale of agricultural land (a further 12% said it was too long and 3% that it was unnecessary) while only 31% felt that this was too short (11% did not know). Similarly, 41% of Poles supported the government's

[13] This position was determined primarily in response to German and Austrian misgivings about large potential migratory flows from the East.

[14] Cited in: K. Montgomery. 'Im szybciej, tym lepiej.' *Gazeta Wyborcza*. 11 June 2001.

[15] Cited in: 'Sojusz za integracją z UE.' *Rzeczpospolita*. 11 June 2001.

[16] Cited in: 'Im szybciej, tym lepiej.'

[17] Cited in: 'Elastyczność, ale bez przesady.'

[18] See: P. Apanowicz, J. Bielecki and A. Stankiewicz. 'Będziemy inaczej rozmawiać z Uni'.' *Rzeczpospolita*. 15 November 2001; and D. Pszczółkowska. 'Skokiem do Unii.' *Gazeta Wyborcza*. 15 November 2001.

[19] See: J. Bielecki. 'Ziema szybciej na sprzedaż.' *Rzeczpospolita*. 20 November 2001; and J. Bielecki. 'Kolejne gesty wobec Brukseli.' *Rzeczpospolita*. 21 November 2001.

proposed seven year transition period for the sale of recreational land (11% said it was too long and 4% that it was unnecessary) and only 32% felt that it was too short (12% did not know). However, 56% of Poles opposed the three year transition period on the sale of farm land to foreign leaseholders (which the government was subsequently forced to modify, see below) while only 32% supported it (12% did not know). 71% opposed the policy of no transition periods on the sale of land for investment and only 21% supported it (8% did not know), while 81% opposed removing restrictions on the sale of domestic dwellings and only 13% supported it (6% did not know).[20]

Moreover, this mixed public reaction was exacerbated by the fact that the government unveiled its new negotiating strategy in a rather clumsy way. As noted above, it was announced in two stages, with some of the detailed concessions (particularly the very controversial one on the sale of farmland to foreign leaseholders) only announced by the Foreign Minister on his subsequent visit to Brussels. This provoked an extremely hostile political reaction not just from Eurosceptics but also from the broadly pro-EU opposition parties, the liberal Civic Platform (Platforma Obywatelsak: PO) and conservative Law and Justice party (Prawo i Sprawiedliwoœæ: PiS), and even from SLD-UP's government coalition partner, the Polish Peasant Party (Polskie Stronnictwo Ludowe: PSL).[21] This, in turn, meant that the new government squandered one of its strongest assets: the bank of goodwill and trust that it enjoyed immediately after the election and which appeared to give it more room for manoeuvre in the accession negotiations than its deeply unpopular predecessor. For example, an October 2001 ISP survey found that, in spite of its 'tough' rhetoric, 49% of Poles felt that the previous AWS led government had given in to the EU's demands. Only 9% of Poles felt that it had stoutly defended Polish interests and 27% felt that it had skilfully combined the two. In contrast, 38% felt that the incoming government would be able to combine the two, 24% that it would be a tough defender of Polish interests and only 13% that it would make too many concessions.[22] However, a subsequent December 2001 CBOS survey found that 44% of Poles felt that the new SLD led government was making too many concessions while only 27% felt that it was proceeding correctly (5% thought it was too tough and 24% did not know).[23]

Perhaps even more worryingly for the new government, other polling evidence suggested that the generally negative public reaction to its new negotiating strategy was underpinned by a more basic lack of understanding of the rationale on which the new approach was based. In particular, most Poles did not appear to accept the new government's argument that political and economic advantages would flow from early EU accession, particularly the opportunity to advance Polish interests within the EU's decision making structures, but that achieving this involved making some concessions. In other words, they did not appear to fully appreciate that the accession negotiations would require reciprocity in order to be swiftly completed and

[20] See: CBOS. Stosunek do integracji Polski z Unią Europejską po ogłoszeniu nowego stanowiska negocjacyjnego. Warsaw: CBOS. January 2002.

[21] See, for example: 'Będziemy inaczej rozmawiać z Unią'; E. Olczyk, A. Stankiewicz and M. D. Zdort. 'Posłowie wyzwają ministrów.' *Rzeczpospolita*. 22 November 2001; A. Stankiewicz. 'Ziemia pod ochronę.' *Rzeczpospolita*. 23 November 2001; and A. Stankiewicz. 'Przyspieszenie na ostatniej prostej.' *Rzeczpospolita*. 30 November 2001.

[22] See: B. Roguska and J. Kucharczyk. *Wybory 2001 a integracja Polski z Unią Europejską*. Warsaw: ISP. 2001. p 28.

[23] See: Stosunek do integracji Polski z Unią Europejską po ogłoszeniu nowego stanowiska negocjacyjnego.

that Poland was very much the weaker negotiating partner.[24] For example, a February 2002 CBOS survey found that 57% of respondents felt that Poland should only join when it could benefit from all the possibilities associated with EU membership. Only 19% felt that Poland should join as quickly as possible even if this meant giving up some of the advantages with EU membership (13% said should Poland not join at all and 11% did not know). Even 61% of those who supported EU membership in principle rejected the idea of early accession if this involved making concessions.[25] Similarly, a June 2001 OBOP/Polityka survey found that 69% of respondents felt that Poland should not make any concessions in the accession negotiations, even if this meant delayed EU entry. Only 18% felt that Poland should make concessions in order to join the EU as quickly as possible (13% did not know).[26]

A more specific example of this kind of thinking could be seen in the public's reaction to the European Commission's January 2002 proposals on agriculture, the other major development that has occurred since the election that was likely to have influenced Polish opinion towards the EU. The Commission proposed to phase in agricultural subsidies to Polish farmers (and other candidate states) over a ten-year period. They would begin by receiving only 25% of the proportion paid to farmers in member states, increasing to 35% in 2005, 35% in 2006 and then 100% in 2013.[27] Not surprisingly, this proposal met with a hostile reaction from the across the Polish political spectrum as well as from the general public. A February 2002 CBOS survey found that 59% of Poles felt that the Polish government should demand full subsidies from the moment of accession even if this led to the breakdown of the negotiations and Poland failing to join the EU (25% disagreed with this and 16% did not know).[28]

This belief that Poland could secure EU membership on more favourable terms if it was prepared to countenance some delay was linked to a more fundamental and ongoing concern (evident in Polish attitudes towards the EU for some time) that Poland was 'not ready' for EU membership. This was, in turn, based on a broader de-coupling of the economic modernisation and EU accession processes, rather than viewing them as complementary. For example, a February 2002 CBOS survey found that 52% of respondents felt that Poland was not ready to join the EU and should modernise its economy first compared with only 32% who felt that such economic modernisation was actually conditional upon swift EU entry (17% did not know).[29] Similarly, a May 2001 OBOP survey found that 75% of respondents felt that Poland should first carry out necessary reforms and only then join the EU. Only 15% felt that Poland should join the EU as quickly as possible (10% did not know). Even 67% of those who said they would vote Yes in an accession referendum felt that Poland needed to carry out reforms first.[30]

---

[24] See, for example: F. Gawryś. 'Do Unii bez ustępstw.' *Rzeczpospolita*. 2 July 2001; and 'Bez entuzjazmu.'

[25] See: CBOS. Opinie o integracji Polski z Unią Europejską. Warsaw: CBOS. March 2002.

[26] See: 'Bez entuzjazmu.'

[27] See: J. Bielecki. 'Większe ustępstwa za mniejsze pieniądze.' *Rzeczpospolita*. 31 January 2002. The Commission also proposed lower production quotas than the Polish government had requested.

[28] See: CBOS. Poparcie dla wejścia Polski do Unii Europejskiej i opinie o negocjacjach w sprawie rolnictwa. Warsaw: CBOS. February 2002.

[29] See: Opinie o integracji z Unią Europejską.

[30] See: OBOP. *Opinia społeczna o członkostwie Polski w Unii Europjeskiej*. Warsaw: OBOP. June 2001.There are, however, some potential grounds for optimism for the pro-EU camp here because these figures also suggest that there is a substantial segment of the anti-EU camp who do not actually oppose Polish membership in principle but simply lack faith that Poland will join on advantageous terms. For example, a May 2001 CBOS survey found that 47% of those who were against EU membership also said Poland should only join if it could benefit from

Another obstacle to the further acceleration of the accession negotiations was the fact that, as Table 3 shows, the SLD-UP coalition fell 15 seats short of winning the 231 seats required for them to have an overall majority in the Sejm (the more powerful lower house of the Polish parliament). The equally strongly pro-EU PO refused to join the SLD-UP in a coalition and they were thus forced to form a government with the PSL, their erstwhile partner during the 1993-97 parliament. The PSL, in turn, adopted a very tough stance on the EU accession negotiations, particularly where the interests of its core rural-agrarian constituency were concerned. This gave the SLD less room for manoeuvre to compromise on certain negotiating issues than it would have enjoyed had it been able to govern on its own. Firstly, at the end of November PSL leader and Agriculture Minister Jarosław Kalinowski announced his intention to introduce a new law on the turnover of agricultural land that would introduce the right of primary purchase for neighbours and the state. The law also envisaged that permits be issued to farmers stipulating minimum qualifications, minimum residence requirements and a requirement that those purchasing the land cultivate it themselves.[31] Secondly, due to pressure from the PSL, the government was forced to modify its original proposal that there should only be a three-year transition period on the sale of Polish land to foreign leaseholders of farmland. In December 2001, the government announced that a seven-year transition period would apply for these farmers in the eight Western Polish provinces (it would continue to be three years in the eight Eastern provinces).[32] Then, after the Commission accepted this modified proposal the agreement on this 'chapter' nearly unravelled in February 2002. The PSL initially refused to accept the SLD's compromise proposal that the transition period for current foreign leaseholders of farmland begin in April 2002 and for the remainder from the date of Polish accession. (the Commission wanted it to begin for all foreigners from the moment that they began leasing the land, the PSL for all of them from the moment of Polish accession).[33]

Similarly, the participation of the PSL in the government means that it will be much more difficult to agree to a compromise on the Commission's proposals on agriculture, given the importance of this issue to the party's core electoral constituency. A possible precursor of future disputes came when Kalinowski ignited a row with the head of the Polish Committee for European Integration Danuta Hubner following a February 2002 speech in Brussels when he threatened that Poland would suspend talks on the liberalisation of agricultural trade. He also said that Poland was considering maintaining customs duties on EU imports if the current member states did not agree to 100% direct payments for Polish farmers from the date of accession.[34]

---

full membership. Consequently, achieving a satisfactory outcome to the accession negotiations could, potentially, significantly reduce the number of opponents of Polish accession. See: *Opinie o integracji z Unią Europejską*. June 2001.

[31] See: 'Ziemia pod ochronę.' *Rzeczpospolita*. 23 November 2001. Such a law could, potentially, bring Poland into conflict with the Commission.

[32] See: A. Stankiewicz. 'Na zachodzie siedem lat.' *Rzeczpospolita*. 19 December 2001; and D. Pszczółkowska and J. Pawlicki. 'W ziemię wbici.' *Gazeta Wyborcza*. 19 December 2001.

[33] See: K. Naszkowska. 'Integracja z PSL.' *Gazeta Wyborcza*. 27 February 2002. In the event, the PSL actually accepted the Commission's proposal with the caveat that the transition period would only start from the beginning of the leasehold for individual farmers and not companies. Kalinowski claimed that this, together with his law on the turnover of land, would be sufficient to prevent Polish land falling into the hands of foreign speculators. See: K. Naszkowska. 'Sukces Kalinowskiego, ferment w PSL.' *Gazeta Wyborcza*. 6 March 2002.

[34] See: J. Bielecki. 'Dopłaty albo cła.' *Rzeczpospolita*. 19 February 2002; and 'Jako lider PSL, a nie minister.' *Rzeczpospolita*. 26 February 2002.

Moreover, as well as the return to government of the SLD the September 2001 Polish parliamentary election also saw parties and political groupings that were critical of, or openly hostile to, Polish EU membership win a significant share of the vote and substantial bloc of parliamentary deputies. As Table 3 shows, of the six parties and groupings that secured representation in the Sejm two of them, winning 18.07% of the vote and 91 seats, might be described as having adopted a hard Eurosceptic stance of *de facto* outright opposition to EU membership.[35] The most openly and unambiguously anti-EU grouping was the League of Polish Families (Liga Polskich Rodziń: LPR), a coalition of various parties and organisations on the Catholic nationalist right that won 7.87% of the vote and 38 seats.[36] The other hard Eurosceptic political grouping that secured parliamentary representation was the radical-populist Self-Defence (Samoobrona) party led by Andrzej Lepper that emerged as the third largest parliamentary grouping winning 10.2% of the vote and 53 seats. Unlike the LPR, Samoobrona did not state explicitly that it was against Polish EU membership, but made its support conditional upon securing an unachievable set of conditions (effectively exemption from the provisions of the Single Market).

Table 3. September 2001 Polish Parliamentary Election Results

	Votes (%)	Seats
Democratic Left Alliance-Labour Union (SLD-UP)	41.04	216
Civic Platform (PO)	12.68	65
Self-Defence (Samoobrona)	10.20	53
Law and Justice (PiS)	9.50	44
Polish Peasant Party (PSL)	8.98	42
League of Polish Families (LPR)	7.87	38

Source: Polish State Electoral Commission.

Although they avoided opposing Polish EU membership in principle, two of the other four groupings elected to the Sejm, PiS (9.5% and 44 seats) and the PSL (8.98% and 42 seats), also adopted a critical tone towards the EU in their election programmes and campaign rhetoric. For example, the leaders of both groupings failed to attend the signing ceremony of the "Pact for Europe", an attempt to develop an all-party consensus in support of EU membership during the election campaign.[37] In fact, both parties were primarily concerned with highlighting the need for the Polish government to maintain a 'tough' negotiating strategy. This kind of rhetoric did, however, contain an implicit message that the EU was

[35] On the distinction between hard and soft Euroscepticism see: P. Taggart and A. Szczerbiak. *The Party Politics of Euroscepticism in EU Member and Candidate States*. Sussex European Institute Working Paper No. 51/Opposing Europe Research Network Working Paper No. 6. Brighton: Sussex European Institute. May 2002.

[36] Critical to the LPR's success was the backing of the Catholic nationalist broadcaster Radio Maryja whose charismatic director, Father Tadeusz Rydzyk, used its airwaves to convey a strong anti-EU message. Radio Maryja had 2.7 million listeners and was closely aligned to the "Our Daily" (Nasz Dziennik) newspaper with 600,000 readers. See: '"Claudia" z "Przyjaciółką".' *Rzeczpospolita*. 11 December 1998.

[37] PSL leader Jarosław Kalinowski had previously agreed to attend the ceremony while the PiS leadership had delegated their election organiser Ludwik Dorn to attend, but neither of them actually turned up. See: 'Pakt na rzecz integracji z Unią,' *Rzeczpospolita*. 23 August 2001; and 'Europa ich łączy,' *Gazeta Wyborcza*. 23 August 2001.

attempting to exploit Poland and, therefore, often came close to shading into a kind of soft Euroscepticism.[38]

While it would be far too simplistic to interpret the September 2001 election as representing some kind of 'Eurosceptic backlash',[39] it clearly meant that the new Polish parliament would contain a much larger bloc of deputies that are either critics or outright opponents of EU membership. The two most successful grouping (the SLD-UP and PO) were the two who were the most supportive of Polish EU membership and there was still a strong consensus in favour of the principle of EU membership. However, the presence of a sizeable anti-EU bloc meant that the new government faced a more openly critical parliament. It quickly emerged that debates on EU related issues would be much less consensual and that the government would face much tougher scrutiny of its EU policy. Enjoying, for the first time, a real public platform to put across its views, the anti-EU camp was able to set much of the tone for, and therefore polarise, many of the post-election parliamentary debates on EU issues. For example, in the first few months of the new parliament they: attacked the government's new negotiating strategy, (unsuccessfully) moved a motion of no confidence in Cimoszewicz for his failure to properly inform parliament of the new stance and proposed (again unsuccessfully) pre-emptive referendums on EU accession and the sale of Polish land to foreigners.[40]

This put the two broadly pro-EU opposition groupings, the PO and PiS, in an awkward position. On the one hand, the logic of opposition forced them to attack the government on a broad policy front. With the EU negotiations being a prominent political issue it was (and will continue to be) very tempting for them to attack the new government when they perceived them to be on weak ground. For example, even the strongly pro-EU PO voted against the government when it presented its modified negotiating strategy to parliament on the grounds that it was making concessions with no guarantee that this would secure reciprocity from the EU in other areas.[41] In his reaction to the new strategy, PO leader Maciej Płażyński argued that, "it would be safer if, in exchange for agreeing to the EU's position when it comes to access to EU labour markets, we could have obtained advantages in other areas such as structural funds, regional policy or agriculture…The government's new position will certainly speed up the negotiations, but it is not just a case of being in the Union in 2004, but to be in it on the best possible conditions. As a Polish citizen I would prefer to be sure that our concessions are in exchange for their concessions. And I would also like to know what they are."[42] Similarly, although the grouping abstained in the LPR and Self-Defence sponsored vote of no confidence on Foreign Minister Cimoszewicz, it criticised the government's proposal for a three-year transition period on the sale of farmland to foreign leaseholders. It also said that it would move such a motion itself if it did not feel that his performance had

[38] Soft Euroscepticism can be defined as where concerns on one (or a number) of policy areas lead to the expression of qualified opposition to the EU, or where there is a sense that 'national interest' is currently at odds with the EU's trajectory. See: *The Party Politics of Euroscepticism in EU Member and Candidate States*.

[39] See: A. Szczerbiak. 'A Eurosceptic backlash in Poland? The September 2001 parliamentary election,' *European Studies: A Journal of European Culture, History and Politics*. Vol 20. forthcoming, 2003.

[40] See: 'Przyspieszenie na ostatniej prostej.'; K. Niklewicz. 'Techniczny czy fatalny błąd.' *Gazeta Wyborcza*. 30 November 2001; 'Cimoszewicz zostaje.' *Rzeczpospolita*. 15-16 December 2001:D. Pszczółkowska. 'Cimoszewicz nieodwołany.' *Gazeta Wyborcza*. 15-16 December 2001; 'Referendum będzie, ale później.' *Rzeczpospolita*. 11 January 2002; 'Prereferendum.' *Gazeta Wyborcza*. 11 January 2002; and 'Jak Liga polskiej ziemi broniła.' *Gazeta Wyborcza*. 16-17 March 2002.

[41] See: 'Przyspieszenie na ostatniej prostej.'

[42] Cited in: 'Będziemy inaczej rozmawiać z Unią.'

improved within the next three months.[43] However, using the EU issue to attack the government in an opportunistic way breeds the cynicism that is the anti-EU camp's strongest potential ally given, as discussed below, that a low turnout could render an accession referendum invalid. In this sense, even a subsequent call on their supporters to vote 'Yes' to EU membership in the referendum may come too late if, by opportunistically attacking the government in the months leading up to it, they contribute to fostering resentment and hostility towards the EU accession process.[44]

TOWARDS THE ACCESSION REFERENDUM: GROUNDS FOR CAUTIOUS OPTIMISM?

However, as Table 1 shows, the Polish public appears to have been relatively unmoved by the recent high profile controversies surrounding the government's new negotiating strategy and the Commission's controversial proposals on limiting agricultural subsidies to Polish farmers. Public support for EU membership appears to remain stable at around 55-60% while the level of opposition remains stuck at around 25%. Moreover, there are number of reasons for the pro-EU camp to remain cautiously optimistic that it is very likely to win the autumn 2003 accession referendum.

Firstly, there is evidence that the Polish public has a fairly realistic, if somewhat schizophrenic, attitude towards the costs and benefits of EU accession. On the one hand, as the data on public attitudes towards the accession negotiations cited above shows, Poles appear to be very sensitive about the prospect of joining the EU on a 'second class' basis and without certain vital national interests being protected. This is something that the anti-EU camp will no doubt attempt to exploit in order to try and win over undecided Poles and detach the 'softer' elements from pro-EU camp. On the other hand, in spite of their unwillingness to make concessions in the accession negotiations, most Poles appear to have a realistic appreciation of the distance that still exists between Poland and most EU member states. They also appear to be aware that joining the EU will involve making certain sacrifices and have fairly modest expectations of the material benefits that are likely to accrue from it.[45] For example, an October 2001 ISP survey found that 60% of Poles (including 50% of those who supported Polish EU membership) believed that the country would be a second class member when it joined the EU, while only 30% thought that it would join with full membership rights.[46] A June 2000 ISP survey found that 81% of Poles acknowledged that the financial costs of EU accession would be substantial while only 10% thought that they would be minimal. 42% thought that Poland would have to bear the bulk of these costs, 40% that they

---

[43] See: 'Cimoszewicz zostaje.'

[44] See: 'Nie wolno graæ Uni¹: Z profesorem Len¹ Kolarsk¹-Bobiñsk¹, dyrektorem Instytutu Spraw Publicznych, rozmawia Andrzej Stankiewicz.' *Rzeczpospolita*. 21 November 2001; and C. Lewanowicz. 'Eurosceptyczny język eurozwolenników.' *Gazeta Wyborcza*. 6 December 2001.

[45] See: J. Kucharczyk. 'Club class Europe? The examination of socio-political conditions for a Eurosceptic backlash in Poland'. Paper prepared for the PSA Annual Conference. University of Manchester. 10-12 April 2001. p9; and L. Kolarska-Bobińska. 'Introduction: the Poles before the great change' in L. Kolarska-Bobińska, ed. *Before the great change: Polish public opinion and EU enlargement*. Warsaw: ISP. 2001. pp3-10.

[46] Wybory 2001 a integracja Polski z Unią Europejską. pp26-27.

would be spread equally and only 8% thought that they would be borne mainly by the EU.[47] Moreover, most Poles also appear to understand that the full benefits of EU accession are not likely to become apparent for some time. For example, a June 2000 ISP survey found that only 4% of Poles believed that their country would benefit from EU membership immediately, 51% after a few years and 30% after more than ten years.[48] The key point here is that, in spite of this realistic but rather negative perception of the costs and benefits of EU membership, most Poles remain broadly pro-EU as long as they continue to believe that the *overall* balance of political and economic costs and benefits will be advantageous.[49] For example, an June 2000 ISP survey found that as many as 57% of those who intended to vote Yes in an accession referendum would do so in spite of the fact that they believed Poland would be joining the EU as a 'second class' member.[50]

Some commentators have argued that one of the main factors accounting for the continuing support for Polish EU membership in spite of the rather pessimistic evaluation of the immediate benefits, could be that most Poles support accession for political rather than economic reasons. In other words, they see joining the EU as a civilisational choice that will help Poland 'catch up with the West.'[51] For example, a June 2000 ISP survey found that when discussing their 'hopes' associated with Polish EU membership, most respondents mentioned political rather than economic factors. While 59% of respondents felt that EU membership would mean aid for Polish agriculture (26% disagreed), only a minority (41%) thought that it would lead to improved living standards for ordinary people (46% disagreed). However, most respondents felt that it would bring about an improvement in international security (70% to 18%), greater opportunities to live and work in other European countries (65% to 19%) and better law enforcement and observance of human rights (61% to 22%).[52] In a similar vein, a December 2001 CBOS survey found that 48% of respondents felt that joining the EU would "reduce the distance" between Poland and other EU members (21% said it would make no difference, 9% said it would increase it and 22% did not know).[53]

However, as Table 4 shows, a more recent February 2002 CBOS survey of the motives given by those supporting Polish EU membership found a somewhat more mixed picture. Large numbers of respondents cited the economic benefits flowing from Polish EU membership, although most of these tended to be couched in very general terms such as a reduction in the level of unemployment (26%), general benefits for the economy (19%) and an improvement in living standards (18%). On the other hand, 26% of Poles simply stated that Polish EU membership would mean a "change for the better." Other respondents pointed to the 'historical necessity' of membership: 12% felt that due to globalisation Poland could

---

[47] See: M. Strzeszewski. 'Adaptation to the European Union: hopes, fears, and costs,' in *Before the great change*. pp89-126 (114-115).

[48] See: Ibid. p105 and L. Kolarska-Bobińska. 'Nie liczymy na pieniądze.' *Gazeta Wyborcza*. 12 July 2001. The figures in Table 2 showing that most Poles believe that current EU member states will benefit most from Polish accession, together with the figures cited above on how individuals are uncertain about how much they will gain personally from the process, can also be interpreted as evidence of this 'realistic' approach.

[49] See: 'Club class Europe' p10.

[50] See: J. Kucharczyk. 'Poland the EU - Unequal partnership.' in *Before the great change*. pp67-88 (71). Indeed, on another occasion Kucharczyk has argued that Poles' pessimistic view of their prospects as EU members was more related to a negative assessment of the current state of Poland than hostility towards the EU as such. See: 'Club class Europe, p13.

[51] See: 'Nie liczymy na pieniądze.'

[52] See: 'Adaptation to the European Union.' p108.

[53] See: Stosunek do integracji Polski z Unią Europejską po ogłoszeniu nowego stanowiska negocjacyjnego.

not afford to be isolated internationally, 10% felt that there was a lack of alternatives and 7% that EU membership provided better prospects for future generations. Similarly, a March 2001 CBOS survey found that 49% of Poles believed that the Polish economy would benefit from EU membership and only 33% felt that it would not (18% did not know). 45% felt that it would improve the competitiveness of Polish firms compared with 26% who felt that it would not (14% did not know).[54] In other words, it appears that economic benefits are certainly evident in underpinning support for Polish EU membership but that Poles view them in much more general terms rather than relating them to improvements in specific sectors or linking them to the precise terms of accession. For example, as Table 4 shows, only 4% of respondents cited the benefits for farming and the countryside as a specific reason for supporting EU accession. Similarly, a March 2001 CBOS survey found that only 13% of Poles felt that Polish farmers would benefit most from EU membership while 50% felt that farmers in EU member states would derive the most benefit (24% felt that the benefits would be evenly spread and 14% did not know).[55]

Table 4. Motives for Supporting Polish EU Membership, January 2002

General benefits	26%
Benefits for specific areas	
Reduction in unemployment, job opportunities	26%
Benefits for the economy, economic development	19%
Improvements in living standards, quality of life	18%
Open borders	5%
Benefits for agriculture and the countryside	4%
Positive impact on domestic public affairs	3%
Common currency, the euro	2%
Integration as a historic necessity	
Globalisation, need to avoid international isolation	12%
General - necessity of, lack of alternatives	10%
Better perspectives for future generations	7%
Only hope for rescuing the country	4%
Don't know	2%

Source: CBOS. Argumenty zwolenników i przeciwników integracji Polski z Unią Europejską. Warsaw: CBOS: February 2002.

A second reason why the pro-EU camp are more likely to win an accession referendum is that evidence suggests that supporters of Polish membership are more likely to turn out to vote than opponents. For example, a March 2002 CBOS survey found that (as Table 1 shows) the number of Poles supporting EU membership was 55% to 29% (16% did not know). However, of those who would turn out in a referendum 67% said that they would vote Yes and only 25% No (8% did not know).[56] Similarly, an June 2000 ISP survey distinguished between 'potential' and 'referendal' supporters and opponents, that is: those who had a pro or

[54] See: CBOS. Przewidywane skutki integracji Polski z Unią Europejską. Warsaw: CBOS. March 2001.
[55] Ibid.
[56] See: CBOS. Poparcie dla integracji Polski z Unią Europejską i opinie o konwencje Europejskim. CBOS: Warsaw. March 2002.

anti EU orientation and those who said that they would actually turn out to vote to vote Yes or No in a referendum. The survey revealed that 59% of Poles had a broadly pro-EU orientation while 30% were broadly anti-EU. However, more than eight out of ten of the broadly pro-EU segment (49% of the total sample) were classified as more solid, 'referendal' supporters while only one third of the anti-EU bloc (10%) were 'referendal' opponents.[57]

Thirdly, the fact that Polish elites are overwhelmingly pro-EU could have an enormous impact on the referendum outcome. Polish elites (particularly political ones) do not enjoy particularly high levels of public trust. However, as Kolarska-Bobińska has pointed out, if they speak out with one voice and come out solidly in favour of EU membership then most Poles will perceive that there is "something in this."[58] In particular, the fact that the influential Catholic Church hierarchy has become increasingly vocal in its support for EU membership has helped to counter the influence of Radio Maryja on the Catholic rank-and-file, and will continue to do so. Indeed, on his most recent visit to Poland in June 1999 the Pope used his address to the Polish parliament to spell out explicitly the Church's pro-EU stance. Supporters of EU membership will, no doubt, be hoping that he does so again on his next visit scheduled for August 2002.[59] Moreover, there is some evidence, that the pro-EU camp is beginning to make some serious efforts to mobilise support among the Polish public. One example of this was the appointment of political communications specialist Sawomir Wiatr to co-ordinate the government's promotion of the case for and benefits of EU membership.[60] Indeed, if the pre-accession aid that Poland is currently receiving from the EU is invested wisely and properly promoted then it could also help to strengthen support for the pro-EU camp in the way that regional aid has in some current member states. At the same time, although, as noted above, the anti-EU camp now has a sizeable bloc of parliamentary deputies, it still lacks a sufficiently credible or authoritative political figure capable of standing at the head of and mobilising a majority for a No vote.

In particular, if the main Polish parties and groupings could agree to undertake a non-partisan Yes campaign then this would undoubtedly provide a significant boost for the pro-EU cause. The future attitude of the two main pro-EU opposition parties, the PO and PiS, will be particularly important here. It is certain that the PO will support Polish EU membership in an accession referendum. However, in many ways the more important factor is how the party conducts itself during the remainder of the accession negotiations. As became apparent during the parliamentary debate on the new government's change of negotiating strategy and the no confidence vote on Foreign Minister Cimoszewicz, the logic of being in opposition can force the PO to make critical statements which, however measured, can lead to increased public cynicism about EU membership. This is an even greater problem for PiS whose precise response will be more difficult to predict. On the one hand, in spite of their misgivings about the potential terms of Polish membership, the party leadership appears to be broadly pro-EU

---

[57] See: X. Dolińska. 'Poland's Membership of the European Union: From Support to Rejection.' in *Before the Great Change*. pp11-52 (33).

[58] See: 'Nie liczymy na pieniądze.'

[59] Indeed, there has been some speculation that the new SLD government has reached a tacit arrangement with the Church hierarchy. The former communists will refrain from promoting certain aspects of their social agenda that the Church finds unacceptable (such as liberalisation of the abortion law) in return for the bishops' support in the run up to the accession referendum. See: M. Janicki. 'Czerwone i czarne.' *Polityka*. 16 February 2002; and E. Olczyk. 'Nie drażnić biskupów.' *Rzeczpospolita*. 15 February 2002.

[60] See: A. Stankiewicz. 'Kampania ruszy w maju.' *Rzeczpospolita*. 12 March 2002. Wiatr was previously head of the Polish section of the Gallup organisation and has worked as a media adviser to the SLD on various election campaigns.

and it is very likely that they will eventually come out in favour of a Yes vote. Indeed, polling evidence suggests that PiS voters in the 2001 parliamentary election broadly reflected general public attitudes towards EU membership, with a clear majority in favour.[61] On the other hand, it will be extremely difficult for a right-wing opposition party appealing to former AWS voters (and containing a strong Eurosceptic current) to avoid attacking a government comprising former communists at every conceivable opportunity. This is likely to be particularly true if it senses that concessions in the EU negotiations are viewed as a potential sign of weakness. Indeed, it is likely that those PiS deputies who originated from the Eurosceptic Christian National Union (Zjednoczenie Chrzeœcijañsko-Narodowe: ZChN) party will certainly not waste any opportunity to attack the government to ensure that are not outflanked by the LPR and Samoobrona.[62] The danger for the pro-EU camp is that even if both the PO and PiS do eventually come out in favour of EU membership at the time of the accession referendum this may not be enough to dispel the notion that this is, basically, an 'SLD project.'

Fourthly, and perhaps most significantly, even if most Poles are not particularly enthusiastic about EU membership, the pro-EU camp's strongest card remains the Eurosceptics' lack of a credible or attractive alternative foreign policy. The most frequently cited alternatives to EU membership are an independent foreign policy and closer links with Russia (and Poland's Eastern neighbours) or the USA (specifically membership of NAFTA).[63] However, the first two options are clearly unattractive for obvious historical and geo-political reasons while, even in so far as closer economic and political links with the USA are seen as desirable, NAFTA membership is not widely perceived as a realistic alternative to the EU. For example, an June 2000 ISP survey found that when presented with a range of alternative foreign policy options support for EU membership fell from 54% to 43%, as one would have expected when respondents were presented with a variety of alternatives rather than a straight Yes or No choice. However, it was still a much more popular choice than neutrality (21%) and closer links with the USA (13%) or Russia (11%).[64]

Finally, the fact that the fact that there has been a lively public debate on Polish EU membership, including the voicing of openly Eurosceptic views, and concomitant hardening of public attitudes may (ironically) also be good news for the pro-EU camp.[65] This means that polling data provide a more solid and accurate representation of the true state of Polish public opinion and, therefore, a more reliable indicator of what is likely to happen in the actual accession referendum. In this sense Poland compares favourably with other post-communist candidate states, such as Hungary, were much less attention and public scrutiny has focussed on this issue.[66]

---

[61] See: Wybory 2001 a integracja Polski z Unią Europejską. p13.

[62] See: M. D. Zdort. 'Prawica tradycyjna czy nowoczesna.' *Rzeczpospolita*. 25 September 2001.

[63] See, for example: Europe as a realigning issue in Polish politics?

[64] See: 'Poland's Membership of the European Union.' p15. Similarly, an earlier December 1998 survey found that when presented with a range of possible Polish foreign policy options the number of supporters of EU membership fell from 64% to 55%. However, EU membership was still much more popular than isolationism (12%), forging an alliance with the USA (6%) or developing closer links with Poland's Eastern neighbours (5%) CBOS. *Na drodze do Unii Europejskiej*. Warsaw: CBOS. January 1999.

[65] For example, an October 2001 ISP survey found evidence of a crystallisation of public attitudes with a fall in number of Poles who did not know who would gain or lose as a result of Polish EU membership between June 2000 and October 2001. See: *Wybory 2001 a integracja Polski z Unią Europejską*. pp23-25.

[66] See, for example, the description of the paucity of the Hungarian euro-debate by Agnes Batory in 'Current and Future Issues in European Integration: Public Opinion and EU Enlargement: Proceedings of a seminar in a series

However, in spite of this broadly optimistic scenario for the pro-EU camp it still faces two potentially serious obstacles. Perhaps, the greatest threat to securing a Yes vote is if the accession referendum becomes transformed into a broader plebiscite on the socio-economic transition as a whole. EU membership could then be seen to benefit mainly an elite of already privileged transition winners: those narrow elite groups that people feel are the beneficiaries of this process. In other words, there is a danger that the Polish public, a majority of whom already feel that they have lost out from the transition, sees EU accession as an elite driven process from which it will gain little and simply lead to a further deterioration in their living standards. ISP polling data has shown that attitudes towards the socio-economic transition were the single most powerful variable explaining attitudes towards Polish EU membership. The highest levels of support for EU membership were to be found among those who supported the transition process in its broadest sense as well as specific policies such as privatisation and encouraging foreign investment. For example, an October 2001 ISP survey found that 70% of those who strongly agreed that post-communist Poland was a better place to live than pre-1989 Poland intended to vote Yes in an accession referendum compared with only 34% who strongly disagreed with this proposition.[67] At the same time, most Poles perceived themselves to be 'transition losers' and this is a perception that has increased markedly in recent years. For example, the same October 2001 ISP survey found those who believed that post-communist Poland was a better place to live in than pre-1989 Poland fell from 55% in June 2000 to 44% in October 2001. Those who felt that it was not increased from 37% to 48% over the same period.

Table 5. Motives for Opposing Polish EU Membership, January 2002

General disadvantages	18%
Impact of distance between Poland and EU countries	
Poland is unprepared, too weak to be an equal partner	20%
Loss of sovereignty, fear of becoming vassals	20%
General fear of second class membership	12%
Threats to specific areas	
Negative impact on agriculture	13%
Negative impact of the economy, industry, trade with the EU	13%
Negative impact on employment, opportunities to work abroad	6%
Negative impact on living standards	4%
Other factors	
Lack of information	10%
Disapproval of accession negotiations	6%
General lack of trust towards the EU	4%
General uncertainty, fear of the future	5%
Don't know	2%

Source: CBOS. Argumenty zwolenników i przeciwników integracji Polski z Unią Europejską. Warsaw: CBOS. February 2002.

of meetings on current issues in European integration organised by the Centre of International Studies, Cambridge University and sponsored by the Foreign and Commonwealth Office, held at Pembroke College, Cambridge'. 14 June 2001' at www.intstudies.cam.ac.uk/fco/fco-pubop.html.

67 See: *Wybory 2001 a integracja Polski z Unią Europejską*. p20. For more on this see: 'Poland's Membership of the European Union'. pp26-28; and 'Nie liczymy na pieniądze.'

Not surprisingly, therefore, fear of the possible negative consequences of Polish EU membership were rooted primarily in socio-economic factors, particularly the impact on certain sectors of the economy such as agriculture and small and medium-sized businesses. For example, an June 2000 ISP survey found that 56% of Poles believed that EU accession would mean the collapse of many small and medium sized enterprises and increased unemployment (28% disagreed). Similarly, although, as noted above, a majority felt that EU accession would mean more money for Polish farmers, a substantial minority (40% to 44%) also felt that it would lead to a collapse of Polish agriculture when exposed to EU competition. Moreover, only 41% of Poles believed that their standard of living would increase when Poland joined the EU.[68] Similarly, as Table 5 shows, a February 2002 CBOS survey also revealed that the potentially negative impact of EU membership on the Polish economy was the most frequently cited motive for opposing accession. Such concerns about the economic impact of EU membership, particularly the idea that Poland was not yet ready to compete with the more economically advanced current EU member states, were also likely to have underpinned the anxieties (noted above) of those who opposed what they saw as 'premature' accession on unfavourable terms.[69]

As Table 6 shows, this link between attitudes towards the socio-economic transition and EU accession was also reflected in the demographic profile of the pro- and anti-EU camps, particularly the correlation between attitudes towards Polish EU membership and age, place of residence, education, distribution of income, assessment of personal financial prospects and certain occupations. The highest levels of support for EU membership were evident among groups that one could consider to be transition winners or potential winners: younger and better-educated Poles who lived in larger towns or cites, had the highest incomes and were most optimistic about their own personal financial position. It was also particularly evident among certain occupational groups such as managers (75%), white collar workers (68%), businessmen (64%) and particularly students (74%). Opposition or ambivalence to EU membership, on the other hand, was particularly high among the transition losers: older, less well-educated Poles living in rural areas, lower income groups who were most pessimistic about their financial prospects, and, particularly, farmers. Indeed, those Poles who made their living from agriculture were the only occupational group where there was a majority opposed to EU membership (65% to 19%).[70] This pattern was reflected in a June 2000 ISP survey which found that when asked who would gain from EU accession the most frequently cited groups were: educated people (73% to 5%), the political elite (70% to 7%) and big business (59% to 17%). Smaller majorities thought that consumers (45% to 27%) and the unemployed (37% to 29%, with 20% unsure) would also benefit. The groups most frequently cited as accession losers were owners of small and medium sized businesses (45% to 22%), workers (40% to 23%) and farmers (48% to 29%).[71]

---

[68] See: 'Adaptation to the European Union.' p108.

[69] The positive side of this was, of course, that many opponents of EU membership were not necessarily anti-EU *per se* but simply concerned that Poland was not ready to join and, if they were convinced that it was ready, could be persuaded to join the Yes camp. See note 28.

[70] Roguska and Kucharczyk found a similar pattern (See: *Wybory a integracja Polski z Unią Europejską*. pp11-12) as did Dolińska, although she argued that this correlation was much weaker than the one with subjective support for or opposition to socio-economic transformation (See: 'Poland's Membership of the European Union.' pp23-28).

[71] See: 'Adaptation to the European Union.' p113. A majority (43% to 26%) also thought that swindlers would benefit from EU membership!

Table 6. Socio-Economic Profile of Supporters/Opponents of Polish EU Membership, March 2002

Age	Pro	Anti	Don't know
18-24	67	21	12
25-34	56	32	12
35-44	59	37	15
45-54	55	23	21
55-64	57	27	16
Over 65	48	30	23
Place of residence	**Pro**	**Anti**	**Don't know**
Villages	40	42	18
Less than 20,000 inhabitants	66	20	14
20-100,000	59	20	21
101-500,000	63	23	14
Over 501,000	68	19	13
Education	**Pro**	**Anti**	**Don't know**
Primary	46	32	22
Vocational	50	34	16
Middle	61	24	15
Higher	75	17	18
Occupation	**Pro**	**Anti**	**Don't know**
Managers	75	18	7
Intellectual workers	68	15	17
Intellectual-physical workers	49	30	21
Qualified workers	43	39	17
Unqualified workers	57	20	24
Farmers	19	65	16
Businessmen	64	20	16
Pensioners	37	43	21
Retirees	59	21	20
Students	74	18	8
Unemployed	57	30	13
Housewives	54	26	20
Weekly earnings	**Pro**	**Anti**	**Don't know**
Less than 299 z³oties	40	33	27
300-399	51	35	13
400-599	51	32	17
600-800	66	24	9
More than 800 z³oties	74	16	9
Assessment of own position	**Pro**	**Anti**	**Don't know**
Bad	45	37	18
Average	55	28	17
Good	77	11	12
Church attendance	**Pro**	**Anti**	**Don't know**
Several times a week	39	34	27
Weekly	53	30	18
Several times a month	60	29	11
Several times a year	64	23	13
Never	52	29	19

Source: CBOS. Poparcie dla wejścia Polski do Unii Europejskiej i opinie o konwencji Europejskim. Warsaw: CBOS. March 2002.

However, the key point here is that while attitudes towards EU membership overlapped with those towards the transition and (although to a somewhat lesser extent) those socio-economic groups that one could classify as actual or potential transition winners and losers, they did not do so completely. In other words, there was clearly a substantial group of Poles who were still pro-EU in spite of the fact that they were (or perceived themselves to be) transition losers. For example, as noted above, a June 2000 ISP survey showed (predictably) that 70% of those who felt that they were transition winners intend to vote for EU membership. However, it also revealed that a plurality of those who said that were transition losers, 34%, also intended to vote Yes compared with only 20% who said that they would vote No. Similarly, as Table 6 shows, even among most of those socio-economic groups that perceived themselves to be transition losers, there were majorities for EU membership in almost every case. This was, perhaps, because they identified Polish EU membership with economic advancement more generally or perhaps because they saw joining the EU as part of a broader 'civilisational choice' not necessarily linked to their specific socio-economic 'class interests'. Whatever the reason, the fact that the two issues, the perception of being a transition loser and opposition to EU membership, were (to some extent at least) de-coupled, accounts for this substantial segment of pro-EU transition losers. This, in turn, ensured that a majority of Poles continued to support EU membership.

The anti-EU camp's best hope (and the pro-EU camp's greatest fear) is, therefore, to link the two processes so that the EU accession referendum becomes a proxy for a referendum on the transition as a whole. It is, therefore, socio-economic arguments, the fear that Poland will not be able to cope successfully with accession and have to pay huge social costs, which are most likely to strike a chord with the Polish public and provide the most fertile recruiting ground for the Polish anti-EU camp. On the other hand, the strategy adopted by some Polish Eurosceptics (such as Łopuszański and Wrzodak) of stressing the threat to national sovereignty posed by EU membership is unlikely to make much headway with the majority of Poles nor provide any serious threat to the pro-EU camp. A June 2000 ISP report found that most Poles did not believe that the EU would lead to a loss of independence (only 13% compared to 77%) nor a weakening of Polish traditions and culture (only 31% compared to 60%).[72] Similarly, as Table 5 shows, only 20% of those opposed to Polish EU membership cited 'ideological' factors rather than economic ones.[73] One explanation for this phenomenon is the unambiguously pro-EU stance adopted by the Pope and Catholic Church hierarchy (noted above) which makes it very difficult for Catholic nationalists, such as those clustered around Radio Maryja, to evoke the possible 'loss of national identity' as an argument against EU membership.[74]

However, a much bigger threat to the pro-EU camp than a No vote is the danger of a low turnout in an accession referendum, particularly if the conduct of the Polish Euro-debate over

72 See: Ibid. p108.

73 Obviously, it is difficult to completely separate economic issues from those relating to national sovereignty. However, it is possible to distinguish between those anti-EU Poles who are primarily motivated by fears of loss of sovereignty (and who, implicitly, would oppose EU membership even if they accepted that the net economic effects were beneficial) are and those who are mainly fearful of the economic consequences rather than any loss of sovereignty *per se*. Polish opponents of EU membership are, I would argue, principally located in the latter category.

74 See: 'Club class Europe'. pp9-10. As Table 6 shows, those attending Church services several times a week (the core of the 'religious right') were more likely to be anti-EU. However, apart from that relatively small group there was no clear link between religiosity and attitudes towards EU membership.

the next eighteen months serves to breed apathy and resentment towards the whole European project. According to the Polish Constitution, a referendum is only valid if more than 50% of eligible voters participate in it.[75] On the face of it, opinion poll evidence suggests that securing a 50% turnout for an accession referendum should not be too onerous a task. A May 2001 OBOP suggested a 70% turnout,[76] an October 2001 ISP poll 65%[77] and a March 2002 CBOS survey 66%.[78] However, the experience of previous referendums and parliamentary elections suggests that the propensity to declare a willingness to vote systematically overstates the real likely turnout so that one must approach these figures with extreme caution. For example, polling evidence in the run up to the February 1996 referendum on mass privatisation indicated a turnout of 52% while the actual turnout was only 32.4%. Similarly, polls taken in the run up to the May 1997 referendum to ratify the Constitution itself (that, interestingly, did not require a 50% turnout) indicated that two thirds of Poles would vote while actual turnout was only 42.9%. Again, immediately prior to the September 2001 parliamentary election an OBOP survey predicted a 60% turnout while only 46% in fact voted. Indeed, three out of the four parliamentary elections held since the emergence of multi-party politics in 1989 have had turnout levels of below 50%.[79] In reality, a more accurate indicator of turnout is likely to be the number who say that they will *definitely* vote and in the case of both the OBOP and ISP polls cited above this was only 43%.[80] Only the March 2002 CBOS survey was somewhat more optimistic in this respect, with just over half (51%) of respondents saying that they would definitely participate in an accession referendum.

If, as the evidence above appears to indicate, the average Pole does not really understand what impact EU membership will have on their lives then this is sure to depress turnout. Similarly, the fact that it is rather general economic and abstract political motives that underpin support for EU membership could be a problem as these may have a less powerful capacity to mobilise voters than more specific economic factors. Moreover, there is also some evidence that propensity to turnout in an accession referendum is affected by attitudes towards the socio-economic transition. For example, an October 2001 ISP survey found only 19% of those who considered themselves transition winners said that they would definitely not participate in an accession referendum, while this figure increased to 35% among perceived losers.[81] Asking this question in a slightly different, and more future oriented, way 50% of those who said that Poland would be a worse place to live in five years time said that would they would definitely not vote in an accession referendum. This compared with only

[75] In fact, according to Article 90 of the Polish Constitution, it is also possible to ratify an accession treaty by a two-thirds majority vote in both houses of parliament (sitting as the National Assembly). However, Poland's political leaders have committed themselves to a referendum, a commitment that it will be virtually impossible for them to retract. Theoretically, they could fall back on the parliamentary option if, for example, turnout fell just short of 50% but an overwhelming majority of those participating voted 'Yes'. However, such a decision would be open to challenge both on legal grounds and (perhaps more importantly) on the dubious political legitimacy that it would confer on a decision of such historic proportions. See: P.Winczorek. 'Głośniej nad tą urną.' *Polityka*. 8 December 2001.

[76] See: Opinia społeczna o członkostwie Polski w Unii Europejskiej.

[77] See: Wybory 2001 a integracja z Unią Europejską. pp5-6.

[78] See: Poparcie dla integracji Polski z Unią Europejską i opinie o Konwencji Europejskim.

[79] Only presidential elections, where voters can identify more clearly with an individual candidate, have consistently secured turnouts above 50%.

[80] Even here the ISP figure may be an exaggeration as it was based on a poll taken just after an election when there is a tendency for such figures to increase.

[81] See: Wybory 2001 a integracja z Unią Europejską. p20.

14% non-voters among those who said that it would be a better place.[82] Consequently, any further negative shifts in attitudes towards the transition (and its future impact) are also likely to negatively affect the referendum turnout. At the same time, some commentators claim to have detected signs that, although still broadly supportive of EU membership, even transition winners are losing enthusiasm about Polish accession and will also be less likely to turn out and vote.[83]

CONCLUSION

Recent years have seen a significant fall in support for Polish EU membership and the emergence of a sizeable bloc of anti-EU public opinion. The September 2001 parliamentary election also saw parties and groupings critical of, or even hostile to, Polish EU membership win a significant share of the vote and secure substantial parliamentary representation. Moreover, as predicted, the new SLD-led government actually adopted a new, more flexible attitude towards issues such as access to Western labour markets and sale of land to foreigners in order to accelerate the accession negotiations. This produced a mixed public reaction, primarily because most Poles did not really accept or understand the government's argument that delaying Polish EU accession would be a disaster and it was necessary to make certain concessions in order to facilitate early Polish entry. Moreover, the clumsy way in which the new negotiating strategy was announced also produced an extremely hostile political backlash even from within the government and the pro-EU opposition parties. Indeed, the SLD-UP coalition fell short of an overall majority in the election and was forced to form a government with the PSL, a party that will be extremely reluctant to agree to concessions that do not satisfy its core rural-agrarian constituency. This has constrained its room for manoeuvre and will continue to do so during the negotiating endgame. The anti-EU parties have also exploited their newly gained parliamentary platform and attempted (with some success) to shift the terms of and polarise the Polish Euro-debate.

However, the public appears unmoved by the controversies surrounding the change of negotiating strategy and EU proposals for agricultural support, and overall levels of support for Polish EU membership remain at the relatively high levels at which they stabilised in the middle of 1999. Although it may suffer some further slippage, it is still extremely likely that a majority of Poles will vote Yes in the accession referendum. Poles have a fairly realistic attitude towards the costs and benefits that will flow from EU membership and pro-EU voters are more likely to turn out to vote than those who are against. All of this does not mean that Polish Euroenthusiasts should get too complacent or that the accession referendum will not be a hard fight. A lot will obviously depend on how the negotiating endgame works itself out and precise 'deal' that the Polish government is able to secure. However, it is also critical how the Polish political elite conducts itself, particularly if the SLD led government and pro-EU opposition can form a relatively united front on the issue. The extent to which the Catholic Church hierarchy actively engages in mobilising the faithful or, at the very least, neutralising the impact of the influential anti-EU Radio Marjya broadcaster will also be an important factor.

[82] Ibid. p21.

[83] See: 'Nie liczymy na pieniądze'; and : D. Zagrodzka. 'Teraz albo wcale.' *Gazeta Wyborcza*. 30 October 2001.

It is also critically important how the debate on the accession referendum is framed. The pro-EU camp's strongest argument remains the Eurosceptics' lack of an attractive or realistic alternative foreign policy. Their most promising strategy, therefore, would be to present the accession referendum primarily in historical terms as representing a major civilisation and geo-political choice, with the economic benefits forming a strong complementary second strand, focussing on pre-accession aid as a precursor of more to come. On the other hand, the anti-EU camp's only real hope of victory is to present the accession referendum as a plebiscite on the socio-economic transition as a whole, portraying EU membership as something that will only benefit the minority who perceive themselves to be transition winners. The greatest danger for the pro-EU camp, therefore, is that a stereotype develops of the kind of person and socio-occupational groups that are likely to benefit from it with certain segments of the population clearly defined as, and perceiving themselves to be, winners and losers. However, if the anti-EU camp frames its arguments in ideological terms, focussing on the perceived threat to Polish sovereignty and culture, then it will almost certainly lose. Nevertheless, even if the pro-EU camp secures a convincing Yes vote, then there is still a (probably even greater) danger that the referendum will fail to achieve the 50% turnout required by the Polish Constitution for it to be valid. This could happen if the conduct of the Polish Euro-debate creates an image of EU membership as simply a regrettable necessity or if the average Pole comes to view EU membership as an elite-driven process that will not have any positive impact on their day-to-day lives.

INDEX

A

B

C

D

E

F

G

H

I

J

K

L

M

U

V

W